RECORDS

OF THE

COURT OF NEW CASTLE

ON DELAWARE

VOL. II

1681-1699

LAND AND PROBATE ABSTRACT ONLY

BY THE COLONIAL SOCIETY OF PENNSYLVANIA

Southern Historical Press, Inc.
Greenville, South Carolina

This volume was reproduced from
A personal copy located in the
Publisher's private library.

All rights reserved. No part of this publication may be reproduced,
stored in a retrieval system, transmitted in any form, posted
on to the web in any form or by any means without
the prior written permission of the publisher.

Please direct all correspondence and orders to:

www.southernhistoricalpress.com
or
**SOUTHERN HISTORICAL PRESS, Inc.
PO BOX 1267
375 West Broad Street
Greenville, SC   29601
southernhistoricalpress@gmail.com**

Originally published: Lancaster, PA. 1934
Reprinted by: Southern Historical Press, Inc.
Greenville, SC
ISBN #0-89308-022-5
All rights Reserved.
Printed in the United States of America

octob: 28th 1682 — 261

B 437

On the 27th day of october 1682, arrived before ye Towne of New Castle in Delowar from England William Penn Esq: Propriet:r of Pensilv: who produced two Certaine deeds of ffeofment from ye Illustrius Prince James Duke of Yorke & Albany &c: for this Towne of New Castle and twelve miles about it, and also for ye Two Lower Counties of Whorekills and St Jones's; w:ch s:d deeds bore date 24 august 1682, and pursuant to the true Intent Purpose and meaning of his Roy:ll highniss in ye same deeds hee ye s:d William Penn Received possession of ye Towne of new Castle ye 28th of octob:r 1682 —

Copia Vera

B 438

By the Comander in Cheife & Councell —
Whereas his Roy:ll highnesse hath been Graciously pleased by Indenture under his hand & Seale bearing date ye 24th day of augus:t Last past for ye Consideracon therein mentioned to Bargain Sell Enfeofe and Confirme unto William Penn Esq:r his heires & assignes for Ever; all that the Towne of New Castle otherwayes called Delowar and all that tract of Land Lying within the Compasse or Circle of twelve miles about the same with all Islands and ye River and Soyle thereof Lying north of ye Southern

William Penn's First American Landing, at New Castle, Delaware, October 28, 1682, as described on page 261, of the Original Manuscript Book of the Records, here reproduced.

INTRODUCTORY NOTE

The first volume of *Records of the Court of New Castle on Delaware, 1676-1681*, was published, with some few unindicated omissions, by The Colonial Society, in 1904; it is an octavo book, of 547 pages, limited to an edition of 200 numbered copies. The printing was from a modern transcript in the collection of The Genealogical Society of Pennsylvania, in the Library of The Historical Society of Pennsylvania, in Philadelphia, made, in 1902, by the late Jacob Martin, of Marshallton, Chester County, Pennsylvania, from the original manuscript preserved in the Office of the Prothonotary of the Superior Court for New Castle County, in the Court House, City of Wilmington, Delaware.

The original manuscript, in the handwriting of the contemporary court clerk and surveyor, Ephraim Herman, of New Castle, may still be seen in the Office of the Prothonotary; it consists of two folio books,—Liber A, October 19, 1676-December 3, 1678, and Liber B, January 7, 1679-December 12, 1681.[1]

The present printed volume of the *Records*, covering the years 1681-1699,—and the second to be published by The Colonial Society,—is, of necessity, limited to such extracts from the original court minutes as were ordered made by the Government of The Three Lower Counties on Delaware, in the year 1770, of all items respecting land titles and probate proceedings. These extracts are the only survivals of the original records for the period named.

The hiatus in the original court minutes is as follows:

(1) After page 382, in Liber B, about 56 pages, for the period December 12, 1681–November, 1682.

(2) All of Liber C, of at least 537 pages, for the period November 2, 1682–March 23, 1688.

(3) All of Liber D, of 68 pages, for the period May 5, 1688–March 16, 1689.

(4) A volume or volumes, the lettering unknown, for the period June 17, 1690–November 21, 1699.

The whole of the original court minutes for the period 1676-

---

[1] A photostatic copy of the original has since been placed in the Manuscript Division of The Historical Society of Pennsylvania.

1699, under resolutions of the years 1768 and 1769, and an enactment of the year 1770 of the Assembly of Delaware,[2] was extracted for the land and probate references, which, after being "carefully compared with the original records", were certified as "true copies" by a Committee of two Delaware Assemblymen from New Castle County, Evan Rice and Thomas McKean (Lawyer, later Signer of the Declaration of Independence for Delaware and Governor of Pennsylvania).

These extracts of land and probate references, certified at the end by the signatures of Evan Rice and Thomas McKean, fill a large folio (10 x 15½ x 2⅜ inches), manuscript, broken-backed, calf-bound volume of 530 pages, lettered on the front cover of the book:[3]

> Old Records
> Transcrib'd

This book of "Old Records", cited by Dr. George Smith, in his *History of Delaware County*, Pennsylvania (Philadelphia, 1862), page 287, and by J. Thomas Scharf, in his *History of Delaware* (2 volumes, Philadelphia, 1888), Volume II, pages 612-613, was among the public archives of New Castle County, as late as the year 1902, according to a letter of the late Jacob Martin, of 1909. In the disorganization of the County records, as a consequence of removal and building operations, the old volume disappeared. It was finally discovered by the Editor to be in the possession of the late Walter G. Tatnall (1856-1929), of Smyrna, Delaware. By the courtesy of the latter the volume was made available for the personal historical use of the Editor and also for The Colonial Society in its present publication of that portion of it beginning with February, 1681-2, not previously printed. The proof of the printed work has been critically compared with the original manuscript book "Old Records Transcrib'd".

ALBERT COOK MYERS,
Editor.

[2] *Votes of the Assembly of Delaware*, Wilmington, Delaware, 1770, pages 154, 202, 216, 219-229, 231; *Laws of Delaware, I*, New Castle, Delaware, 1792, pages 457-458.
[3] A photostatic copy of the book has been placed in the Manuscript Division of The Historical Society of Pennsylvania.

RECORDS

OF THE

COURT OF NEW CASTLE

february 7^(th) 16$\frac{81}{82}$;—

Att a Co^(rt): held in the Towne of New Castle by his May^(ties): Authority february the 7^(th). 16$\frac{81}{82}$—

P^(r)sent;—
M^(r). Peter Alrichs
M^(r). Gerret Otto
M^(r). Joh: D'haes
M^(r). Will Sempill
} Justices

B 384.

Capt^(n). Edm: Cantwell h: Sherrife

The Co^(rt): Granted unto Daniell Pagg & Thom: Smith to take up w^(th):in this County 300 acres of Land, w^(ch): heretofore hath not ben Granted taken up or Improoved by others they Seating & Improoveing y^(e) same; according to Lawe & regulacons. B 386.

The Co^(rt): Granted unto Rich: Noble to take up a Lott w^(th):in this Towne of New Castle upon Condition of Settlem^(t): as others and also Twoo hundred Acres of Land w^(th):in y^(e) County— B 386.

The Co^(rt): adjorned till y^(e): first Teusday in March next

March y^(e) 6^(th): 168$\frac{1}{2}$

The Justices of this Co^(rt): thougt it fitt to adjorne y^(e) Co^(rt). untill y^(e) first Teusday in y^(e) month of Aprill next Ensung and after y^(e) Co^(rt): was opened proclamation was made occordingly;— B 387.

Aprill y^(e): 4^(th): 1682. Justice John Moll Peter Alrichs M^(r): Joh: D'haes & Will: Sempill, thougt good to adjorne ye Co^(rt): till y^(e) first Teusday of y^(e) month of May next the Cheef occasion thereof being that y^(e) Clark Eph: herman was Imployed by the Dep^(ty): Govern^(r): of New Yorke to Collect y^(e) Quit rents etc:— B 387.

May 2^(d): 1682.—

Att a Co^(rt): held in the Towne of New Castle by his May^(ties): Authority on Teusday the 2^(d): of May Annoq Dom: 1682

P^(r)sent
M^(r). John Moll
M^(r). Gerret Otto
M^(r). Joh: D'haes
M^(r). Will: Sempill
} Justices—

Capt^(n). Edm: Cantwel H: Sherrife

B 388.	Upon the Peticon of Oele Poulsen, The Co^{rt}: Granted him to take up wth:in this County 200 acres of Land and 25 Acres of Marsh not Granted or taken up before he the Peticon^r: Improoving & Seating the Same according to Law & orders—

B 388.	Upon the Peticon of Will: Osborne The Co^{rt}: Granted him to take up wth:in this County 200 acres of Land not Granted or taken up before by others, hee ye Peticon^r: makeing Improovem^t: thereon & Seating according to Law & orders;—

B 388.	Upon the Peticon of James Beswike and francis his Mate Granted them to take up 400 acres of Land not Granted before upon Condition of Settlement as hereabove

May 2^d: 1682.—

B 389.	Lewis Dauis Shewing by his Peticon that Even Salisburry deceased was Justly indebted to the peticon^r: for one whole Years Service p^{r}formed ye sume of 2500℔ of tobbacco & Caske, and that there was noe Vissible Estate of ye s^d. Even Salisburry but one peece of Land wth:in this County desiering Sence there was noe heir nor p^{r}son putting in for administration: that the Peticon^r might bee admitted to administr^r: upon ye s^d: Estate of Even Salisburry;

The Co^{rt}: hauing duely Examined the Case Doe thinke fitt to Authorize and appoint the s^d. Lewis Dauis Administ^r: of all the Estate of ye s^d: Even Salisburry wth:in this County hee makeing and bringing in a true & Exact Inventory and p^{r}forming according to Lawe,

Lewis Dauis binds ouer his s^d: debt of 2500 ℔ tobb to the Co^{rt}: and all his other Estate for Security of his due administration on ye s^d: Estate of Even Sallisburry according to Lawe;—

B 390.	Lewis Dauis Proveing in Co^{rt}: by the witnesses Symon Whitwell Tho: Gilbert and Mist^{rs}: Anna Young that Even Salisburry deceased Stands Justly and Truely indebted unto him for one Years Service P^{r}formed, the full and Just Sume of 2500 ℔ of tobbacco & Caske

The Co^{rt}: doo Grant him an order against the Estate of ye s^d:

Even Salisburry deceased for ye Payment of ye s^d: debt w^th: ye Costs—

May 2^d: 1682.
Upon the Peticon of henry Ward Sheweing that hee hath formerly taken up & Seated a peece of Land below this Towne of New Castle at Reeten Point, for w^ch: hee hath also a Patent B 390. of Confirmation from Govern^r: Edmund Andros; and the Peticon^r: Suspecting that the quantity of acres mentioned in ye s^d: Pattent did not agree with the bounds did therefore humbly Intreat ye Co^rt: to Grant him an order for a Resurvey, on the Same, and if any Greater quantity of acres bee found w^th: in the bounds of ye s^d: Pattent, then therein is Exprest that hee ye Peticon^r might haue P^rferrence and a Grant to take itt up; The Co^rt: haueing taken the premises into Consideracon doo grant the Peticon^r his s^d: Request, and doe order the Surveyo^r: to make a Resurvey accordingly—

Apeared in Co^rt: Elizabeth Pouls daughter—widdow of B 391. Moens Poulsen deceased whoe then & there produced the Laest Will & Testam^t: of hur s^d: deceased husband and prooved the Same in Co^rt: by the oaths of Mathias Mathias de Vos & Jacob Vander Veer wittnesses to the Same: Itt was by the Co^rts: ord^rs: that the s^d: will be Translated and Recorded and that the Widdow bee admitted administratrix and Shee bring in an Inventory & p^rforme all things according to Lawe & Custome.

followeth the Laest will & Testament of Moens Poulsen deceased:
Copia & Translt:
In the name of o^r Lord & Sauior Jesus Christ and in the Yeare 1680 the 3^d: of decemb^r: appeared before us—underwritten Moens Poulsen aged Seventy Years, being in good and p^rfect health and desired to hauve his Laest will & Testament made, and Considering the frailty of o^r Lyves the Certainty of B 391. death and the uncertaine houre thereof, did therefore think fitt (:before hee d[e]parted this Lyfe:) to dispose of his Temporall Estate w^ch: God almighty had bestowed upon him & Elizabet

Pouls daughter his wyfe; therefore when Almighty God Shall haue taken him out of this world, hee recommends his Soull in ye hands of allmighty God, & his boddy to the Earth to bee decently burried; and next that his wyfe Elizabeth whoe Lykewyse was p^{r}sent Shall haue and Inherrit it after his decease, the one half of what shall bee Left, houses & Land Cattle, and Moveables nothing att all Excepted and the remaining halfe of his Estate hee Gives and bequeaths unto his Children w^{ch}: hee has by p^{r}sent wyfe Elizabeth afores^d, as for his other Children Poull and Margriet whoe this Testator has begott by his former wyfe, they Shall haue nothing more to demand, Either of his p^{r}sent wyfe or hur Children; Except Margrieta whoe Yett must haue thirty & fyve Gilders; This Testator haueing as hee declares Given his s^d: dauter Margret a wedding and Soe mutch as hur part or Sheare came to, with a Cow and a Calfe & a Sowe; and his Son Poull he Sayes to haue Given him soe mutch as Contented him; This Soe don & past in the p^{r}sence of these underwritten witnesses to witt Mathias Mathiasse John Schaegen Cornelis Vander Veer & Jacob Vander Veer datum Utsupra;—

May 2d: 1682.—

B 395.　Upon the Severall Peticons of the hereafter named P^{r}sons; the Co^{rt}: haue Granted them to take up wth:in this County; the quantitys of Land hereafter mentioned, wth: this Condition that they and Each of them doe Settle build & Improve the same according to Lawe & the Governo^{rs}: Regulacons; the s^d: Lands so to bee taken up are to bee Cleare of any former Grants or Surveys; and the Surv^r: is hereby ordered to Survey and Lay out the same; according to Custome;—

　　Granted to—
　　John Jarvis to take up 200 acr: of Land
　　Andrew Love to take up 200 acr: of Land—
　　John Smith Junior & Sam: Bercker Each 100 acr:—
　　William Sempill the Lott w^{ch}: was formerly Granted to hans Coderus & not Improoved. hans Coderus a Lott to take up in Towne—

Poull Gerritzen 100 acr: of Land—
hans hansen Miller to take up 400 acr: of Land
Sybrant Mathiass to take up one Lott:—
William Picket 200 acr: of Land.

John Smith ye Carpender this day appeared in Co^{rt}: and did then & there aknowledge a Certain deed and Conveigance Signed Sealed and delivered by him ye s^d: John Smith to the use of John Gerritzen Verhoof of a Certaine house and Lott of Ground Scituate & being within this Towne of New Castle att y^e. Strand or watersyde hauing to y^e. East ye house and Lott of ground of John hendrixon ye Torner on ye west the house & Lott of Will Osborne of Long Island Contening in breath before on the front forthy & twoo foott and in Lengt Equall wth: ye other Lotts hee ye s^d: John Smith aknowledged to have Received full Sattisfaction from ye s^d: John Gerritzen for ye same; as by ye s^d: deed bearing date ye 26 of March 1682 may more att Large appeare;— B 396.

Doctor Gerrardus Wessells was this day appointed to adminst^r: upon ye Estate of Matheus Beekman deceased (:hee being the Greatest Credito^r: and none other being willing thereunto:) and the Co^{rt}: doe hereby authorize him thereunto hee bringing an Inventory and p^rforming all things according to Lawe;— B 397.

Nota Justa Andries has Co^{rt}: disanuld relinequist this deed & Conveigance as by ye records ye 5 S^{mr}: 1682 wil appear

Jonas Arskin ye son and heir of John Arskin deceased appeared in Co^{rt}: and aknowledged a deed & Transport of a Certaine peece of Land wth:in this Towne of New Castle next to ye Land of Gerrit Gerritson Containing about 4 acres of Ground as by ye deed thereof baring date 2^d: May Instant doth more att Large appeare;— B 402.

Upon ye request of Arent Johnson of bread & Cheese Island the Co^{rt}: haue Confirmed and allowed of a Certaine Survey made by Philip Pocock ye Late Surveyo^r of one hundered acres of Land as by ye Certificate of Survey baring date the   of   167   will more att Large appeare:— B 402.

B 403. Ambroos Baker produced a Resurvey of Severall Lotts Lying togeather w^th: in this Towne of New Castle, by him bougt of Severall p^rsons, and ye desired ye Co^rts: approbation thereon, ye s^d: resurvey bears date ye 27th decemb 1681 and ye Lotts Lying w^th:in this Towne of New Castle as above neare ye midle there of haueing to ye South ye marked place to ye west Wood Street to ye North ye brewers Street, and to ye East ye house and Lott of Geo: Moore and Contayn[ing] in brath 343 foott & in Lengt 169 foott etc; The Same Resurvay was allowed of;—

The Co^rt: adjorned till the first Teusday in June next.

June 6th: 1682.—

B 404. Att a Court held in the Towne of New Castle in Delowar by his May^ts: Authority the 6th and 7th: dayes of June Annoq Dom: 1682.—

P^rsent
Mr. John Moll—
Mr. Gerrett Otto— } Justices
Mr. William Sempill
Captn: Edmund Cantwell   h: Sherrife

B 406. Appeared in Co^rt: Dirk Williamsen of Appoquenemen Creeke whoe produced the Laest Will and Testament of his partner and mate Dirk Laurentsen Late of appoquenemen deceased; and desired that ye Witnesses thereunto might bee Examined, and ye will prooved to the End that y^e: s^d: will might Stand good and take Effect according to Lawe;—

Whereupon hendrik Walraevens & Peter Abrink being Examined and Sworne that that will hereunder annext was the Laest will and Testament of s^d: dirk Laurens deceased and that hee ye Testator all y^etyme of makeing s^d: will was & had his full and perfect Senses Speech and Knowledge, w^ch: Justice Gerret Otto whoe alsoe had ben p^rsent in Cort: also declared; The Co^rt: therefore thougt good and doe approove and allow of ye s^d: will, and doe order y^t: the Same Shall bee Recorded The partee deceased being not any wayes Indebted; Itt was therefore ordered that Each Should Sheare ye Estate according to ye will w^th:out further Charge of takeing out Lett^rs: of administration;—

followeth ye Laest will and Testament of dirk Laurens deceased produced & prooved in Co^rt:

Copia & Translt.
In the Name of o^r: Lord Jesus Christ; has dirk Laurens (:being Cast by God into his Sike bed:) w^th: full and perfect Knowledge;—premediately Made this his Least will & Testament hereby disposing of his Estate as followeth—hee makes and bequeaths unto his Mate dirk Williams, his Land and all whatsoever is Standing thereupon, and all his horses w^ch: are his owne w^ch: I the s^d: dirk Laurens doe hereby Give and bequeath unto ye s^d: dirk Williamson; And as for ye Cattle and hoggs w^ch: are myne owne; hee Gives and bequeaths them unto his brother huybert Laurens and to his Sister Grietie' Each ye halfe, and this is my Laest Will and Testament Given under my hand & Seale this 27th: of aprill 1682 att appoquenemen in ye p^rsence of the undernamed wittneses;—

As Wittnesses in ye Margent	(was Subscrybed)
(Signed)	of
Gerret Otto—	The mark × Dirk L S
hendrik Walraevens—	Laurenson
Peter Abrinck—	

June 6th: 1682.—
Upon ye Severall Peticons of the hereafter named p^rsons; B 408. The Co^rt: haue Granted Every of them ye Quantitys of Land hereafter named to take ye same up, provyded itt bee Cleare Land and that they and Every of them doe Seate and Improove ye same according to Lawe and the Governo^rs: Regulacons
    Granted to take up to—
Samuell Land 300 acres of Land—
Gerrett Ott Roelof Andries hans hanson Adam Pieters John Walker Junr: dirk Williams & Rich: hudden granted the Mill Land 200 acr: for to build a water Mill on where ye former was begun w^th: Inclusion of Caspar herman and other neigbours if they will haue a Sheare therein;—
William Croesie (als) Lorayne a Lott being a Slipe of Land w^th:in this Towne next to Gysberts Land:—

hendrik doll 100 acr: of Land:
Justa Andries 400 acr: of Land—
John Mathiass one Lott in Towne—
Pieter Johnso 150 acres of Land
Sampson and Richard atkins 400 acr: of Land
Gyles Barrott Masson 300 acr: of Land
George Moore. ye Carpend^r 300 acr: of Land

Upon ye Peticon of John Watkins & Charl. Rumsey ye Co^{rt}: doe Grant them to Resurvey their Land bougt of Jonas Erskin according to Pattent and ye Surv^r: hereby ordered to Resurvey ye same:—

B 244. The Co^{rt}: adjorned till tomorrow ye 7 Sep^t:

June ye 7th: 1682.—

B 409. The Co^{rt}: have nominated and appointed M^r. Caspares herman & M^r: John Walker apraizers to appraize the Estate of Even Salisburry deceased they to bee Sworne by one of ye Justices & to make a true returne of their s^d: appraizm^t: according to Lawe;

B 411. The Co^{rt}: did this day nominate & appoint Gerret Otto to bee administrato^r: to administ^r: upon ye Estate goods and Chattles of Philip Teunisse, Laete of this County deceased; hee to act therein and Give a Just and true accompt thereof according to Lawe:—

B 411. John Walker Junior of appoquenemen this day produced an Acct^t: in Co^{rt}: whereby it appeared that he had paid unto William Philips the husband whoe married . . . . ye daughter in Lawe of John Siericx deceased & Wybregh his his wyfe, ye sume of 795 gilders w^{ch}: s^d: acc^t: was by him ye s^d: Philips owned in Co^{rt}: and for ye remaining 362 gilders yet due to ye s^d: Philips upon ye acc^t: of his s^d: wyfes Portion from hur s^d: father in Lawe John Sierix deceased; Itt was agreed on by the partees & ordered by the Co^{rt}: that ye Just halfe thereof Should bee paid to his s^d: wyfe & ye other halfe unto Will Philips himselfe; and out of Will: Philips halfe s^d: Philips ordered John Walker in ye p^{r}sence of ye Co^{rt}: to pay doctor followeth ye Laest will and Testament of dirk Laurens deceased produced & prooved in Co^{rt}:

Copia & Translt.

In the Name of o^r: Lord Jesus Christ; has dirk Laurens (:being Cast by God into his Sike bed:) wth: full and perfect Knowledge;—premediately Made this his Least will & Testament hereby disposing of his Estate as followeth—hee makes and bequeaths unto his Mate dirk Williams, his Land and all whatsoever is Standing thereupon, and all his horses w^{ch}: are his owne w^{ch}: I the s^d: dirk Laurens doe hereby Give and bequeath unto ye s^d: dirk Williamson; And as for ye Cattle and hoggs w^{ch}: are myne owne; hee Gives and bequeaths them unto his brother huybert Laurens and to his Sister Grietie Each y^e halfe, and this is my Laest Will and Testament Given under my hand & Seale this 27th: of aprill 1682 att appoquenemen in y^e p^{r}sence of the undernamed wittneses;—

As Wittnesses in y^e Margent   (was Subscrybed)
  (Signed)   of
Gerret Otto—   The mark $\times$ Dirk   L S
hendrik Walraevens—   Laurenson
Peter Abrinck—

June 6th: 1682.—

Upon y^e Severall Peticons of the hereafter named p^{r}sons; The Co^{rt}: haue Granted Every of them y^e Quantitys of Land hereafter named to take y^e same up, provyded itt bee Cleare Land and that they and Every of them doe Seate and Improove ye same according to Lawe and the Governo^{rs}: Regulacons

B 408.

   Granted to take up to—

Samuell Land 300 acres of Land—

Gerrett Ott Roelof Andries hans hanson Adam Pieters John Walker Junr: dirk Williams & Rich: hudden granted the Mill Land 200 acr: for to build a water Mill on where ye former was begun wth: Inclusion of Caspar herman and other neigbours if they will haue a Sheare therein;—

William Croesie (als) Lorayne a Lott being a Slipe of Land wth:in this Towne next to Gysberts Land :—

hendrik doll 100 acr: of Land:
Justa Andries 400 acr: of Land—
John Mathiass one Lott in Towne—
Pieter Johnso 150 acres of Land
Sampson and Richard atkins 400 acr: of Land
Gyles Barrott Masson 300 acr: of Land
George Moore. ye Carpend^r 300 acr: of Land

Upon ye Peticon of John Watkins & Charl. Rumsey ye Co^{rt}: doe Grant them to Resurvey their Land bougt of Jonas Erskin according to Pattent and ye Surv^r: hereby ordered to Resurvey ye same:—

B 244. The Co^{rt}: adjorned till tomorrow ye 7 Sep^t:

June ye 7th: 1682.—

B 409. The Co^{rt}: have nominated and appointed M^r. Caspares herman & M^r: John Walker apraizers to appraize the Estate of Even Salisburry deceased they to bee Sworne by one of ye Justices & to make atrue returne of their s^d: appraizm^t: according to Lawe;

The Co^{rt}: did this day nominate & appoint Gerret Otto to bee administrato^r: to administ^r: upon ye Estate goods and
B 411. Chattles of Philip Teunisse, Laete of this County deceased; hee to act therein and Give a Just and true accompt thereof according to Lawe:—

John Walker Junior of appoquenemen this day produced an Acct^t: in Co^{rt}: whereby it appeared that he had paid unto William Philips the husband whoe married . . . . ye daughter in
B 411. Lawe of John Siericx deceased & Wybregh his his wyfe, ye sume of 795 gilders w^{ch}: s^d: acc^t: was by him ye s^d: Philips owned in Co^{rt}: and for ye remaining 362 gilders yet due to ye s^d: Philips upon ye acc^t: of his s^d: wyfes Portion from hur s^d: father in Lawe John Sierix deceased; Itt was agreed on by the partees & ordered by the Co^{rt}: that ye Just halfe thereof Should bee paid to his s^d: wyfe & ye other halfe unto Will Philips himselfe; and out of Will: Philips halfe s^d: Philips ordered John Walker in ye p^{r}sence of ye Co^{rt}: to pay doctor

Spry one hundred Gilders next faall—the Whole Acct^t: is as followeth Viz^t:

Will Philipps &c:—

D^r:—
To John Walker for ye following perticulars paid viz:

	gild^{rs}:
1 Cowe & Calfe	" 200:
1 Coat & Cassiag for his wyfe	" 100:
1 bed 1 pot 1 Sowe & a boare	" 100:
to John hayly p^d for him....	" 10:
1 p^r Shoes for his wyfe......	" 10:
to his bill to ye Surv^r: for £2: 5:s or	" 90:
to Eph: herman by acc^t:.....	" 127:
2 Months dyet for his girle formerly	" 20:
wintering above	" 20:
dyet of himselfe & girle now Laest 5 w̄:	" 60:
p^d. henry Grubb	" 52:
1 pr: Shoes for his wyfe from h:Grub	" 16:
nayles to finish his house 3 ℔	" 4:
	g 819
deducted for 2 weekes dyet & Charg^d:	" 24:
	g 795:

Cred^r:
for his wyves portion of hur father in Lawe John Siericx deceased as p^r:

	gild^{rs}:	
ye records may apeare	1175:	**1681.**
deducted 18 gild^{rs}: for y^e: Charges of appraizm^t:	18:	
rest g	1157::	
paid as in debet	795:	
remains g	362	

½ of this for Philips 181 gilder Each deducted 100 gild^{rs}: for Spry rest for Philips his halfe from John walker 81 gild^{rs}:—

This day apeared in Co^{rt}: Roelfe Andries of appoquenemen Creeke whoe then & there did aknowledge to haue bargained Sould alienated Enfeofed Transported and made ouer unto Huybert Lourentsen his heirs and assignes for Ever y^e: one Just halfe of a Certaine Pattent from Governo^r: Ed̄m: Andros bearing date ye 25th of march 1676 Granted unto Caspares Herman for 330 acres of Land and Called ye good neighbourhood, Lying and being on y^e: west syde of Delowar River, and on ye north East syde of S^t: Augustines Creeke, butted and bunded as by s^d: Pattent may more att Large apear; w^{ch}: s^d: Land was Sence to witt on ye first day of march 1679, Sould

B 412.

& made ouer by the s^d: Caspares herman unto Jan Biske, Marten Gerritzen and Mathias Mathiass de vos as by ye Assignm^t: on y^e: bake of s^d: Pattent may more att Large appeare and Mathias Mathiassen did afterwards Sell and make ouer his Right and Intrest therein unto Jan Biske and Marten Gerritzen aforenamed Soe that they the s^d: Jan Biske & Marten Gerritz became Invested Equally Conserned in all ye Land in ye s^d: Pattent; Sence w^{ch}: Marten Gerritze did sell and alien all his Right Tytle and Intrest of ye Just halfe of all ye Land in ye said Pattent, unto Poelof Andries first abovement Soo that hee ye s^d. Roelf did this day Sell alien and make ouer unto ye s^d: huybert Lourens his heirs and assignes, all his Right Tytle & Intrest to ye one halfe of all ye s^d: Land and Pattent, and aknowledged to haue received full Sattisfaction to Content for the Same;

B 413.
Grietie Siericx this day produced an order upon a Peticon: from Governo^r: Edmund Andros about a Certain peece of Land Lying & being neare ye Paerden hoek, formerly bougt by M^r: Will: Tom deceased, but noe sattisfaction made nor Conveigance given; and Captn: Edmund Cantwell being asked in Co^{rt}: did acquite any Clayme hee has as administrato^r: of ye Estate of M^r: Will: Tom had thereon, Itt was therefore by the Co^{rt}: ordered; that Shee Should, bee reposest of y^{e}s^d: Land and appurtenances according to y^e: Governo^{rs}: orders;—

The Co^{rt}: adjorned till ye 1st Teusday of August next, (noe Sooner) by reason of the harvest;—

August ye 3d: 1682. The Magestrates thougt good to adjorne the Co^{rt} Sitting till ye first Teuesday of ye month of Septemb^r: next;—

Sept^r: 5th: 1682.—

B 415.
Att a Co^{rt}: held in the Towne of New Castle by his May^{ties}: Authority Septemb^r: ye 5th & 6th: 1682.—

P^{r}sent.
M^r. John Moll—
M^r. Peter Alrichs—
M^r. Gerret Otto— } Justices
M^r. Joh: D'haes—
M^r: Will: Sempell—

Captn: Edm: Cantwell h: Sherrife

Upon Severall Peticons of ye hereafter named P^rsons the
Co^rt: haue Granted them to take up w^th:in this Co^orts: Jurisdiction, ye quantitys of Land hereannex Exprest the s^d: Land to bee cleare of former Grants or Incumberances and is to bee Seated and Improoved according to Lawe & the Governo^rs: Regulations:—

Granted to take up to—
John hermsen 500 acres of Land—
Andrew Tilly 200 acres of Land—
John Mathiassen 200 acres of Land—
Richard Smith 400 acres of Land—
Jonas arskin 200 acres of Land—
John Wilkinson & Benit Starr 300 acr: of Land
John Nummersen 100 acres of Land—
Joseph Barnes 200 acres of Land—
Isacq Sauoy 200 acres of Land—
John Grubb 200 acres of Land—
Dauid hendrix 200 acres of Land—
Thomas Bell 200 acr: of Land—
William Skart 200 acr: of Land—
John Darby 400 acr: of Land—
Robberd Parke 400 acr: of Land—
John Smith 200 acr: of Land—
Joseph Cookson 200 acr: of Land—
Joseph Moore 100 acr: of Land
John Smith of Whyt Clayes Creeke 200 acr: of Land—
Anthony Wallis 150 acr: of Land—
Coenraet Constantinus 150 acr: of Land—
hendrik Gerritzen 150 acr: of Land—
Gyles Barrot 100 acr: of Land—
Edmund Linsy 200 acr: of Land—

James William
Gyles Barrott—
John Cann—
Eldert Egberts forsben
} Each of these 4 p^rsons Granted a Lott of Ground in this Towne—

James Taylor 400 acr: of Land
Pieter Claassen 200 acr: of Land and one Lott in Towne

henry Wattkinson 200 acr: of Land
John Staalcop—
Samuel Peters— } 200 acr: of Land betweene them three
Andries Staalcop—

Sept^r: 5th: 1682.—

B 420. Apeared in Co^{rt}: John Wattkins of Christina Creeke Sawyer, whoe then & there did aknowledge Confesesse and declare, to make ouer Sell alien & Transferr, unto John Can of ye Towne of New Castle his heirs and assignes for ever (:according to a Certaine deed, of Conveigance & alienation, from under ye hand & Seale of him ye s^d: John Watkins bearing date y^e: 11th: day of february 168½. Now also by him ye s^d: Watkins produced and aknowledged in full Co^{rt}: :) a Certaine parcell or tract of Land of twoo hundred acres Lying and being on ye westsyde of delowar River nigh unto ye Upper End of Bread and Cheese Island in Christina Creeke afores^d: and on a brainch thereof called whyt Clayes Creeke w^{ch}: divydeth this from ye Land formerly belonging unto John Edmunds; beginning att a Corn^r: marked Popler standing by the Creeke Syde in apeece of Lowe Land night unto ye upper End of bread & Cheese Island and soe for Lenght & breath according to ye Pattent, Soe that this aboves^d: twoo hundred acres is ye Lower most part of a Certaine p^{r}cell of Land of 570 acres Granted unto Charles Rumsey and walraeven Jansen by a Pattent from Governo^r: Edmond Andros bearing date y^e: 25th: of March 1676 and ye s^d: John Wattkins did aknowledge to haue Received full Sattisfaction from ye s^d: John Cann for the same to Content—

Sept^r: 5th: 1682.—

B 421. Apeared in Co^{rt}: Charles Rumsey of Cristina Creeke in Delowar River whoe then and there did aknowledge Confesse and declare to Sell alien Transferr and make ouer unto Samuell Berker also of Christina Creeke in Delowar River his heirs and assignes for Ever (:according to a Certaine deed of Conveigance & alienation from under y^e hand and Seale of him

y^e s^d: Charl: Rumsey & Catherin his wyfe bearing date y^e 26th day of Jannuary 16$\frac{78}{79}$, Now also by him y^e s^d: Charles Rumsey produced and aknowledged in full Co^{rt}: :) a Certaine parcell of Land of one hundred acres, being part of a larger tract of 570 acres, Granted unto y^e s^d: Charles Rumsey and Walraeven Jansen by a Pattent from y^e: Right hon^{rble}: Governo^r: S^r: Edmund Andros bearing date 25th of March 1676, and Sence by s^d: Walraeven Jansen made ouer whole unto Charl: Rumsey as by the assignm^t: on ye bake of ye s^d: Pattent bearing date y^e: 24th: day of May 1679 may more at Large appeare The afores^d: one hundered Acres hereby made Ouer being Scituated and Lying in whyte Clayes Creeke in Cristina afores^d: and is ye next a^{l}nd adjoyning to 200 acres also by him y^e: s^d. Charl: Rumsey made ouer unto John Watkins Soe that the s^d: 100 acre, by these p^{r}sents sould and alienated as afores^d: bounds upon y^e: 200 acres of Land of John Watkins on ye Lower or East Syde, and on ye west or upper Side upon ye Land and Plantation of him ye s^d: Charles w^{ch}: hee hath Sould unto M^r: John Moll of New Castle; as by ye first aforementioned deed bearing date as above May more att Large appeare; and ye s^d: Charles Rumsey did also aknowledge to haue Received full Sattisfaction to Content from ye s^d: Samuell Barker for ye Same;—

Sept^r: 5th: 1682.—

Appeared in Co^{rt}: Justa Andries of the Towne of New Castle Inholder whoe then & there did declare to Cancell disanull & to all intents & purposes to make Void a Certaine deed and Conveigance of 4 acres of Ground wth:in this Towne of New Castle, Sould and made ouer unto him by Jonas Arskin ye son & heire of John Arkin deceased, y^e: 2^d: of may Laest past, delivering all his Right Tytle and Intrest bake againe unto the s^d: Jonas Arskin wth:out any Reservation   B

Apeared in Co^{rt}: Jonas Arskin ye son & heir of John Arskin deceased; togeather wth: his Mother Jeane ye widdow & Relict of ye s^d: John Arskin deceased, whoe then & there aknowl-   B 423.

edged a Certaine deed & assignm^t: upon ye bake of a Pattent from Governo^r: francis Louelace for y^e: Transferring and makeing ouer unto John Moll of y^e: Towne of New Castle his heirs and assignes for Ever a Certaine parcell or small peece of Land first Granted by S^r: Robberd Carr unto John arskin Contain about Six acres mentioned at Large in ye s^d: Pattent, bounded by ye East wth: Gerrit Gerritsen to ye North ye high way & to ye west wth: that w^{ch}: was formerly Reynier Vander Coelens wth: in this Towne of New Castle, only Reserving and Excepting out of ye same Six acres of Land fower Erves or Lotts of Ground next to ye Land of Gerrit Gerritson, w^{ch}: is made ouer unto Joh: D'haes & Eph: herman Executo^{rs}: of ye Estate of Marten Roosemond deceased also mentioned att Large on ye bake of ye s^d: Pattent Soe that all ye remaining part of ye s^d: Six acres Let there bee more or Lesse, is Sould & made ouer unto ye s^d: John Moll, as by the s^d: assignm^t: on ye bake of ye s^d: Pattent bearing date ye 26th: of august 1682, under ye hands and Seales of ye s^d: Jonas Arskin & Jeane his Mother May more att Large appear—

B 425. Apeared n Co^{rt}: John Can of this Towne of New Castle and Mary his wyfe whoe then & there did aknowledge & Confesse to haue bargained Sould Transported and made ouer unto Joseph Barnes of whyte Clayes Creeke his heirs and assignes for Ever (:according to a Certaine deed of Conveigance from under ye hand and Seale of them ye s^d: John Can and Mary his wyfe bearing date ye 5th: day of Sepemb^r: 1682. now also by them ye s^d: John & Mary produced and aknowledged in full Court:) a Certaine parcell or peece of Land Lying and being in ye whyte Clayes Creeke in Cristina, beginning from a marked poplar Standing in a Little Valley and a Little nould thereby w^{ch}: Lyeth on ye weft syde of ye Plantation of Late by Charles Rumsey Sould unto M^r. John Moll, and Soe along ye maine run of ye Creeke unto the Land of John Nummersen Containing in breath along ye s^d: Creeke Syde 260 Yards and Soe the Same breath up for Lengt into ye woods along ye Land of John Numers aforenamed; This aboves^d:

parcell or peece of Land being ye uppermost part or Slipe of a Certaine parcell or tract of Land of 570 acres Granted unto Charles Rumsey and Walraven Johnson by a Pattent from Governo^r Edm̃: Andros bearing date ye 25th: March 1676 togeather w^th: a dwelling house and other appurtenances by him ye s^d: J^o: Can built thereon; as by ye first abov^d: deed respect thereunto being had may more att Large appeare, and they ye s^d: John Can & Mary his wyfe did aknowledge to haue received full Sattisfaction to Content for ye same,—

Appeared in Co^rt: Saumell Barker togeath^r: with agnis his B 426. wyfe, whoe then and there did aknowledge Confesse and declare to haue bargianed Sould aliened Enfeofed Transported and made ouer unto John Cann of this Towne of New Castle his heirs and assignes for Ever (:according to a Certaine deed and Conveigance from under ye hands and Seales of them y^e: said Samuell Berker & agnis his wyfe bearing date y^e: 28th of July 1682: Now also by them ye s^d: Samuell Barker produced and aknowledged in full Co^rt: :) a Certaine parcell of Land of one hundred acres, Lying and being in whyte Clayes Creeke, in Cristina; Itt being all and ye same 100 ac̅r̅: of Land w^ch: hee y^e: Samuell Barker bougt of Charl: Rumsey and was aknowledged in this Co^rt: of New Castle by Charles Rumsey this 5th of ye Instant month of Septemb^r: as by this Records herebefore will appeare, togeather w^th: all and Singular y^e: Plantation housing fencing & all other Improovem^t: of him ye s^d: Samuel Barker thereupon; and they the s^d: Samuel & agnis did aknowledge and Confesse to haue received full Sattisfaction & Content from ye s^d: John Can for the Same; as by the aboves^d: deed bearing date as above more att Large may appeare—

Septemb^r: ye 6th. 1682.—

Johannes D'haes and Ephraim herman as Executo^rs: of ye B 427. Laest will & Testament of Martin Roosemond deceased did this day in Co^rt: aknowledge the makeing ouer of a Certaine house & Lott of ground w^th:in this Towne of New Castle unto

John Can his heirs and assignes for Ever, as by a deed under the hands & Seales of them ye s^d: Johannes & Ephraim bearing date the 6th: of Septemb^r: 1682 may more att Large appear;

B 428. Apeared in Co^{rt}: John Nommersen of Whyte Clayes Creeke Planter whoe then and there aknowledged a deed by him Signed Sealed and delivered, for the Transporting and makeing ouer unto Joseph Barnes also of ye Whyte Clay Creeke his heirs and assignes for Ever of a Certaine parcell or peece of Land being part of a Pattent Granted by Governo^r: Edmund Andros unto him ye s^d: John Nomers ye 25th: of March 1676 y^e: s^d: Land Lying on ye North syde of whyte clayes Creeke beginning att a Marked poplar att ye syde of ye maine Run, being a Corner tree of ye Land of Charl: Rumsey and Walraeven Jansen d'vos, and up by their Lyne N:W: 232 perches to a marked whyte oake & from y^e: s^d: whyte oake S: W: 158 perches by a Lyne of marked trees to a Corner marked whyte oake Standing on a high bank att the North Syde of ye Creeke; of w^{ch}: s^d: Land att ye north Syde of ye Creeke or Run ye s^d: John Nummers doth hereby Sell and make ouer unto Joseph Barnes the one Just halfe part thereof and noe more as for ye remaining halfe part of the Northsyde of ye Creeke ye same is Sould unto Thomas Woollaston, and the rest of ye Land of ye s^d: Pattent on ye South Syde of ye Creeke ye s^d: John Nomers reserves for himselfe, as by ye s^d: deed bearing date ye 5th: day of Septemb^r: 1682 may more att Large appeare—

B 429. The Co^{rt}: adjorned till the first Teusday of ye month of octob^r: next;—

Octob: 3^d: 1682.—

B 430. Att a Co^{rt}: held wth:in the Towne of New Castle by his May^{ties}: Authority October, the 3^d: 1682.—

P'rsent.   M^r. John Moll—
          M^r. Joh: D'haes—   } Justices
          M^r. Will: Sempill
          Captn Edmund Cantwell   h: Sherrife

Upon the Severall Peticons of the hereunder named p'rsons B 431.
the Co^{rt}: Granted unto Each of them to take up wth:in this
County, the Severall quantityes of Land, hereannex Exprest,
the s^d: Land to bee not Granted taken up or Improoved before
by others, and ye severall peticon^{rs}: seating and Improoveing y^e
same according to Lawe & Regulations;—

Granted to take upto;—
John Manday 300 acres of Land—
Isacq Warner & Edward Eglinton Each 200 acres
George Andrews 200 acres—
hans Coderus Cooper 200 acres—
John Radford 200 acres
Broer Sinnexen 100 acres—
Carsten Lourensen 200 acres—
Hendrick Vanden Burgh 400 acres—
Garrardus Wessells—300 acr:—
Thom,: harris & William Osborne 200 acr:
William Ridger 200 acres;—
Hendrik Lemmens 300 acres—
Dirk and Hendrik huyberts Each 200 acr:

Octob^r. 3^d. 1682.—

Upon the Peticon of John Staalcop, Itt was ordered that B 433.
hee Should forthwth: Seate and Improove his Land formerly
by him taken up and Surveyed by Walter Wharton called
Southern Land according to Lawe & regulacons, otherwayes
hee to forfeit ye Same, and those as now haue Surveyed y^e
Same, are to quit itt;—

Appeared in Court John Taylor of appoquenem, whoe ak- B 434.
nowledged and declared to haue bargained Sold aliened Transported and made ouer unto Thomas Snowding also of appo-

quenem Creeke Planter his heirs & assignes for Ever (:according to a Certaine deed of Conveigance from under the hand and Seale of him ye s^d: John Taylor bearing date ye 2^d: of octob^r: 1682; now also by him produced and aknowledged in full Court:) a Certaine peece or parcell of Land Lying on ye North Syde of one of ye brainches of appoqumeme Creeke called ye drawjers Creeke, and on ye north syde of a Creeke or brainch of ye s^d: drawjers Creeke, called ye Secund drawjers Creeke, beginning at a Certaine Small run or brainch wch Lyeth above ye s^d: Taylors brainch, and Soe up northerly along the Creeke to another brainch thereof called Snowdings brainch, Soe that all the Land Lying between ye s^d: twoo brainches is hereby Sould and Made ouer Containing one hundered & Seventy acres more or Less This Land being part of a Greater Tract of 620 acres Resurveyed for John Taylor the 21th of octob^r: 1681. as by the first aforementioned deed may more att Large appeare, and the s^d: John Taylor aknowledged to haue Received full Sattisfact: to Content from s^d: Snowding for ye same;—

B 435.   This day appeared in open Court Hans Oelsen and helena his wife, the s^d: hans Oelsen & helena, did then and there aknowledge Confesse and declare, before ye Co^{rt}: that for and in Consideracon of a Certaine Valluable Sume of monny to them in hand paid by Morgan Druit of this River of dellowar and for other Reasons and Consideracons them thereunto mooveing, they haue Given Granted Bargained Sould allienned assigned Transported and made ouer, and by these p^{r}sents doe fully Clearly and absoluthly Give Grant Bargaine Sell allien assigne Enfeofe Transport and make ouer unto y^e s^d: Morgan Druit his heirs and assignes a Certaine peece or parcell of Land Scituate and Lying on y^e West Syde of this River of Delowar in y^e bougt above y^e Verdity=hook haueing to y^e west y^e boght Kill and to the East a Small Gut or Run w^{ch}: parts this from y^e Land whereon formerly Oele Coeckoe Lived Containing by Estimation about 100 acres of Land, togeather wth: all & Singular y^e houses fences plantation and other the appurtenances thereupon; To haue and to hold the s^d: peece or parcell of Land Plantation and premisses wth: all and singular the appurtenances, as also all the Right Tytle and Intrest of them the s^d: hans Oelsen and helena his wyfe therein unto the s^d: Morgan druit his heirs and assignes unto the Soale and proper use and behoofe of him ye s^d: Morgan Druit his heirs and assignes for Ever;—This Land was the 4th of octob^r: 1681 made ouer unto hans Oelsen by Evert Aldrets as by this Records ye same date will appear;—

The Co^{rt}:adjorned till the first Teusday of ye month of Nov^r: next— B 436.

Octob^r: the 23^d: 1682. Did Justice Johannes Dehaes and Justice Will: Sempill upon ye Earnest Request of Will: Geuest, Grant unto him ye s^d: William Geuest to take up wth:in this County fower hundred acres of Land not Granted or taken up before upon Condition of p^rsent Settlem^t: as ye others,— B 437.

And also was then by them Granted unto John Mettland to take up 400 acres of Land upon Condition as above Exprest;— B 437.

Octob^r. 28th: 1682.—

On the 27th: day of october 1682; arrived before ye Towne of New Castle in Delowar from England William Penn Esqr: Propriet^{ry}: of Penliuania, whoe produced twoo Certaine deeds of feofement from ye Illustrius Prince James Duke of Yorke & Albany etc: for this Towne of New Castle and twelve myles about itt, and also for ye Twoo Lower Counties, ye whoorekills and St: Jones's; w^{ch}: s^d: deeds bore date 24 august 1682, and pursuant to the true Intent Purpose and meaning of his Roy^{ll}: highnesse in ye same deeds hee ye s^d: William Penn Received possession of ye Towne of New Castle ye 28th: of octob^r. 1682.— B 437.

Copia Vera

By the Comander in Cheefe & Councill—

Whereas his Roy^{ll}: highenessee hath ben Graciously pleased by Indenture under his hand & Seale bearing B 438.

date ye 24th: day of augus Laest past for ye Consideracon therein mentioned to Bargain, Sell Enfeofe and Confirme unto William Penn Esqr: his heirs & assignes for Ever, all that the Towne of New Castle otherwayes called Dellowar and all that tract of Land Lying w^th:in the Compasse or Circle of twelve myles about the same w^th: all Islands and ye River and Soyle thereof north of ye Southernmost part of s^d: Circle and all Rents and Services, Royalties franchizes, Duties, Jurisdiction Priviledges and Liberties thereunto belonging. And by another Indenture of ye same date for ye Consideracon: therein Lykewyse mentioned hath alsoe bargained Sold Enfoefed and Confirmed unto ye s^d. William Penn Esqr: his heirs and assignes for Ever all that tract of Land upon Delloware River and Bay beginning twelve myles South from ye Towne of New Castle otherwayes called Delloware and Extending South to ye Whoore kills otherwayes called Cape inlopen w^th: all Isles Rivers Rivulets Bayes and Inletts, Royalties, franchizes Powers Priviledges and Immunitys whatsoever, and in and by the s^d: Indentures appointed and authorized John Moll Esqr: and Ephraim herman Gent: to deliver to him ye s^d: William Penn free & actuall possession of ye premisses, as by ye s^d: Indentures here produced and Shewen to us and by us well approved of and Entred in ye Publicq Records of this Province doth and may more att Large apeare, And wee being thereby fully Sattisfied of ye s^d: William Penns Right to ye possession and Injoyment of ye premisses haue therefore thought fitt and necessary to Signify and declare the Same to You to prevent any doubt or trouble that migt arrize, and to give you o^r: thenkes for yor: good Services done in yor: severall offices and Stacons, during ye tyme you remayned under his Roy^ll: highnesse Governm^t. Expecting noe further account then that you Reddily Submit and Yeeld all due obedience & Conformity to The Powers Granted to ye s^d: William Penn in and by ye s^d: Indentures, in ye performance and Injoyment of w^ch: wee wish you all happinesse, Dated in New Yorke the 21th: day of november annoq. Dom̃: 1682.

(t' was Subscrybed)

To ye Severall Justices of the   Antho: Brockholls
Peace Magistrates and other
officers att New Castle St:
Jones Deale (Als) Whoorekills
att Dellaware or wth:in any of
ye bounds & Limits above, mentioned;—

By ord^r: in Councill
(Signed)
      John West
          Cl^r: Coun.
            Finis —— (of Book B)

Novr. 2^d: 1682.

Begins Book C

Att a Co^{rt}: Held in the Towne of New Castle upon Delloware in the Name of o^r: Soueraigne Lord Charles the 2^d: by the Grace of God of England Scotland France & Ireland King defend^r: of the Faith, and by Commission and Appointment of William Penn Esqr: Propriet^{ry} & Governo^r: of Pensilvania etc: on Thursday the 2^d: of Nouemb^r: in y^e: 35th: Yeare of his May^{ts}: Raighne Annoq Dom̃: 1682.

The R^t. Hono^{rble}: Propriet^{ry}: etc—
P^{r}sent
- Captn: Will: Markham —
- Mayo^r: Thom̃: Holms —
- M^r: William Haigh —
- M^r: John Simkock —
- M^r: Thomas Brasie —

} of The Councill —

- M^r: John Moll —
- M^r: Johannes De Haes —
- M^r: William Sempill —
- M^r: Arnoldus De Lagrange
- M^r: John Cann . . . .

} Justices of ye Peace

The Right Hono^rble: Propriet^ry: William Penn by his publicq Speech directed to y^e: Inhabitants in Genner^ll: Did in open Co^rt: declare that hee had appointed and called this Co^rt: 't Cheefly to Signify and declare unto them in a more publicq manner;—

The Propriet^ry:^s Speech wherein he declares.

First—That itt had Graciously pleased ye Illustrious Prince James Duke of Yorke and albany etc: to Give & Grant Unto him this Towne of New Castle & itts p^rcincts wth y^e: County of St: Jones's and Whoorekills downwards And that therefore hee was Resolued for the Incouragem^t: of all ye Inhabitants thereof and for y^e: Better Settlement quiet and Sattisfaction of them, first to State and Settle their Lands, & possessions, and therefore hee willed and desired them to bring in att y^e: next Court to bee held w^th :in this Towne of New Castle all their Pattents Surveys Grants and Claymes, w^ch: they had to their Lands Livings Tennements & Possessions promising to a certaine adjust and Confirme not only those as had a Sufficient Tytle & Right, but also those as yett wanted a Certaine Right to ye same: Soe far forth as Equity Justice and Reason could Requiere;—

1: the Dukes feoffment of N: Castle etc unto him.—

2dly: that for ye quiet of y^e: Inhabit^ts: hee intended to Settle their Lands

and therefore willed y^m: to bring in View their Pattents Surveys etc

and promises to Confirme all as had a good Tytle & also those as wanted a tytle etc

2dly: The Propriet^ry: Recommended itt to ye Magistrates and desired them, to take inspection, View and Looke ouer their Towne plott, to See and find out what vacant Roome may bee found therein for ye accommodating & settling of New Commers Traeders and handicrafts men, therein, and for ye Gener^ll: & publicq good and Incouradgem^t: of ye Place and parts of w^ch: hee desired y^t: an Account might be Given him;—

3^d a Recommendat: to y^e: Justices to Looke ouer their Towne plot for room for New Commers

3ᵈˡʸ That if any persons had requests or Peticons to pʳsent unto him, hee willed them to doe itt for an answer att yᵉ next Coʳᵗ: day;—

4ᵗʰˡʸ: any hauing requests to pʳsent them—

4ᵗʰˡʸ: In Regard that for want of a pʳsent assembly there are not as yett fitting Lawes Regulacons orders and by lawes for yᵉ Contry provyded Hee yᵉ Proprietʳʸ: therefore recommended the magistrates in yᵉ Interim to follow and take the Lawes of his Royˡˡ: highnesse provyded for the Province of New Yorke for their Guyde Soe farr Forth as they are Consistent and not Repugnant to yᵉ: Lawes of England assuring yᵉ Inhabitants of this and the other twoo Counties downwards that they Should haue and Injoy full Equall, and yᵉ same Priveledges wᵗʰ: those of those of yᵉ Province of Pensiluania, and that for the future they Should bee Governed by Such Lawes and orders as they themselves by their deputys and Representatiues Should Consent to, and that hee would call an assembly for yᵉ purpose as soon as Conveniently might bee: etc;

The Migistrates Recommended to observe yᵉ dukes Lawes till an assembly should provyde new ones

6: The Proprietʳʸ: assures yᵉ Inhabitants that they shall Injoy Equall Priviledges wᵗʰ: Pensilvania—

and yᵗ: henceforth to bee Governed by Lawes of yᵉ assemblies owne making

The Coʳᵗ: adjorned till yᵉ first Teusday of yᵉ: Month of decembʳ. next;—

Novⁿ. 9ᵗʰ: 1682.

Att a Meeting of the Deptʸ. Governʳ: and Justices in yᵉ Towne of New Castle Novembʳ: yᵉ: 9ᵗʰ: 1682.—

Pʳsent.

Captⁿ: William Markham Deputʸ: Govʳ:
Mʳ: John Moll—
Mʳ: Wiꞁꞁ: Sempill—
Mʳ: Arnoldus D'Lagrange
Mʳ: John Cann—
} Justices—

C 7.

a Comission for ye Keeping of a market

Upon a Commission directed by the Right Hono^rble: Propriet^ry: to y^e: Deputy Gouerno^r: and Court touching the keeping of a weekly Constant Market w^th:in this Towne of New Castle etc; Itt was this day Resolued, by ye Dept^y: Govr.

and by ye Magistrates Resolued upon Satturday to bee the Market day—

& Justices aboves^d:, that Satturday being the 18th: day of this Instant month of Novemb^r: Shall bee ye first Marked day and Soe Every Satturday following, Shall from henceforth bee ye Sett marked days for this Towne of New Castle & precincts; and all p^rsons Conserned are hereby desired to take notice hereof

and y^t Sherr: cause proclamat: to bee made thereof—

and to Repair w^th: their Commoditys to to ye forte in ye marked place att p^rsent appointed for ye same, and that ye Sherrife Shall proclayme ye same to begin at 10 of ye Clocq in ye morning and Continue till 4 of ye Clocq in ye afternoone;—

1: Jannua^m: 168⅔.

Att a Court Held in the Towne of New Castle by ye Kings Authority and by Commission Received from Will Penn Esqr: Propriet^ry: etc. The first and 2^d: dayes of ye Elleventh month called Jannuary Annoq Dom̄: 168⅔.

C 8.

P^rsent

The R^t: Hono^rble: Propriet^ry: etc—
Captn: William Markham
M^r: John Moll—
M^r: Arnoldus DeLagrange
M^r: John Cann—
M^r: James Walliam—
} Justices

Captn: Edmund Cantwell high Sherrife—

The Laest will of Will Sempil produced in Co^rt:

The Laest will and Testament of William Sempill Late of New Castle deceased was produced in Co^rt: The Witnesses thereunto were Examined Viz^t:—

and proved in C0^{rt}:   John Biske and Jonas Arskin doe
by 2 wittnesses,— Solomly declare in C0^{rt}: that they were personally P^{r}sent and did heare and See William Sempill Declare, Signe and Seale this as his Laest will and Testament;—

Administrac͞on Granted to Josyn ye widdow and ye will ordered to bee Recorded wth: a momento about ye word Executo^{rs}:
    Itt was this day by ye C0^{rt}: ordered C 9. that ye aboves^d: Will Should bee recorded, and y^t: Administration bee Granted to Josyn ye Widdow of s^d: William Sempill deceased wth: this momento that ye word (Executors touching James Walliam & Samuel Land) mentioned in ye s^d: will is and Shall bee understood only as overseers & assistants to ye widdow in ye p^{r}formance of hur said husbands Will; The widlow makeing appeare y^t: that was ye Intent and meaning of hur s^d: deceased husband

    Followeth the Laest will and Testament of Wm: Sempil

Will: Sempills Will Recorded Verbatim
    In the Name of God amen this 11th: day of december in ye Yeare of o^r: Lord God 1682. I:William Sempill Inhabitant of New Castle upon deloware River being Sick and weake in Boddy but of perfect mind & memory thenkes be Given unto God, Therefore calling unto minde the mortality of my Boddy and knowing that itt is appointed for all men once to dye, Doe make and ordayne this my Laest will and Testament in manner and forme following   That is to say first and Principally I: give my Soule into The Hands of God and Gaue itt mee and for my boddy I: commend itt to y^e: Earth, to bee burried in decent Christian manner, nothing butt att ye Genner^{ll}: Resurection I: shall Receave ye same againe by ye mighty power of God, And as touching Such worldly goods as itt hath bin pleased God to blesse mee in this Lyfe tyme wth: I: Give devyse bequeath and dispose the Same in manner & forme following Viz^t: first I: give devyse and bequeath unto my dearly beloved wyfe Josyn Sempill and my Little daughter Margaret wth: Rest of my wyfes Children all my p^{r}sonall Estate as goods and Chattles & moveables to bee Equally divyded and distributed to my wyfe and daughter margret and y^e: rest

of my wyves Children to use occupy and dispose of as Shee my
said wyfe Shall See neccessary and Convenient for ye use of
my s^d: wyfe and daughter Margaret and my wyves Children,
only Excepted I: doe devyse and bequeath & Give unto my
Little daughter Margaret all my Estate in Christina Creeke or
upon a brainch of ye said Creeke boath Reall & personall
moveables and imovables goods and Chattles wth: all y^e: Increase to ye Soale and proper use and behoofe of she my said
daugter Margaret itt being my will that first of all my wyfe
Josyn Sempill puts on and upon y^e: Plantation in Christina
or brainch of ye s^d: Creeke for ye use of my daughter Margaret Soe manny Cowes Sowes and other CHattell and What
Els I:am allreaddy obliged to put upon ye afores^d: Plantation
all being for ye Soale and proper use and behoofe of my
daughter Margret, until Shee Marryeth or Comes of adge
the Increase to bee att ye disposall of my wyfe Soe Long as
She remaines a widdow provyded She my wyfe Keepes ye old
Stoke good, and in ye next place, if itt please God to call mee
out of this world I: doe ordaine Constitute and appoint my
beloved friends M^r. James Walliam & Samuell Land of the
Towne of New Castle, to bee Executo^{rs}: of what worldly
Estate I shall Leave behind mee, and to use the best of their
Indeauors for ye bennefitt of my wyfe my daughter Margret
and my wyves Children, with all that my wyfe Josyn Sempill
pay all Just debts due from mee, to others, and that Shee Receive all debts due from others to mee, and I: doe hereby
utterly disallow Revoake & Annull all and Every other former
Testaments wills, Legacies, bequeaths Executo^{rs}: by me in any
wise before this tyme named willed or bequeathed, Ratifying
and Confirming this and none other to bee my Laest will &
Testament in wittnesse whereof I haue hereunto Sett my hand
& Seale the day & Yeare above writtn—

      (& was Subscrybed)
        Will: Sempell (LS)

Signed Sealed published
pronounced declared by
ye s^d: William Sempill

as his Laest will & Testament in yᵉ Presence of
us :—
 J : D'haes
 Jan Bisck—

Primo Jannuʳᵒ : 168⅔.

<small>A Peticon Entred by yᵉ Children of Mathias Eskelson agˢᵗ: their Eldʳ: brother about their fathers Land—Swanwyk, etc—</small>
 Upon the Peticon of Symon Eskelson John Eskelson, & Margaret Eskelson Children of Mathias Eskelson deceased, desiering to haue a Sheare and part of their fathers Land now possessed by their Elder brother Peter Eskelson of

C 11.

<small>The Coʳᵗˢ order and determination on yᵉ above Peticon.</small>
 Itt was ordred by the Proprietʳʸ: & Court, that Peter Eskelson Shall bring in att yᵉ net Coʳᵗ: Accompt of what he has paid & disburst on Yᵗ: accompt of his sᵈ: fathers Estate, adn how all is disposed of and that hee produce an Inventory; and itt is ordered and allowed that hee yᵉ sᵈ: Peter Eskelson as yᵉ Eldest Son Shall haue a double Portion, and all yᵉ other Children a Singell Portion according to his Royˡˡ: highnesse yᵉ duke of Yorkes Lawes, provyded for yᵉ Province of New Yorke, wᶜʰ: were here in force att yᵉ decease of yᵉ aboveˢᵈ: Mathias Eskelson;—

<small>Æmilius D'Ring by his Peticon Sues for administ: upon yᵉ Estate of his wyves father Gybert direxen deceased—</small>
 Æmilius D'Ring of yᵉ Towne of New Castle, hauing married Susanna yᵉ daughter of Gysbert Dircksen Late of this Towne deceased; apeared in Coʳᵗ: and by his Peticon, Shewed, that his aboveˢᵈ: father in Lawe by his Will made before his decease did Give all his Estate, unto his three Children, provyded that Cattalyntie his wyfe during hur naturall Lyfe Should haue hur maintainance out of yᵉ moveable Estate of yᵉ sᵈ: Gysbert and after hur decease to Returne to yᵉ sᵈ: Children; and that now yᵉ sᵈ: widdow being also deceased, yᵉ Peticoʳ therefore Craued in behalfe of yᵉ sᵈ:

C 13

Children Power to administr. upon ye sd: Estate, to ye: End ye Estate may be Secured, ye Creditors: paid and ye Children

and produce ye Will— Lookt after and thereupon produces in Cort: ye Will of ye said Gysbert

Rynier Vandr: Coelen by peticon Sues for ⅓ of ye Estate of Gysbert— Rynier Vander Coelen, ye son of Cattalyntie ye Late widdow of Gysbert dirksen deceased, appearing in Cort: did by his Peticon in ye behalfe of his Younger Brother and twoo Sisters demand one third part of all ye Estate of ye sd: Gysbert dirksen deceased; and Sayes that his

& alledges that his Mother brought in Marriadge Severll: things of Vallue— Mother at hur marriage wth: Gysbert brought in wth: hur, Several things of a Considerable Vallue;—

Em. D'Ring replyes that Shee brougt in nothing wch: hee prooves— Æmilius D' Ring pleades, that ye sd: Cattalyntie brougt in nothing wth: hur att ye time of hur sd: marriadge wch: hee prooves by a Certaine matrimoniall Contract etc:—

The Laest will & Testament of Gysbert dirksen deceased being Read in Cort: was as followeth Vizt:—

Copia & Translt: of Gisberts will;— In the name of God amen, In the Yeare of or: Lord and Sauior Jesus Christ 1682; the 3d: of december apeared before ye afternamed wittnesses, Gysbert Dirksen Inhabitant att New Castle; whoe being Sike and weake in boddy but of perfect minde and memory as outwardly did apeare and calling to minde the mortallity of menkinde and being desirous not to depart this Lyfe before hee had disposed of his worldly Estate; Therefore Recommending his Soule into ye hands of allmighty God that Gaue itt him; and his boddy ye Earth to bee decently burried and as touching Such temporal and worldly Goods as hee shall Leaue behind him; hee puts and places as his only and universall heirs, his three Childeren; named Susanna, Anna & Aeltie, of all his goods & Estate as well Immooveables as moveables; of what Kind soever and hee doth desire that his daughter Susanna Shall haue So Soon as ye Testato^r: Shall bee deceased one Cowe and a great pewter bason; and the Testator does moveover desire that his wyfe Cattalyntie Gerrits Shall remaine in full possession so Longh as Shee Shall Live, and that Shee doe bring up and maintaine his twoo under adged Children; and when Shee (:his s^d: wyfe:) Shall bee departed out of this world, then Shall his above s^d: three Children Enter upon ye whole Inheritance; and hee willeth, that his Immooveable Estate Shall not bee deminished, as also ye Cattle, of w^ch: Shee his wyfe is to haue only ye use & benefit;—

The will prooved by 3 witnesse in Co^rt: Captn. Edmund Cantwell Josyn ye widdow of Will: Sempill and Justice Arnold: De Lagrange apearing in Co^rt: doe Solemnly afirme that they heard Gysbert Dircksen deceased pronounce & declare ye above will to bee his Laest will and Testament;—

The will allowed of &   The Co^rt: upon a full hearing and due Examination of ye Case doe allow of ye above s^d: will, to stand good and doe order the Same to bee recorded; and doe allow that hee ye s^d: Emilius d' Ring

Administration Granted unto Æmil: D' Ring   Shall administer upon ye Estate of ye s^d: Gysbert dirksen in behalfe of his wyfe and ye other twoo orphants and that hee Exhibit and bring in a true Inventory to bee recorded and give Security for his due administration according to Lawe;—

Followeth the Coppy of ye matrimoniall Contract made between Gysbert Dircksen & Cattalyntie Gerritz this day produced in Co^rt: by Emilius D' Ring;—

Copia & Translaet of Gisberts matrimonial Contract; Recorded.   In the Name of God Amen in the Yeare C 14. of o^r: Lord and Sauior Jesus Christ 1678; in ye 30th Yeare of ye Raighne of his most Roy^ll: May^tie: Charles ye 2^d: King of Great Brittaine etc the 14th: day of august, appeared before ye afternamed witnesses Gisbert Dirksen borne att hop Emert, widdower of annettie Jans, new bridgroom, on ye one and Cattalyntie Gerritz born in the Citty of Bommell Widdow of Reyniersen Vander Coelen, being boath of them well Knowne unto us underwritten wittnesses; and Sence they the above^d: parties doe Intend in ye feare of God to Joyne themselues in Mattrimony, and for p^{r}venting of all future Inconveniencies; and to ye End that ye partees may Live peaceably and Comfortably togeather they haue mutually agreed and Consented to make this their matrimoniall Contract in manner and forme following; first that Every one Shall brng in what Estate, hee hath, and out of ye Same Each party to pay out of their s^d: proper owne Estate what debts they owe, w^{ch}: were created by their former marriadge before this date, and hee ye s^d: Bridgroom doth declare, that his Estate is worth in moveables and Immooveable goods and also in debts, in all according to appraizment & Computation ye Sume of Eight thousand Gilders of this Contry pay, and in Contra the s^d: Cattalyntic Gerritz doth declare (as is well Knowne unto us in what State hur former husband Left hur:) to bring in nothing more then y^e: Cloaths belonging to hur boddy, ye wich Shee wth: hur owne hands Sence the departure of hur s^d: husband has Earned, and Shee declares that Sence his s^d: departure Shee hath not Received one penny of his, wich Shee desires, in case any Creditor^{rs}: Should come upon hur, the Magistrates & Justices to take notice hereof and to free hur accordingly; and hee ye s^d: Bridgroom doth further declare, by these p^{r}sents, that hee will not any wyse Conserne himselfe, nor haue any thing to doe, wth: his brides former Estate; but disannuls the same wholy as to himselfe; This they declare to bee their full Intent and doe desire Justice Peter Alrichs & D'haes, as also fopp Outhout; whoe are by ye bride Chosen for hur assistants to bee wittnesses hereunto and In Confirmation thereof they haue hereunto Set thier hands In New Castle datum Utsupra:—

(:was Subscrybed by.)

In Margine Testor. Gysbert Dirksen &
(Signed) Cattalyntie Gerritz—
Peter Alrichs— In ye absence of ye Clarke
fop Outhout— Signed)
J: D'haes—
                                        fop Outhout.

Jannuar^ry: 2^d: 168⅔.

a Grant to Timothy Pead to take up 200 acr: of Land—

Upon the Peticon of Timothy Pead, desiering a Grant and order to take up w^th:in this County 200 acres of Land etc.—

The Propriet^ry: & Co^rt: Doe Grant ye Peticon^r: to take up w^th:in this County 200 acres of Land not Granted or taken up before, under Condition of Settlement;—   C 16.

a Peticon of Engeltie Vandiemen to ye Propriet^ry: for 120 acr: of Land

Engeltie ye widdow and relict of Will: Vandiemen deceased Haueing p^rsented a peticon to ye Right Hono^rble Propriet^ry: desiering an Order and Grant for to take unto possession a Certain peece of Land formerly Granted unto hur s^d: deceased husband by the dutch Governo^r: and by him then also for Sever^ll: Yeares had in Possession, and a plantation had thereon w^ch: throug casualty of fyre then was burned & ruined and Soe hath for Severall Yeares Sence Laine Vacant, ye s^d. Land Lying bake of this Towne neare ye place called ye Landerijen, Containing 60 morgan or 120 acres and is knowne to this day by ye name of Vandiemens Land etc:—   C 19.

The Propriet^rys Grant to ye s^d. Engeltie of ye same:—

The Propriet^ry: was pleased to order that itt Should be here Enterred that hee Granted ye Petition^r: ye s^d. Land as desiered;—

Grietie Siericx peticon about Land att Pardenhook

Upon the Request of Grietie Siericx Conserning a peece of Land Lying att ye Paerden hook formerly bought by M^r: Tom deceased, but noe payment made ordered that ye Peticon^r: may haue ye Land againe and that Captn: Cantwell y^e: Administ^r: of s^d: M^r. Tom doe pay ye quit rent for ye Tyme M^r. Toms & hee had itt;—   C 20.

The Co^rts: order—

George Moores Peticon ag^st: Edm: Cantw^ll: about Whartons Estate & ye CO^rt. order

Upon a Peticon and Complaint of George Moore ag^st: Edmund Cantwell administrat^r: of Walter Whartons Estate etc: Ordered that Captn: Cantwell deliver in an accompt of Whartons Estate, w^th: ye first Conveniencie—   C 22.

C 22. Lewis Dauis administ[r]. of Even Salisburry produces y[e] acc[t]. & appraizm[t] of ditt[o]. Estate er[ll]: acc[t]: of y[e] s[d]: Estate of Even Salisburry; desiring that hee y[e] Petico[nr]: might haue y[e] Plantation & Land made Sure unto him etc

Apeared in Co[rt]: Lewis Dauis administrato[r]: of y[e] Estate of Even Salisburry deceased whoe produced y[e] appraizem[t]: of y[e]: Land and plantation of y[e] s[d]: Even amounting to 25 pounds; and also a Gen-

ordred y[t]: y[e]: appraizeme[t]: bee recorded & y[t]: Lewis haue ye Land of Even Salisburry, hee makeing good the appraizement—

Itt was ordered, that y[e] s[d]: acc[t]: & appraizm[t]: Should bee recorded; and that hee y[e] s[d]: Even Sallisburry shall haue hold and Injoy the s[d]: Land & plantation

D[r]:	Even Salisburry		Credito[r]:
1681		℔ tobb:	℔ tobb
The acc[t]. To 1 Years wages recorded— To y[e] Indian Purchase		" 2500: " 200:	P[r]: assignm[t]: from Geo Beaston upon Thom Spry...... } 450
To Capt[n]: Cantwel 90 gild[rs]: at 5 sty		" 360:	P[r] y[e] plantation called Salisburry playne & y[e] Land appraized at 25 pound w[ch] makes 1000 gild[rs]. Reduced to tobb at 5 sty[rs]: p[r]. lb.... } 4450
To doct[r]. Spry for accommoda[t]: for him 53 gild[rs]: 10 sty at sty[r]: p[r]. w.. }		" 214:	
To paym[t]: for wryting & attorn fees		" 100:	
To 3 wittnesses Sworne 15 gild[rs]:		" 60:	℔ tobb: 4450
To y[e] funer[ll]: Charges.......		" 800:	
By my Ingagemt: for him to Hend: v:Burgh 83 Gild[rs]..		" 332:	
To 4 Yeares q[t]: rent at 3 Bush p[r]. Yeare yet to pay......		" 600:	
To y[e] Clr: fees as p[r]: acc[t]: 20s or		" 130:	
To a bill paid M[r]. Wooleston by Mist[rs]: Young on Evens acc[t]:		" 400:	
	℔ tobb:	5696:	

A Grant to Arnold: De Lagrange for a Resurvey of Veuren hook Land—	Upon the Request of Arnold D'Lagrange, the Propriet^ry Granted him Liberty to make a Resurvey upon his Land att Veuren hook;—	C 23.
a grant to Will: Sherwood to make a Survey upon his 150 arc: Land—	Upon The Peticon of Will: Sherwood The Propriet^ry: Granted unto ye Peticon^r: to make a Survey upon his former Grant from this Co^rt: of 150 acres of	C 23.

Land Long since by ye Peticon^r: Seated on ye Southsyde of blackbirds Creeke

a Provisionall Regulacon for Surveyo^rs: fees;—	The Propriet^ry: was pleased to make a provisionall regulacons for for ye Surveyo^er: fees as followeth, Viz^t:—	C 23.

all P^rsons for Surveying of New Lands to pay after the rate of 8^s: 4^d: p^r. hundered, in Corne Cattle or Silver;—And for all resurveys or Land that hath been alreddy before Surveyed to pay after ye Rate of 10 Shillings p^r: hundred— Any haueing occasion for the Surveyo^r: are oblidged to fetch and bring him home againe Either by boate or horse and to find him w^th: dyet & Lodging during his aboade; all payment is to bee made p^rsent att y^e: delivery of y^e Certificate;—

The Co^rt: adjorned till y^e 21th of y^e 12 month Called february next

feb: 21: 168$\frac{2}{3}$;—

Att a Court Held in the Towne of New Castle by his May^ties: C 25.
Authority and Commission Received from William Penn Esqr: Propriet^ry: and Governo^r: of Pensiluania etc; the 21 and 22th dayes of y^e month of february being y^e 12th Month Anno Dom: 168$\frac{2}{3}$;—

The R^t: Hono^rble: Propriet^ry: Will: Penn—
Captn: William Marckham—Deputy Govern^r:—

P^rsent:
- M^r. John Moll—
- M^r: Arnold: D' Lagrange
- Mr John Cann—
- M^r. Peter Alrichs—
- M^r: James Walliam—
- M^r. Caspares Herman—

} Justices—

C 25.

the Prioprietar[s]:
Speech to y[e] People about their Lands—
1: all Lands of 1681 & 1682 are to bee Seated in 12 mo: or Ells to bee forforfeited—
2[dly]: all warr[ts]: not yet Surveyed are to bee Surveyed & Seated in 12 mo next—
3[dly]: that all those in arrier of q[t]: rent shall pay ½ this & ½ next yeare
4: that all are to pay noe more then 1 bush: Wheat p[r]: hundred acres upon alienation of Town Lotts Each ordinary Lot to pay 1 bushel afterwards

C 26.

The Propriet[ry]: makes a forme for those to bee Naturalized—

The forme is

The Propriet[ry]: William Penn was this day pleased in open Co[rt]: to declare to all y[e] Inhabitants & People

First that for all Lands that are Granted & taken up in the Years 1681 & 1682, are to bee Seated w[th]:in 12 months next otherwayes to forfeit the Same;—

Secondly all Warrants Granted in 1679 & since and not yett Surveyed are to bee Surveyed and Seated forthwith before y[e]. Latter End of next Summer, and all warrants Granted Sence & not yett Surveyed haue a twelue months tyme for to Survey and to Settle.—

Thirdly thatt P[rs]ons in arrier of Quit Rent Should pay the the one halfe thereof this Yeare and y[e] other halfe next Yeare following;

Fou[r]thly and Laestly That all the aforementioned p[r]sons, Should pay in quantity noe more for a Yearly Quit Rent then one Bushell p[r]: hundred acres as formerly, And that incase of allienation of Towne Lotts Each ordinary Lott to pay a bushell of wheat yearly after such allienation;—

The Proprietar[ry]: was pleased to State y[e] following forme, for those as wanted Naturalization according to act of Assembly past att Chest[r]: (als) upland—

I: A: B: doe Solemnly promise to keep faith and alleigiance to y[e] king of England & his heirs and Successo[rs]: fidelity and Lawfull obedience to William Penn Proprietary & Governo[r]: of the Province of Pensiluania and its Territorys and to his heirs & Successo[rs]: according to y[e] Lawe of Naturalization past in Assembly in y[e] month of december Laest att Chester (als) upland in y[e] Province afores[d]:—

The names of p^r sons naturalized—	Followeth the names of those whoe desired to bee Naturalized in Co^rt :—	
Peter Alrichs	Jacob Clementsen	Jan Pietersenproot
Arnold: De Lagrange	Samuel Pietersen	Hendrik fransen
Hendrik Van den Burgh	Jan hendriksen	Hendrik Lemmens
John Nummers	Harmen Laurier	Petrus Tesschemaker
John Barentsen	Nieles Neelsen ripat	Engelbert Lott:
Ambroos Baker	Michiel Oelsen	Claas Danielson Pruys
Broer Sinnexen	Dirk huybertsen	Jan Valck
Hendrik Gerritzen	Peter Abrinck	Sybrant Valck
Adam Petersen	Oele Clemensen	Isacq Tayne
Jacob Vand^r: veer	Æmilius D'Ringh	Lulof Stiddem
Gerrit Jansen van Beek	Jan Boeyar	Carell Petersen
Jan hermensen	Jan Andriesse Stalcop	Jan Moensen
Mary Blocq	Huybert Lourensen	Erasmus Stiddem
Gerrit Otto	Evert hendrickson	Adam Stiddem
Jsacq Sauoy	Jan Gerritsen Verhoof	Samuell Samuells
Mathias deNos	Gerrardus Wessells	Carell Staalcop
Dauid Bilderbeek	Hendrik Wallraven	Jan Staalcop Junior
Hans Petersen	Dirk Willemsen	Sybrant Jansen
Hendrik Evertsen	Jacob Claassen	Claes Andriessen
Oele or Oliver Thomassen	Tymen Stiddem	Harmen Jansen
Arent Jansen V: Burgh	Pieter Maesland	Lasse Andries Gubban
Pieter Jacquet	Jan Bisck	Mathias Laersen Tossen
Justa Andries de haen	Christopher Myer	Cristiaen Andriessen
Peter de Coomink	Cornelis Jansen Vries	Peter Bayard
Abram Eenloos	Jan Jacquet Junior	Peter Volckertsen—
Roelof Andries	Hendrik Andriessen	
Jacob Aertsen	John Willemsen Neering	
Sick Oelkens	Reynier Vander Coelen	
Oele Toersen	Moses De Gam	
Jurian Boatsman	Oele Poulsen	
Coenraet Constantin	Poul Laersen	
Oele Oelsen Tossen	Lucas Stiddem	
Lasse Oesen Tossen	Mathias Vander heyden	
Peter Claassen	Josyn Sempill	
Peter deWitt	Matheus De Ringh	
Peter Eskelsen Cock	William Croesie	
Andries Staalcop	Peter Jegou	
Poul Gerritzen	Symon Eskelsen Cock	
Hans hansen Miller	Jan Eskelsen Cock	
Justa Poulsen	Eldort Egbertsen forsben	
Henry Doll	Anthony Bryant	
Jacobus Andries	Hans Marckussen	
Hans Coderus	Gysbert Walraeven	
Cornelis Vand^rVeer	Eph: Herman	The Co^rt: adjorned
Joseph Barens	Casp^r herman	til tomorrow att 8 of y^e
Jean Paul Jacquet	Hendrik dulgar	Clocq—

The Co^rt: adjorned til tomorrow att 8 of ye Clocq—

feb^ry: 22th: 168⅔.

The Co^rt: Sits the Proprietry: absent and ye Co^rt: opened & Sate— The 22th of ye 12 mo: at 8 of ye Clock The Deputy Governo^r: & Justices all met The Propriet^ry: was absent—

C 29.   James Sanderlin attor: for Proprietry: agst: Roelof Andries & Jacob Aertsen   Upon the Peticon of James Sanderlins as attorney for ye Proprietary & in behalfe of Marmaduke Randall his heirs or assignes; about ye s^d: Marmadukes 300 acres of Land in S^t: Georges against Roelof Andries and Jacob Aertsen the p^rsent possesso^rs: thereof.

Referred to a Jury   The case was Referred to a Jury Viz^t: Abram Mann Gyles Barrott, William Geust Thom: Woollaston, Morgan druit, Gerrardus Wessells Jan hermsen, Isacq Sauoy Mathias de Vos fabian orme John Taylor Richard Smith whoe Returning their Verdict doe find

Their Verdict   ye Land for the heirs of Marmaduke Randall;—

C 30.   Judy Crawford Sues for administracon on hur husband James Crawfords Estate; etc:—   Upon the Request of Judy Crawford widdow and Relict of James Crawford Late of this County deceased desiering to bee admitted administrat^x: of hur said husbands Estate Goods & Chattles, and that hur husbands nuncupative Laest will attested by Ann Young might bee recorded;—

w^ch: y^e: Co^rt: Grant hur Shee Giving Security

on ord^r: for ye noncupative Will to bee recorded   The Co^rt: doe Grant unto ye s^d: Judy Crawford Power to administer upon hur s^d: husbands Estate goods and Chattles, Shee Exhibiting an Inventory to bee recorded ye next Co^rt: Giving Security for hur due administracon and performance according to Law, and that the nuncupative will attested as above Shall bee recorded—

Followeth the aboves^d: noncupative Will Viz^t:

C 30.   The above s^d: will recorded accordingly   I: did heare James Crawford deceased Say that itt was his Laest will That y^e: two Boyes Should haue two hundred acres of Land apeece and the two Girles one hundered acres a peece, and further that the Boyes when they come to age that they might build where they pleased upon their Land, but they must not mole[s]t his wyfe their mother upon his plantation during hur Lyfe, and for his p^rsonall Estate hee Left itt wholy to hur disposing this I: am reddy to Testify, wittnesse my hand february the 17th, 168⅔;—

(was Signed),
Anna Young.

Will: Grant & Justa Andries Enterthemselves Securitys for Judy Crawfords administ:

William Grant and Justa Andries did p^rsonally apeare in Co^{rt}: and did then & there put and bind themselves their Executo^{rs}: & administrato^{rs}: as Securitys for ye due administrato^{rs}: as Securitys for ye due administracon of Judy Crawford; on hur husbands, Estate according to Lawe w^{ch}: the Co^{rt}: did to bee Soe Recorded:—

The Proprietry: States & Gives a forme instead of an oath to ye Jury

The forme to bee Used in ye Roome of ye Oath for ye Jury as the Same was delivered in Co^{rt}: by ye Hono^{rble}: Propriet^{ry}: William Penn Viz^t:

C 34.

The aboves^d: forme

You Solemly promis in ye p^resence of God & this Co^{rt}: that you will Justly try & deliver in yor: Verdict in all Cases—depending, that shall bee brought before you during this Session of Court, according to Evidence and ye Lawe of this Government to y^e: best of yor: understanding;—

A: 2^d: Peticon Entred by ye Children of Mathias Eskelson about their fathers Estate:—

Upon the Peticon of Symon Eskelson Jan Eskelson and Margret Eskelson touching their fathers Lands and Estate etc—Itt is ordered that Peter de Witt, Peter Maesland & Matheus de Ring, Shall appraize ye plantations of Mathias Eskelson deceased ye one Lying att Swanwyk

C 34.

The Co^{rt}: appoints 3 p^{rs}ons to appraize ye Land & State ye acc^t:—	the other att paerden hoek and to Settle and State ye whole accompt of Mathias Eskelsen their father deceased and make Returne thereof all ye next Co^{rt}:—

C 36. Gyles Barrotts peticons for 50 acr: of Land

Upon the Peticon of Gyles Barrott, The Co^{rt}: haue Granted him to take up as an addition to his other Land 50: acres of Land hee Conforming himselfe and paying for y^e s^d: fifty acres after the rate of one penny p^r: acres as a quit rent,—

C 38. Captn: Cantwell adm: of W^m. Tom brings in Co^{rt}: the appraizem^t: & acc^t: of s^d: Estate

Captn: Ed$\widetilde{m}$: Cantwell administrato^r: of M^r: William Tom deceased, this day delivered in Co^{rt}: the apraizment and accompt of y^e s^d: Estate; w^{ch}: the Co^{rt}: will if ocasion peruse, and in y^e: meantyme, The Same is to bee Recorded;—

Apraized this 11 & 12 of July 1678:—

the appraizm^t. recorded

		gild^{rs}:
3 Cowes wth: 3 Calues	ƒ	600: =
1 Cowe wth:out Calfe	"	180: =
1 heiffer & Calfe	"	180: =
2 oxen	"	440: =
2 Yearlings	"	160: =
1 Yearling bull	"	60: =
1 Great pot & 1 Small pott & pott hookes	"	70: =
1 Yron porringer 1 Grid Yron & 1 hang Yron	"	10: =
3 small pewter dishes old	"	8: =
6 woodden boules	"	8: =
1 brasse Candelstike	"	10: =
1 Cullender A old peale 1 funnel of tinue	"	8: =
2 woodden Peales	"	6: =
3 old hilling howes 1 grubbing howe 2 wiedding howes Som Yron for y^e Axeltree of a Cart & harrow 4 old Sythes 1 hammer	"	60: =
1 Cherne	"	8: =
1 Yron Gun Stike	"	7: =

acres of Land apeece and the two Girles one hundred acres a peece, and further that the Boyes when they come to age that they might build where they pleased upon their Land, but they must not mole[s]t his wyfe their mother upon his plantation during hur Lyfe, and for his p^rsonall Estate hee Left itt wholy to hur disposing this I: am reddy to Testify, wittnesse my hand february the 17th, 168⅔;—

(was Signed),

Anna Young.

Will: Grant & Justa Andries Enter- themselves Securitys for Judy Crawfords administ:	William Grant and Justa Andries did p^rsonally apeare in Co^{rt}: and did then & there put and bind themselves their Executo^{rs}: & administrato^{rs}: as Securitys for ye due administrato^{rs}: as Securitys

for ye due administracon of Judy Crawford; on hur husbands, Estate according to Lawe w^{ch}: the Co^{rt}: did to bee Soe Recorded:—

The Propriet^{ry}: States & Gives a forme instead of an oath to ye Jury	The forme to bee Used in ye Roome of ye Oath for ye Jury as the Same was delivered in Co^{rt}: by ye Hono^{rble}: Propriet^{ry}: William Penn Viz^t:	C 34.
The above^{sd}: forme	You Solemly promis in ye p^resence of God & this Co^{rt}: that you will Justly try	

& deliver in yor: Verdict in all Cases—depending, that shall bee brought before you during this Session of Court, according to Evidence and ye Lawe of this Government to y^e: best of yor: understanding;—

A: 2^d: Peticon Entred by ye Children of Mathias Eskelson about their fathers Estate:—	Upon the Peticon of Symon Eskelson Jan Eskelson and Margret Eskelson touching their fathers Lands and Estate etc—Itt is ordered that Peter de Witt, Peter Maesland & Matheus de Ring, Shall appraize ye plantations of Mathias Eskelson deceased ye one Lying att Swanwyk	C 34.

	The Co^rt: appoints 3 p^rsons to appraize ye Land & State ye acc^t:—

the other att paerden hoek and to Settle and State ye whole accompt of Mathias Eskelsen their father deceased and make Returne thereof all ye next Co^rt:—

C 36.	Gyles Barrotts peticons for 50 acr: of Land

Upon the Peticon of Gyles Barrott, The Co^rt: haue Granted him to take up as an addition to his other Land 50: acres of Land hee Conforming himselfe and paying for ye s^d: fifty acres after the rate of one penny p^r: acres as a quit rent,—

C 38.	Captn: Cantwell adm: of W^m. Tom brings in Co^rt: the appraizem^t: & acc^t: of s^d: Estate

Captn: Edm: Cantwell administrato^r: of M^r: William Tom deceased, this day delivered in Co^rt: the apraizment and accompt of y^e s^d: Estate; w^ch: the Co^rt: will if ocasion peruse, and in y^e: meantyme, The Same is to bee Recorded;—

Apraized this 11 & 12 of July 1678:—

		gild^rs:
the appraizm^t recorded	3 Cowes w^th: 3 Calues	f 600:=
	1 Cowe w^th:out Calfe	" 180:=
1 heiffer & Calfe		" 180:=
2 oxen		" 440:=
2 Yearlings		" 160:=
1 Yearling bull		" 60:=
1 Great pot & 1 Small pott & pott hookes		" 70:=
1 Yron porringer 1 Grid Yron & 1 hang Yron		" 10:=
3 small pewter dishes old		" 8:=
6 woodden boules		" 8:=
1 brasse Candelstike		" 10:=
1 Cullender A old peale 1 funnel of tinue		" 8:=
2 woodden Peales		" 6:=
3 old hilling howes 1 grubbing howe 2 wiedding howes Som Yron for y^e Axeltree of a Cart & harrow 4 old Sythes 1 hammer		" 60:=
1 Cherne		" 8:=
1 Yron Gun Stike		" 7:=

1 Little Chist	"	6:=
2 old Clyres 1 brass Lamp & 2 old Sifters	"	20:=

Carried to yᵉ next Leafe...... ƒ1841

Brought ouer from yᵉ other Syde.. ƒ1841:=   C 39.

1 meale tubb	"	8:=
1 Grinstone & Yron worke	"	30:=
1 handmill & Yron work	"	100:=
1 Stew pann	"	30:=
1 old fatt wᵗʰ: feathers	"	10:=
1 Cross Cutt Sawe	"	20:=
1 feather bed & boulster 1 old whyte blancket 1 old blew Rugg	"	120:=
1 old feather bead & boulster 2 whyte blanckets	"	120:=
4 Gunnes & 1 Carrabyn	"	170:=
1 old Sword	"	20:=
1 glasse bottel gallon	"	6:=
1 old dutch Case wᵗʰ: 6: bottells	"	20:=
1 old Chamber pott	"	6:=
1 small Silver beker & 1 Spoone	"	60:=
1 old boate & Grapplin	"	120:=
1 Silver Spoone	"	12:=
1 pʳ: bellowes 1 small cupboard & 1 old Chest	"	30:=
6 Printed bookes	"	20:=
1 old Syne	"	30:=
1 Yron beame 1 old Jack 1 old Sword & Som old Yron	"	25:=
1 deske	"	30:=

ƒ2828:=

The wᵗʰ:in written goods belonging to Mʳ: Will: Tom were appraized the day & date wᵗʰ:in written to twenty Eight hundred & twenty Eigt Gilders as pʳ: yᵉ accompt by—(Signed)

                        G: Dircksen

                        Will: Sempill:—

Debt^r: The Estate of M^r: W^m: Tom;—

C 39. Captn: Cantw^l: administ^r: of Will: Toms Estate his acc^t: recorded—

To Captn: Thoṁ: D'Lauall by Execut: wth. y^e Charge & intrest	ƒ 5565 :=
To y^e Estate of doct^r. Jordins by Mortgage	" 630 :=
To M^r: herman by ord^r: and y^e fees of y^e Vendue..	" 548 :=
To Captn: Nicolls by bill & ord^r: w^th: y^e Charge....	" 229 :=
To my owne debt wth y^e. Charges	" 1655 :=
To boat hyre & a Man to y^e whork^l	" 1655 :=
To Rume att y^e Vendue	" 16 :=
To my Sallary after y^e rate of 10 p^r: C^to: makes...	" 895 :10
	ƒ 9709 :100

Contra Cred^r:—

By Land Sould in y^e Vendue as p^r: y^e Vendu Mast^rs. booke doth apeare	5135 :=
By appraizm^t: by Mr Willam Sempil & gysbert dirkss as p^r. acc^t. under their hands	2820 :=
By 5000 ^lb of toḃḃ: att the Whoorekills Eṅg: w^tt: & tare at 4 Styv^rs: p^r: ℔ makes	1000
	ƒ 8955 :=
Due to ballance	ƒ 853 :10
	ƒ 9708 :10

N:Castle feb 22th: 1682

by Edṁ: Cantwell administ^r:

Phil: Teunis deceased his appraizem^t: recorded	Appraized by us William Grant & Caspares herman The Goods of Philip Teuness deceased in y^e house of M^r: Gerret Otto;—	C 40.

	gild^{rs}:
3¾ Yards of of Carsy .... ƒ	31 :=
1 remnant of broad Cloath............ "	42 :=
2½ yards of whyte Linnen.............. "	6 : 5 :
6¼ Yard^r: of Linning................. "	44 :=
1 goes .... "	2 :=
1 p^r: of Sheares .... "	5 :=
one hatt .... "	8 :=
	ƒ 138 : 5

Will Grant
Casp^r: herman

The Co^{rt}: adjorned untill the first Teusday In the month of Aprill next

The 4th: of y^e 2 mo: 1683:—

The Co^{rt}: adjorned till 1 Teusday in May next—   The 4th: day of y^e: $\frac{2}{mo}$: called aprill 1683. The Justices being mett and y^e Co^{rt}: opened Itt was thought fitt and Resolued that y^e Co^{rt}: Should bee adjorned, untill the first Teusday of the month of May or y^e 3 month next, by reason of y^e Assemblys Sitting att Philadelphia   C 44.

The 1: of y^e $\frac{3}{mo}$: called May 1683.

Att a court Held in the Towne of New Castle by the Kings Authority and by Commission Received from William Penn Esqr: Propriet^{ry}: & Goveno^r: of Pensiluania the first day of y^e y^e $\frac{3}{mo}$: called May 1683.   C 45.

P^rsent   M^r: John Moll
       M^r: Joh: De Haes
       M^r: John Cann— } Justices—
       M^r: James Walliam
Abram Mann High Sherrife—

C 45. Jos: Barnes pro- Joseph Barnes produced in Co^rt: the
duces Sam: fields Laest will & Testament of Samuel field
will & Late of this County deceas^d:

Prooves ye same by John Nummersen and William Ysop
2 wittnesses doe Solemly in Co^rt: declare that they
were p^rsonally p^rsent & did heare & See Samuell field to Sign
Seale and deliver and pronounce ye s^d: will as his Laest will
& Testament for his Estate w^th:in this County of NewCastle;—

The Co^rt: ord^r: ye The Co^rt: ordred that ye s^d: will Should
will to bee Re- bee recorded—
corded—

C 45. The above s^d: Will In the Name of God Amen, Jannuary
accordingly here the 16th: 1682. I: Samuell field Sadler,
recorded Living in whyte clay kill in ye County of
New Castle, being in perfect memory and remembrance,
praized bee God, due make this my Laest Will and Testament, in manner following. In ye first place I: bequeath my
Soull into ye hand of allmighty God, my maker, hopeing
through the merritorious death and passion of Jesus Christ
my only Sauior and redeemer, to receive free pardon of all my
Sinnes, In ye Second place I: give my boddy To the Graue;
In the third place I: give to Joseph Cookson some of my
Carpenders Tooles that I: haue in this County;—

In the fourth place I: make Joseph Barnes of white clay
Kills my Sole Executo^r: of all the Goods Bills and bonds that
I: doe possesse in this County of New Castle, Revoking all
other wills and Testaments, In Wittnesse whereof I haue
hereunto Sett my hand and Seale the day and yeare first-
written, and in ye p^rsence of

(was Subscrybed)
Samuell ffield (LS)

John Nomers
William × Ysops
marke—

a Resolut of ye Co^{rt}: to adjorne till ye 8 of This Instant month because noe Lawes etc.	The acts of ye Laest Assembly held att Philadephia not being come as Yett to ye hands of ye Co^{rt}: wth:out w^{ch}: they could not well act Conformable there unto Itt was therefore by the Co^{rt}: Resolved to

C 46.

adjorne untill y^e: 8th: day of this Instant month; In Expectation of y^e s^d: Acts and Lawes in y^e Interim to come;

The Co^{rt}: adjorned untill the 8th: day of this Instant month of may—

The 8th of y^e $\frac{3}{mo}$: called may 1683.—

Att a Co^{rt}: Held in the Towne of New Castle the 8th: day of the $\frac{3}{mo}$: 1683.—

P^rsent
Mr. John Moll—
M^r. Joh: DeHaes
M^r: John Cann—
M^r: James Walliam—
} Justices   C 47.

Adam Mann high Sherrife

no Lawes y^e Co^{rt}: againe Resolues to adjorne til 1 Teusday of June next—	The acts or Lawes of assembly not as Yett being come, Itt was againe Resolued to adjorne the Co^{rt}: untill the first Teusday of y^e next month called June,—

Proclamation was Made, That ye Co^{rt}: did adjorne untill y^e: s^d: Teusday of y^e: month of June next Ensuing;—

The 5th: of y^e $\frac{4}{mo}$: called June Anno Dom̃: 1683.—

Att a Court Held in the Towne of New Castle By the Kings Authority and Commission Received from Will: Penn Proprie^{try}: and Governo^r: etc: the 5th: day of the 4 mo: called June Anno Dom̃: 1683.

C 49.

P^rsent
M^r: John Moll—
M^r: Peter Alrichs—
M^r: Joh: De Haes—
M^r: John Cann—
M^r: Arnoldus De'Legrange
M^r: James Walliam—
} Justices—

Abram Mann high Sherrife

C 57.

Complaines agst: ye def^{ts}: for hindring him of his Land etc.—

Cornelis Jansen P^{lt}:
Peter DeWtt
and
Jan Barentsen
De^{fts}:

In an action of ye Case

The P^{lt}: complaynes that these def^{ts}: haue hindered him and forwarned ye Surveyo^{r}: to resurvey his Land according to his Pattent Transports and the Governo^{rs}: warr^{t}: of Resurvey—

Sentence y^{t}: hee haue his Land Surveyed etc ye def^{ts}: to pay Costs—

The debates of both partees being heard and ye papers examined, The Co^{rt}: doe order and Sentence that the P^{lt}: Shall Survey his Land according to ye Tennor of ye Pattent and Transports, and that the def^{ts}: pay ye Costs of Suite;—

C 60.

Sam: King brings in Co^{rt}: ye will of Joseph appelthigt deceased &

Apeared in Co^{rt}: Samuell King attorney of his Brother John King, whoe produced ye Laest will and Testament of Joseph Appelthyht Late of this Towne of New Castle deceased, desiering to prove ye Same and that ye will might be allowed of and Recorded,—

Prooves ye same by 2 wittnesses

Thomas Spry and John Maitland doe Solemly declare in Co^{rt}: that they were p^{r}sonally p^{r}sent and did see Joseph Appelthight Sign Seale and pronounce this will as his Laest Will & Testament

an ordery^{t} ye will be recorded

Whereupon the Co^{rt}: doe order that ye s^{d}: will Shall bee recorded Viz^{t}:

April ye 9th 1683

The will recorded

In the name of God amen I: Joseph Appelthight, of ye Kingdom of Yreland, being Sike and weake in boddy but of p^{r}fect Sence and memory thenkes bee to God, and Knowing that death is Common & Certaine to all men, doe make my Laest will and Testament in manner and forme following;—Inprimis I. bequeath my Soule unto the hands of God that Gave itt me, and my Boddy to ye Earth to bee burried in decent Christian manner, and as for what worldly goods God hath been pleased to Endow mee with I: doe give and bequeath all that is Left boath in the

River of Dellaware in Pensiluania or the Kingdom of Ireland (after my Legall debts are paid unto my three Sisters to haue Sheare and Sheare alike, and doe by these p^{r}sents, Constitute and appoint Mr John King of New Castle on Deleware to bee my true and Lawfull Executo^r: and to See this my Laest will to bee fullfilled, and to See my Lawfull debts paid here in America if my Estate here will pay what I: owe, and the remainder Sent to my three Sisters in Ireland, In Confirmacon whereof I: haue hereunto Sett my hand & Seale this day and Yeare above written;—

      (was Subscrybed)
      Joseph Appelthight (LS)

Pronounced declared Signed
Sealed and delivered in ye p^{r}sence
of us
 Tho: Peirce
 John Maitland
 Edmund Varnnun
 James Nevill
 Thom: Spry

Sam: Land and John Whyte appointed apraiz^{rs}: to appraize Joseph appelhights Estate

Samuell Land and John Whyte were by y^e: Co^{rt}: nominated and authorized appraizers to appraize ye Estate of Joseph Appelthight deceased   C 61.

Will: whyte a grant for 200 acr: Land--

Upon the Peticon of William whyte, The Co^{rt}: Granted him to take up wth:in this County two hundred acres of Land not Granted or taken up before, hee complying wth: ye Propriet^{rys}: Tearmes & new Conditions;—   C 63.

The Co^{rt}: adjorned till y^e first Teusday of y^e month called August next

August 7th: 1683
Att a Court Held in New Castle by the Kings Authority and by Commission Received from William Penn Esqr: Pro-   C 64.

C 64.	priet^{ry}: & Governo^r: of Pensiluania and Territo^{rs}: the 7th day of y^e $\frac{6}{mo}$: called August 1683;—

P^{r}sent

    Captn: William Markham
    M^r: John Moll—
    M^r: Peter Alrichs—
    M^r: Arnoldus De Lagrange— ⎫
    M^r: John Cann— ⎬ Justices
    M^r: James Walliam— ⎭
    M^r. Caspar Herman—

C 67.   Thom: Pieterss was naturalized

Thomas Pietersen a Norman was this day upon his request Naturalized, hee haueing p^{r}formed according to Lawe;—

C 69.   Walburgh widdow of Hend: Nielson p^{r}duces hur husbands Laest Will & Testam^t:—

Walburgh ye Widow of Hendrik Nielsen Late of this County deceased appeared in Co^{rt}: and produced ye Laest will and Testament of hur s^d deceased husband;—

and prooves itt by fyve wittnesses in Co^{rt}:

Jacob Vander Veer Oela Tossen Oela Clementsen Carell Pietersen & Jacob Clementss is wittness to y^e: aboves^d: will, apearing in Co^{rt}: did declare that they were p^{r}sent att y^e: Signing and Delivery of ye s^d: Will by Hendrik Nielsen, & that hee was in p^{r}fect minde & understanding;—

The Co^{rt}. allow ye will & Grant hur administ:

The Co^{rt}: did thinke fitt to allow & approove of ye s. Will, and doe order that the Same bee Translated & recorded, And doe further Grant unto ye s^d: Widow, Power to Administer Shee Giving Security and p^{r}forming all things according to Lawe;—

Jan Erikson & Jacob Vander veer Ener Securitys

Jan Eriksen and Jacob Vander Veer doe put themselfes Securitys to y^e: Co^{rt}: for ye due Administ: of Walburgh Nielsen according to Lawe

Copia & Transl^t:

The Laest will of hendrik Nielson Recorded

In the Name of o^r: Lord & Sauior Jesus Christ, and in ye Yeare 1683, the 13th: of Jannua Apeared before us y^e: underwritten wittnesses Hendrik Nealson being Verry Sike in bed but of perfect minde & memory as itt apeared to us whoe Considering ye frayltie of this Lyfe the Certaintie of death and ye uncertaine tyme thereof and being unwilling to depart this Lyfe before hee had disposed of what Worldly Estate hee by Gods Blessing had procured togeather wth: his Walburgh Jans daughter,—Therefore doth hee ye Testator first of all commit his Soul into ye hands of almighty God that Gaue itt him and his boddy to ye Earth to bee decently burried; And further doth hee y^e: Testator desire that his wyfe Walburg Jans Shall haue the one third part of all houses & Land, Cattle mooveables & Inmooveables nothing excepted and moreouer Shee his s^d: wyfe Walburgh Shall haue ouer and aboue, one bed & itts furniture & hur Cloathing as well Linnen as woolling:— Secundly hee bequeaths to his Children, as well to that w^{ch}: his wyfe now bears as to those w^{ch}: hee now att p^{r}sent hath, The twoo other remaining third parts of his Estate, houses & Land Cattle, mooveables & Inmooveable nothing Reserved, Except that my daughter Sara Shall first of all haue as a Legacy one heiffer of twoo Yeare old, a bed and boulster, wth: her mothers Chest, and an Yyron pott, a psalm booke, and a Sweads Booke called ye 12 meditations and twoo other bookes and twoo Coats and a wast coate of ordinary stuff;—Thirdly itt is ye Testato^{rs}: will that when his Son Jan hendricx comes to adge that then hee shall haue ye p^{r}ferrence to buy all ye Land of him ye Testato^{rs}: att a Civill ordinary prys or Sume; and further his Son John Shall haue as a Legacy a Certaine deanish Evangely Booke;

And further itt is ye Testato^{rs}: desire that his wyfe shall remaine in full possession of ye houses and Land cattle any or nothing Excepted Soo Long until the Children Shall be of adge or married, and further the Testato^r: desireth that his Brother Mathias Nealson Shall haue the oversight of his daughter Sara, and that s^d: Mathias and Jan Erikson as the God father Shall haue the oversight of his Son Jan hendrikson; all w^{ch}: being twoo or three tymes Read ouer to him the Testato^r, hee did Reply that itt was well and his Laest will and

Testament in ye p^rsence of ye afternamed wittnesses Viz^t: oela Tossen Oela Clements Carrell Petersen & Jacob Clementss, and therefore in Testimony of the Truth thereof hee hath hereunto Sett his hand in ye p^rsence of all these wittnesses

    In my p^rsence;—   This is the × marke
      Jacob Vander Veer—   of hendrik   Nealson
      Oela × Tossen—   made by himselfe
      Oela × Clementss—
    Carell Petersen × :—
    Jacob × Clementss—

C73. In Regard M^r: Peter Alrichs has and doth refuse to administ: upon y^e: Estate of Ralph hutchinson deceased and Rob: hutchinson the brother of ye deceased now requesting this Co^rt: to grant him ye administracon upon his s^d: Brothers Estate profferring to Give Sufficient Security for his due administracon according to Law; The Co^rt are of opinion that hee ye s^d: Robberd hutchinson may bee admitted administ^r: of ye s^d: Estate Ralph hutchinson deceased, according to his proffer for w^ch: hee must obtaine Lett^rs: of administra: & Give Security to ye honorble: Propriet^ry: or those by him thereunto Impowered;—

The Co^rt: adjorned untill ye first Teusday of ye month of october next Ensuing w^ch: is also to bee an orphants Co^rt:—

C 74. Sept^r: 4th: 1683.

Att a Meeting of the Justices Held in New Castle the 4th: day of Septemb^r: 1683.—

C 75. P^rsent
    M^r: John Moll—
    M^r: Johannes D'haes—   } Justices
    M^r: John Cann—
    M^r: James Walliam—

Copia Vera.—

C 76. To all whome this p^rsent award Shall Come Sendeth Greeting in o^r Lord God Everlasting Whereas heretofore there hath bin divers Stryfes & Variances mooved and are Yett depending betweene hendrick Lemmens of Calcoen Island in Cristina Creeke in delowar

River; on ye one party and hendrick Andriessen Catharin Johnson ye Widdow of Willem Jansen deceased, Eskell Andries & John Matsen of the Craen hooke, in the Same River on ye other party Witnesseth, that for the appealing and fynall Ending whereof the s^d: partees of one Assent and Consent as doth apeare by their obligations Each to ye other haue named and Chosen us John Cann & Ephraim Herman of ye Towne of New Castle, their Arbitrators to award Arbiter and determine, offer upon and Conserning all Stryfes, Variances Cost demadges and demands whatsoever hath mooved between the s^d: partees in any manner of wyse from the beginning of ye world to this day about their Land & Marsh etc; And for as mutch as wee the s^d: John Cann and Ephraim herman haue taken ye Charge of ye s^d: arbiterm^t: upon us and thereupon haue deliberatly heard and Examined all variances betweene ye s^d: partees and their allegations answers and proofes in that behalfe doe now therefore Even this p^rsent day of ye date of these p^rsents make and Give in and by this p^rsent wryting under our hands and Seales o^r: full and fynall award arbitriment in manner & forme following;—

Inprimis as to ye Marsh or meddow Ground between the Bastle kill and Everts Eyland for Soe much thereof as is not allreddy taken up in ye Survey of Everts Eyland the same is to bee and Remaine in common, or Everyone of the Inhabitants of Craenhook is to haue his proportionable Sheare thereof according to the division of their Lotts, only hendrik Everts in Regard hee has bought hendrik Lemmens Symon Jansen & Evert hendriks's parts thereof is to haue Six Sheares and ye others Eight Sheares thereof Viz^t: Hendrik Andries three Sheares for his three Lotts, Catherin Johnson twoo Sheares, Eskell Andries one Sheare, and John Matsen twoo Sheares, in all Eight Sheares, and hendrik Everts Six Sheares, w^ch: is pursuant to ye Co^rt: of New Castles Grant of ye third of october 1677 and as wee Judge most Equitable and Just;—

2dly As for ye Cutting of Timber on y^e: woodland of Craenhooke, in Regard hendrik Lemmens hath twoo Lotts or Sheares Still att ye Craenhook, and hath also Reserved the Cutting of Timber or other wood on halfe Symon Jansens Land Sould to hendrik Everts, wee doe therefore award that hend: Lemmens may freely Cutt wood and Timber upon any part of y^e: s^d: Craenhook Land without the hundred & fifty perches allowed for the home Lotts—

3dly:= As to y^e way in Regard that those of y^e Craenhook haue for this many Years made use thereof there being noe other Convenient Landing, wee doe award that they of y^e Craenhook may have a free waggon way over y^e Eyland to y^e Creeke as formerly—provyded that att any tyme and att all tymes when y^e bridge or way Shall want any mending makeing or repairing that they and Every one of them Shall upon the first notice thereof to them Given by y^e: s^d: hendrik Lemmens bee obliged to come and w^th: the s^d: hendrik Lemens: Repayre make & Compleat, the s^d: Bridge and way upon ye forfeiture and penalty of thirty Shillings for Each person neglecting upon Such notice as afores^d: to bee paid to those as doe worke;—And also ye s^d: Inhabitants, may haue ye priviledge to build a Small house in Some place neare the Creeke where itt may not bee prejudiciall to ye s^d: hendrik, and as to ye old foott way ouer the Marsh, in Regard that itt is ye best of ye s^d: hendrik Lemmens, Marsh and a damadge to him, the Same is to bee Left of, and if they See cause another foott way may bee made heiger up where itt Shall not prejudice ye s^d: hendrik Lemens, and Laestly the Inhabitants of Craenhooke are not any wayes to damnifye o^r prejudice the said hendrik Lemens in his fences or any otherwayes And because Sam: Land hath taken Some paynes in and about this arbitration wee doe award that the above partees, Shall pay unto him Each of them one halfe Crowne or one Shipple of wheat w^ch: is in all ten Shillings or fower Shiple of wheat and that Either of ye partees afores^d: their heyres Executo^rs: and administrato^rs: for their Sever^ll: parts Shall from henceforth Surcease from all Suit and Suits and quarrills in Lawe whatsoever for any matter or difference betweene them att any tyme before ye day of this date about yᵉ premisses, and for the better— Testification and Confirmacon thereof wee yᵉ sᵈ: Arbitratoʳˢ: haue to this oʳ: award Sett oʳ hands & Seales att New Castle upon deloware River this Eight & twentieth day of february 1682.

        (was Signed)
Signed Sealed & delivered John Cann— (LS)
in yᵉ pʳsence of   Eph: Herman (LS)
 James Osborne
 Sam̄: Land—

On the bake Syde of yᵉ aforestanding award was written &   C 79 Subscrybed as followeth Vizᵗ:—

Wee underwritten hendrik Andrews Catharin Johnson yᵉ widdow of William Johnson deceased Eskell Andries and John Matson of Craenhooke in Delowar River; doe owne and aknowledge oʳ Selues to bee well Sattisfyed wᵗʰ: the within mentioned award, and doe accept and stand to itt Resoluing never to Vyolate the Same In Wittnesse whereof wee haue hereunto Sett oʳ: hands att New Castle this 28ᵗʰ: day of february annoq Dom̄: 1682.

        (was Subscrybed)
Testes   The marke × of
 Sam̄: Land— hendrik Andries
       John × Mattson
        his marke
       Eskell × Andries
        marke
       Catherin × Johnson
        hur marke—

Septʳ: 26ᵗʰ: 1683.   C 80.
Copia   To all People To whome this pʳsent
Vera   wryting Shall Come John Hiljard, of Ducke Creeke in Delowar Bay Planter & heir & Execuᵗʳ: to yᵉ Laest will and Testament of John Daston Late of yᵉ sᵈ: ducke Creeke in yᵉ County of Sᵗ: Jones's now of Late called Kent County in delowar Bay aforesᵈ:, Planter deceased; Sendeth

Greeting Whereas the abovementioned John daston deceas^d: did by his Laest will and Testament, produced prooved and allowed of in and by ye Co^{rt}: of S^t: Jones's County aboves^d:, did make mee ye s^d: John hiljard his Lawfull heir, and did give and bequeath unto mee among other things a Certaine peece of Land, Lying allso in Ducke Creeke, behind or backward of francis Whitwells and my Land on ye other Syde of a Swamp and brainch, the s^d: Land Lying betweene twoo Brainches w^{ch}: come up out of s^d: Ducke Creeke, itt being all and the Selfe Same Land, whereon hee ye s^d: John daston Lived att ye tyme of his decease, and itt was formerly Surveyed by Cornelis Verhoofe the then Surveyo^r: and Contaynes according to ye Certificate of Survey Six hundred Acres of Land;—

Now Know Yee that I: the s^d: John hiljard for and in Consideracon of a Certaine Good & valluable Sume of monny, before ye Ensigning and delivery hereof to my full Sattisfaction & Content in hand Received from John albertsen and John Monforde boath of Long Island in ye Province of New Yorke Husbandmen Wherewith I: aknowledge and hold my Selfe fully Sattisfyed contented and paid, and therefore doe hereby for my Selfe my Executo^{rs}: & administr^r:^{s} and also for and in behalfe of any others the heirs of ye s^d. John Daston deceased; fully acquit Exonerate and discharge them ye s^d: John Albertsen and John Monforde of any from ye same and Every part and parcell thereof, I Have Given, Granted, Bargained Sold alliened, Enfeofed Assigned, Transferred, made ouer and Confirmed and by these p^{r}sents doe fully Clearly & absoluthly Give Grant Bargaine, Sell, allien, Enfeofe, assigne, Transferre make ouer and Confirme unto them ye s^d: John Albertsen and John Monforde their heirs and assignes for Ever, all and Singular the Selfe Same abovementioned tract or neck of Land w^{ch}: was ye s^d: John Dastons deceased, Surveyd by Cornelis Verhoofe and Containing Six hundred acres of Land as aboves^d:, togeather wth: all and Singular ye Plantation, housing, fences, woods underwoods, marrishes, and all other the appurtenances thereunto belonging or in any wayes appurtayning

To Have and to hold the s^d: peece or parcell of Land plantation and premisses wth: all and Singular the appurtenances, as also all the Right Tytle Intrest Clayme and propriety of him y^e. s^d. John Daston deceased and of mee ye s^d. John hiljard therein unto y^m: ye s^d: John Albertsen & John Monforde their heirs and assignes, unto ye Soale and proper use behoofe of them the said Albertsen & Monforde their heirs & assignes for Ever, and hee ye s^d: John hiljard doth hereby for himselfe his heirs Executo^{rs}: or administrat^{rs}: further Covenant and agree wth them the Said Albertsen and Monforde their heirs Executo^{rs}: administrato^{rs}: or assignes and Every one of them that hee ye s^d: John hiljard att ye tyme of ye Ensealing and delivery hereof, hath in himselfe and in his owne name full power good and Lawfull Tytle and authority to bargaine Sell & allien all and Singular ye abovementioned Land & premisses in manner & forme as aboves^d: and that hee ye s^d: John hiljard his heirs Executo^{rs}: and administrato^{rs}:; and all or Every of them Shall and will att any tyme keepe harmelesse defend, and maintaine them ye s^d: Albertsen and Monford their heirs and Assignes in ye full and peaceable possession of ye s^d: Land and premisses against all and all manner of p^{r}son or p^{r}sons clayming ye same, and y^t: hee ye s^d: hiljard will further and doth hereby promis, to cleare the Same of all manner of former Incumberances whatsoever according to Lawe, and further hee ye s^d: John hljard doth for himselfe his heires Executo^{rs}: and administrato^{rs}: Covenant promis and agree to & wth: them the s^d: Albertsen and monford that hee the said hiljard Shall and will att ye Proper cost and Charge of them ye s^d: Monford & albertsen their heirs and assignes, make or Cause to bee made any other more fuller and Lawfuller, Tytle, Instrument or wryting as their Counsell Learned in ye Lawe Shall devyse or advyse from tyme to tyme and att all tymes, when demanded also that he will w^t:^{h}in ye Space of one Yeare next Ensuing, procure a Good firme and Lawfull Pattent of ye s^d: Bargained premisses and to cause ye s^d: Pattent ouer upon ye firmest

and Lawfullest way of ye Country to the Partees aboves^d: And that they ye s^d: Albertsen and Monford, their heires and Assignes Shall and may from henceforth for Ever more peaceably and Quietly, have hold and possessee ye s^d: Land and premisses w^th:out any Lett hinderance molestation or Interruption of mee ye s^d: John hiljard my heirs or administrat^rs: or any other p^rson or p^rsons whatsoever clayming by from or under mee In Wittnesse & Confirmation whereof ye s^d: John hiljard hath hereunto Sett his hand and Seale att New Castle in Delowar this 26th: of September in the 35 yeare of his May^ties: Raighne Annoq Dom: 1683   (was Subscrybed)
(in Margine Testor)   John hillyard   (Seale)
  Signed Sealed & Delivered
in ye p^rsence of us—

    (was Signed)
  Gerrardus Wessells
  Reynier Vander Collen
  Eph: Herman.

27th: Sept^r: 1683

C 84.
Copia
Vera

S^r. Edmund Andros Kn^t: Seigneur of Sausmares Lievetnn^t: & Govern^r: Genn^rll: under his Roy^ll: Highnesse James Duke of Yorke and Albany &c: of New Yorke and dependencies &c in America, Whereas there are twoo Certaine parcells of Land on ye west side of Delowar Bay the w^ch: were heretofore Surveyed for, and Granted by Pattent unto John Morgen and John Denny, The former to John morgan Lying on y^e: north syde of Ducke Creeke beginning att a markt oake Standing by a Marsh and running West and by South one hundred and fifty perches to a markt oake Standing in ye Woods, then North and by West 320 perches to another markt oake, then East and by North one hundred & fifty perches to ye marsh, and by ye River and Marsh to ye first markt oake Containing three hundred acres of Land as by ye returne of ye Survey doth & may ap-

(The Seale of ye Province)

peare, The Latter parcell of Land, Granted unto John Denny Lykewyse on ye North syde of Ducke Creeke, beginning att a markt oake by the Marsh, and by ye Land of ye aforenamed John Morgan, and Running West and by South by ye s^d: Morgens Land twoo hundered perches then South and by East one hundred & Sixty Perch: to ye first bounded oake, Containing twoo hundred acres a Survey whereof was Lykewyse returned upon w^{ch}: s^d: Parcells of Land there haueing ben Little or noe Improovem^t: made in Severall Yeares tyme William Pierce made application to ye Co^{rt}: att New Castle, and procured a Grant for ye Same, whereby hee became Invested therein Since, the wich the s^d: William Pierce for a valluable Consideracon by deed under his hand & Seale Transported & Conveiged all his Right Tytle and Intrest in ye premisses unto Ephraim herman of New Castle in Dellowar, and Surrendred ye the old Pattents unto him, whoe had Lykewyse my Grant for s^d: Twoo parcells of Land as they Lay unimprooved, Know Yee that by Vertue of his May^{tis}: Letters Pattents and the Commission, and Authority given unto mee by his Roy^{ll}: Highnesse, I: haue given Ratifyed Confirmed and Granted and by these p^{r}sents doe hereby Give Rattify Confirme & Grant unto Ephraim Herman his heirs and assignes the aforerecited parcells of Land & premisses wth all and Singular ye appurtenances, To haue and to held, the s^d: parcells of Land & premisses unto ye s^d: Ephraim Herman his heires & assignes unto ye Proper use and behoofe of him the said Ephraim herman his heirs and assignes for Ever; hee makeing improovem^t: thereon according to Lawe and Yielding and paying therefore Yearly and Every Yeare unto his May^{tis} use as a quit Rent, fyve Bushells of good Winter Wheat, unto Such officer or officers as Shall bee Impowred to Receive the Same att New Castle Given under my hand & Sealed wth: ye Seale of ye Province in New Yorke this 24th day of September in ye 32th Yeare of his May^{tis}: Raigne Annoq Domini 1680.—

(was Subscrybed)

Examined by mee   E Andross.
Matthias Nicolls Secretary

By the Governo^r:—

Copia Vera

C 86.

Whereas I: haue Given order for the Calling in of twoo Pattents heretofore Granted unto John Morgan & John denny for three hundred acres of Land apeece Lying on ye West syde of Delowar River toward The mouth thereof betweene the Land of Morris Liston and ducke Creecke, the Same haueing never ben Improoved, and ye people dead to whome the s^d: Pattents were Granted,— upon application of M^r: Ephraim herman that hee may haue ye s^d: Twoo pieces of Land Ingageing to make Improovem^t: thereon etc: I: doe hereby Grant ye same, to bee Confirmed unto him by Pattent, When ye s^d: Pattents Shall bee delivered in Given under my hand in New Yorke this 1 day of June 1680.

The Co^{rt}: of New Castle to take order and make returne of ye above Pattents according to Lawe & Costome or practise of the River;—

(was Subscrybed)

E Andross.

C 87.

To all Xpian People To whome this p^{r}sent wryting Shall come William Pierce of Cecill County in ye Province of Maryland Gentlm: Sendeth Greeting. Whereas there was herefore assigned and made ouer unto mee by Arthur Carelton & John Denny, twoo Certaine Pattents from ye Right Honor^{rble}: S^r: Edmund Andros Governo^r: of New Yorke, boath bearing date ye 25th: of march in ye 28th: Yeare of his May^{tds}: Raighne 1676. the one of ye s^d: Pattents was Granted unto John Morgan deceased for three hundred acres of Land in Deloware, and ye other for twoo hundred acres of Land, Granted unto John Denny adjoyning wth: the one Syde upon ye s^d: Land of John Morgan & wth: ye other upon Ducke Creeke in Delowar afores^d:, wch s^d: Assignment was by mee proved att a Co^{rt}: held att New Castle in Deloware ye 4th & 5th: of March 1678/9, and then the s^d: twoo parcells of Land were by ye s^d: Court of New Castle Confirmed unto mee the s^d: Will Pierce as by y⁁ Records of y⁁ s⁁: Co⁁rt⁁: doth more att Large appeare; Now Know Yee that I: the Said William Pierce for a Valluable Consideracon to mee in hand paid by Ephraim Herman of New Castle upon Delloware, wherewith I: aknowledge and Confesse my Selfe fully Sattisfyed & paid, I: haue Given Granted Bargained Sould assigned Transported and made ouer and by these p⁁rsents doe fully clearly and absoluthly Give Grant Bargaine Sell assigne Transport & make ouer unto the s⁁d⁁: Ephraim herman his heirs & assignes all my Right Tytle Intrest Clayme and Properiety to the abovesaid Twoo Pattents and all and Singular the Land and premisses therein contained and mentioned; To haue and to hold the said Pattents Land and premisses w⁁th⁁: all and Singular the appurtenances as allso all y⁁e⁁: Right Tytle and Intrest of him the said William Pierce therein unto the said Ephraim herman his heirs and assignes for Ever, In Wittnesse whereof, the said William Pierce hath hereunto Sett his hand & Seale in Cecill County this 18⁁th⁁: day of August in y⁁e one and Thirtieth Yeare of his May⁁tis⁁: Raighne Annoq Dom: 1680.

Signed Sealed & Delivered
in y⁁e p⁁rsence of us
    (was Signed)
  Philip Burgin
  Casp⁁r⁁: Herman

          (was Subscrybed)
          Will: Pearce (Seale)

Copia Vera.

C 88.

Whereas I: did formerly by Vertue of a grant from y⁁e Co⁁rt⁁: of y⁁e Whoorekills, did Seat my Selfe and did cleare and build upon a certaine peece or parcell of Land Lying and being on the West syde of this River of Delowar Just above Duck Creeke, w⁁ch⁁: s⁁d⁁: Land was formerly taken up by John Morgan deceased, upon w⁁ch⁁: s⁁d⁁: Land I: did Lykewyse Live and Plant for the Space of twoo Yeare, Nok Know Yee that I: William Green of y⁁e River of Delloware Planter for and in Consideracon of twoo Cowes & Calues fifteen hundred of Singletens, and for more other reasons and Consideracons, mee hereunto moveing I: haue

Given Granted Bargained, Sould alliened assigned Transported & made ouer unto Ephraim Herman of New Castle his heirs and assignes, all my Right Tytle and Intrest clayme & propriety to ye aboves^d: tract of Land, and all and Singular my Improovement Buildings clearing & fencing thereon, To haue and to hold the s^d: Land Improovement and premisses wth: all & Singular the appurtenances, as also all my Right Tytle & Intrest therein unto ye s^d: Ephraim Herman his heires and assignes unto ye Soale and proper use and behoofe of him ye s^d: Ephraim herman his heirs and assignes for Ever; and I doe hereby aknowledge to haue Received full Sattisfaction from ye s^d: Eph: herman to Content for the Same Wittnesse my hand and Seale att New Castle In Delowar this 15th day of November 1681.

Signed Sealed and Delivered
in ye p^{r}sence of us
   Æmiluis De Ringh
   Richard Noble

(was Subscrybed)
The marke of
William ✕ Green (Seale)
made wth: his owne hand

C 90.

Know all men by these p^{r}sents and I Meghaeksitt Cheef Sachem of Cohansy and Naturall owner of all ye Land Lying between Ducke Creeke by ye Indians called Quinquingo Cipus, and Appoqueneme Creeke in ye Delowar River, haue for and in Consideracon of twoo halfe Anckers of drinck, one blancket one matscoate, twoo Acxes, twoo knyves, twoo double handfulls of pouder, twoo barrs of Lead and one kittle, before ye Ensigning and Delivery hereof to my full Sattisfaction and Content to mee in hand paid & delivered by Ephraim herman of New Castle in Delowar, Bargained Sould Assigned Transported and made ouer & doe by these presents fully clearly and absoluthly for my Selfe and my heirs & assignes Bagaine Sell assigne Transport & make ouer unto the s^d: Ephraim herman his heirs and Assignes all that tract or parcell of Land wth: the marrishes thereunto adjoyning Scituate Lying and being on ye West syde of Delloware River, att the mouth thereof, beginning att a Creeke, neare ye Land of Morris

Liston by ye Indians called winsacco and Soe up along ye s^d: Creek Trough ye Cedar Swamp to ye head thereof and from ye s^d: head of ye Cedar Swamp upon a Lyne downe threw ye woods to ducke Creeke as farr as the Land formerly taken up by William Sharpe and now possessed By Christopher Ellitt, and from thence downe the s^d: Ducke Creeke to a Creeke in ye marsh w^{ch}: Stryckes toward ye Land of fabian Orme, and from ye head of ye s^d: Creeke Cros the Marsh Easterly by ye End of ye s^d: fabians Island to ye River Syde w^{ch}: place ye Indians caall Appoqueneme where ye s^d: Indians doe use to hall ouer their Canoos into s^d: ducke Creeke, and from thence up ye River to the first mentioned Creeke called Winsacco, To haue and to hold the s^d: Land and Marrishes etc: bounded as afores^d: wth: all and Singular ye appurtenances, as also all ye Right and Tytle of him ye s^d: Mechaeksitt & his heirs and all other Indians Rights therein, unto the s^d Ephraim Herman his heirs and Assigns for Ever. In Wittnesse and Confirmacon whereof hee ye s^d: Machaecksitt hath hereunto Sett his hand and Seale in ye p^{r}sence of Justice Pieter Alrichs Justice Johannes De Haes, Captn: Edmund Cantwell and Caspares herman whoe all of them understand ye Indian Speech att New Castle in Delowar this first day of November in ye 32th Yeare of his May^{tis}: Raigne Annoq Dom 1680—

(:t' was Subscrybed:)

Wittnesses & Interpreters p^{r}sent—
Pieter Alrichs—
J: D'haes—
Edm: Cantwell
Casp^r: herman—

The marke of
Mechaeksit ✕ the Indian
Sachem (Seale)

Copia Vera

I: Underwritten Edmund Cantwell of C 92. the Towne of New Castle, doe hereby for my Selfe and as administrato^r: to ye Estate of Walter Wharton deceased, fully Clearly and absoluthly dessist of any clayme Right Tytle or Intrest w^{ch}: I: as administrato^r of ye s^d: Walter Whartons Estate haue or might haue by Vertue of a Pattent from Governo^r: francis Lovelace bearing date y^e of 1671. on ye Land Ephraim herman now possesses neare ye Rivers mouth betweene Ducke Creeke and Morris Listons Creeke, for w^{ch}: hee hath Pattents from Governo^r: Edmund Andros and is in peaceable possession of ye same, hereby Releassing acquitting and fully discharging the s^d: Ephraim herman his heirs or assignes of & from ye Same claymes as aboves^d: hee to possess occupy and peaceably to Injoy ye same premisses wth :out any manner of Lett hinderance or molestacon of mee ye s^d: Edmund Cantwell administrator as afores^d: or any other p^{r}son or persons whatsoever Clayming by from or under mee, wittnesse my hand & Seale att New Castle in Delloware, this 11th day of Jannuary 1682—,

Sealed and delivered in
ye p^{r}sence of us—
 (:t' was Signed by:)
 H: V. D: Burch
 J: Willems neering
 Jan herms—

(:t' was Subscrybed:)

Ed: Cantwell (Seale)

C 93.   S^r: Edmund Andros Kn^t: Seigneur of Sausmares Liev^t. and Governo^r: Genn^{rll}: under his Roy^{ll}: highnesse James Duke of Yorke & albany &c. of New Yorke and Dependences &c: in America Whereas there were twoo Pattents heretofore granted unto John Asham Junior & Sam̃: Jackson for twoo Sever^{ll}: parcells of Land in partnershipp betweene them Lying on ye Westsyde of Delloware River and on ye Southsyde of a Creeke called Cedar Creeke, the one Called Ashmore beginning att a bounded Red oake by ye River,—Running West north west in breath up ye Creeke one hundred & fifty perches to abounded whyte oake by abrainch then South South west in breath one hundred and Sixty perches, then West North west one hundred perches to abounded Whyte oake by a Small Brainch, then South South west one hundred

Great Seale of y^e Province

Sixty perches, then by a Lyne South East twoo hundred and fifty perches, then by a Lyne North North west three hundred and twenty perches to y^e first bounded Red oake Containing and Laid out for fower hundred Acres as by the Returne of ye Survey doth and may appeare, The parcell of Land called Jacksons neck beginning att a bounded popler by a brainch Running North west one hundred & fifty perches to a bounded Red oake by a Small Brainch then by a Lyne South west three hundered & twenty perches into ye woods, then by a Lyne South East one hundered & fifty perches, and by a Lyne drawne North East three hundered & twenty perches to ye first bounded poplar Contayning and Laid out for three hundered Acres, a Survey whereof hath ben lykewyse Returned, upon w^{ch}: s^d: parcells of Land there hath noe Improovem^t: beene made in Severall years, the partees to whome ye same was granted being dead, and ye old Pattents Returned whereby the Said Land being Vacant and att my dispos and Lasse Cock of Delloware River haueing obtained a grant of mee for ye Same, and being willing to Give Some Consideracon to John Ashman Senio^r: for ye pretences of his Son thereupon, Know Yee that by vertue of his May^{tls}: Letters Pattents & the commission and Authority Given unto mee by his Royall highnesse, I: haue Given Ratifyed Confirmed and Granted and by these p^{r}sents doe hereby, Give Rattify Confirme and Grant unto Lasse Cock, his heirs and assignes the aforereceited parcells of Land and premisses wth: all & Singular the appurtenances, To have and to hold the afores^d: parcells of Land and premisses wth: all & Singular the appurtenances unto ye s^d: Lausa Cock his heirs and assignes unto ye proper use and behoofe of him y^e: s^d Laussa Cock his heirs and assignes for Ever hee makeing Improovem^t: accord: to Lawe & Yielding & paying therefore Yearly and Every yeare unto his May^{tls}: use as a quit rent Seven bushells of good winter wheat unto Such officer or officers as Shall bee Empoured to Receive ye same att New Castle, Given under my hand & Sealed wth: ye Seale of y^e:

Province in New Yorks this 24th day of Septembr: in ye 32th Yeare of his May^tis: Raigne Annoq Dom: 1680—

Exam: by me
Matthias Nicolls Sur:

(was Subscrybed)

E Andross

C 95.   Upon ye bakesyde of ye aforestanding Pattent was written ye following assignment Viz^t:—

Know all men by these presents that I: Laussa otherwayes called Laurens Cock haue for a Valluable Consideracon before ye Signing and delivery hereof in hand Received to full Content, Given Granted Bargain[ed] Sould assigned Transported made ouer and Confirmed, and doe by these p^rsents fully Clearly and absoluthly give grant bargaine Sell assigne Transport make ouer & Confirme unto Ephraim Herman his heirs and assignes the one moyety and full and Just halfe part of all ye Land & premisses in ye: w^th: in mentioned Pattent of Govern^r: Edmund Andros Exprest and Mentioned.

To haue to hold ye said Moyety and halfe of ye s^d: Land Pattent & premisses w^th: all and Singular ye appurtenances as also all the Right Tytle and Intrest of him ye s^d: Lasse Cock therein unto ye s^d: Ephraim herman his heirs and assignes unto ye soale and proper use and behoofe of him ye s^d: Eph: herman his heirs & assignes for Ever; In wittnesse & Confirmation whereof ye s^d: Lasse Cock hath hereunto Sett his hand & Seale att kingsesse in Delowar River this 14th day of october in ye 32th. Yeare of his May^tles: Raigne Annoq Dom: 1680.

Signed Sealed & delivered
in ye p^rsence of us—
   Otto Ernest Coch
   Henry Jones

(: was Subscrybed :)

of
The mark L K Lasse Cock

(Seale)

See further

[C] 96.   To all Xpian People To whome this pressent wryting Shall come Laurens Cock of Passayunck in Delowar River Gentl:

Sendeth Greeting, Know Yee that I: y̅e̅ s̅d̅: Laurens Cock for and in Consideracon of Certaine Sume of monny before ye Enisgning and delivery hereof to mee in hand paid by Ephraim Herman of New Castle in deloware, wherewith I: hold my Selfe fully Sattisfyed Contented & paid, and therefore doe hereby fully acquit Exonerate & discharge ye s^d: Ephraim herman for ye same, as alsoe for more other waighty reasons & Consideracons mee hereunto more Especially moveing, I: haue Given Granted Bargained, Sould Exchanged alienen Enfoefed assigned, Transported, and made ouer and doe by these p^rsents fully clearly and absoluthly give grant Bargaine Sell Exchange allien Enfoefe assigne Transport make ouer and Confirme unto the said Ephraim herman his heirs & assignes, the Remaining one Just halfe part of a Certaine Pattent of Seven hundered Acres of Land; w^ch: was formerly John Ashmans & Samuel Jacksons Lying & being on ye West of Delowar River, att ye mouth thereof in ye neck of Land on ye Northsyde of Ducke Creeke, w^ch: s^d: Land was Granted and Confirmed unto mee by a Pattent from Governo^r: Edmund Andros bearing date ye 24th of September 1680; The one halfe of w^ch: s^d: Land and Pattent I: haue heretofore on y^e: 14th: day of october 1680, assigned and made ouer unto ye s^d: Ephraim herman Soe that I: the s^d: Laurens Cock doe now in Lyke manner assigne & make ouer unto ye s^d: Ephraim herman, the remaining other halfe of ye s^d: Pattent and ye Land therein mentioned and Contained To have and to hold the s^d: Moyety and Remaining halfe part of ye s^d: Pattent & Land togeather w^th: ye remainder and remainders thereof, w^th: all and Singular the appurtenances Prieviledges and benefits thereof as also all the Right Tytle Intrest Clayme and Propriety of him ye s^d: Laurens Cock his heirs and assignes therein unto ye s^d: Eph: herman his heirs and assignes unto ye soale and proper use and behoofe of him ye s^d: Ephraim herman his heirs and assignes for Ever, In Wittnesse and Confirmation whereof the s^d: Laurens Cock hath

Copia

hereunto Sett his hand & Seale in Delloware this 4th day of aprill 1682.

Signed Sealed & delivered
in ye p^rsence of us—
 John hazell—
 Laurens heddings

(was Subscrybed)

Laurens L K Cock (Seal)

his marke —

[C]98. Resurveyd for Ephraim herman a tract of Land called the Good-Land, Scituate Lying and being on the Westsyde of Delloware River neare ye mouth of ye s^d: River between Duck Creeke, and a Creeke & a great Swamp called ye Cedar Sypory Swamp & Creeke Beginning att a Corner marked read oake, being ye Lowermost corner tree of Christopher Ellitts Land, Standing on a point by duck Creeke Marsh Syde, and, and from thence East by North downe y^e: s^d: Marsh and Creeke Syde 316 Perches to a Corner marked hickory Standing upon a point by ye through fayre Creeke, being a brainch of Ducke Creeke from thence N:W:b:N. by a Marsh Syde 120 perches then N:b:W:80 Perches then N:W: 34 Perches to a Corner marked whyte Oake Standing by s^d: Marsh, from thence East by North cros ye s^d: Marsh 110 Perches to a Corner marked Read Oake Standing upon a Point by ye Marsh neare ye River and Plantation Syde of ye s^d: Ephraim herman, and from thence up North by West by ye Marsh and River Syde including 2 or 3 small hommoks of Land in ye Mars 330 Perches to a Corner marked Red oake Standing by ye afores^d: Marsh and River Syde, then west by South 160 Perches to a Corner marked red oake Standing by ye Marsh of Cedar Creeke Syde, then N:W:b:N: by the Said Marsh 120 Perches to a Corn^r: marked Spannish oake Standing on a Point by ye syde of Ceder Swamp and from thence up by ye s^d: Swamp on Severall Courses fyve hundred and therty Perches to a Corner marked whyte oake Standing att ye head of one of the Brainches of Cedar Swamp from thence South West by South by a Lyne of marked Trees one hundred therty Six perches to a Corner marked maple Thee, Standing neare Christopher Ellits South East Lyne and from thence up the said Lyne of Christopher Ellitt South East 310 Perches to ye first mentioned Read oake Contayning, Twelve hundered acres of Land and Eighty acres of Marsh in all Twelve hundered & Eighty Acres; Resurveyd the 5th day of Marsh 168½.

Rich: Noble Dep^ty: Surv^r:

Octob^r: 2^d: 1683.

Att a Court held in the Towne of New Castle by the Authority of ye Kings May^tie. and by Commission from William Penn Esqr: Propriet^ry: and Governo^r: of Pensiluania etc:— C 100.

The 2^d: day of Octob^r: 1683.—

P^rsent M^r: Peter Alrichs
M^r. John Cann— } Justices—
M^r. James Walliam—

The Justices haueing caused proclamation to bee made and ye Co^rt: opened, and finding that they wanted of their number to make a quorum Did therefore thinke fitt to adjorne ye Co^rt: untill Teusday ye 16th: day of this Instant month of october next; — w^ch: was done accordingly by open Proclamation as is Customary;—

Octob^r: 16th: 1683.

Att a Court Held in the Towne of New Castle by his May^tls: Anthority and by Commission Received from Will: Pen Esqr: Propriet^ry: and Governo^r: of of Pensiluania etc: the 16th: 17th: & 18th: day of October Annoq Dom: 1683. C 102.

The R^t: Hono^rble: Will: Penn Esqr: Propriet^ry: etc

P^rsent
M^r. John Moll:—
M^r. Peter Alrichs—
M^r. Joh: D'haes—
M^r. Arnoldus D'Lagrange } Justices
M^r. John Cann—
M^r. James Walliam—
M^r. Carpares herman—
M^r. John White—
M^r. Abram Mann high Sherrife—

| | Abram Mann | P^lt: |
| | Thomas Barecroft | Def^t: |

C 103. The P^lt: demands by his declaration for one house & Lott w^th:in this Towne of New Castle Sould unto ye def^t: ye sume of fifty pound deducting what Barecroft can make apeare to haue paid thereon;

The def^ts: attorney Samuell King not appearing and News being come that ye def^t: dyed att Sea going for Ireland, and that ye heirs of ye s^d: def^t: had appointed an attorney whoe was Lately come ouer into this Country

Itt was therefore ordred by ye hono^rble: Propriet^ry: and Court, That in regard noe boddy Lookes after ye house in ye behalfe of s^d: Barecroft and if the attorney of the heirs of ye s^d: Barecroft doth not w^th:in 20 dayes now next Ensuing apeare and give Sattisfaction to ye s^d: P^lt: That then the P^lt: Shall haue full Power to Enter upon ye s^d: house and Secure itt, and what Ever Charge the P^lt: Shall bee out upon ye same, hee is to bee Reembourst by the def^t: or his heirs, att ye Judgem^t: & award of twoo Indifferrent p^rsons there unto to bee Chosen--

The Co^rt: adjorned till tomorrow at 9 oClocq

Octob^r: 17th. 1683

C 105. Hendrick Lemmens P^lt: Hendrick Andriessen De^ft: } In an Action of Trespasse on ye Case—The def^t: haueing taken In this p^lts: Land at Craen hook Church—

The afternamed twoo wittnesses were Sworne for ye P^lt: Hans Petersen & Charles Petersen Sworne in Co^rt: that they haue ben p^rsent and Seen that the def^t: hath taken in fence att Craenhooke Church yard about ye breath of three paces more then were ye old pales Stood—

The def^t: alleidging that hee could proove that y^e former owners of y^e Land had Given Sufficient power for Inlargeing y^e s^d: Churchyard, and desireing that y^e case might bee Suspended till next Co^rt: for him to Proove y^e aboves^d:— The Co^rt: therefore Suspended y^e same and ordred that the def^t:

bring in y\ :sup:`e` wryting w\ :sup:`ch`: hee Sayes there is, to proove that by y\ :sup:`e` former owners of y\ :sup:`e` Land there was Sufficient power Given for the Enlargeing of y\ :sup:`e` Church yard to ye Church att Craenhooke afores\ :sup:`d`:—

John Cann	P\ :sup:`lt`:	⎫ In an Action of Tres-
Reynier Vand\ :sup:`r`: Coelen	Def\ :sup:`t`:	⎭ passe on y\ :sup:`e` Case

The P\ :sup:`lt`: Complaynes, that this def\ :sup:`t`: hath and doth hinder and Molest yo\ :sup:`r`: P\ :sup:`lt`: in y\ :sup:`e` peaceable & quiet possession of a Certaine Lott of Ground w\ :sup:`th`:in this Towne of New Castle betweene y\ :sup:`e` mincquaes and Bever Streets w\ :sup:`ch`: s\ :sup:`d`: Lott yo\ :sup:`r`: P\ :sup:`lt`: by Vertue of a grant of y\ :sup:`e` Co\ :sup:`rt`: of New Castle bearing date y\ :sup:`e` 5\ :sup:`th`: of Sept\ :sup:`r`: 1682, did take up and was Surveyed to him y\ :sup:`e` 18\ :sup:`th` day of y\ :sup:`e` same month and that y\ :sup:`e` def\ :sup:`t`: claymes a Right to y\ :sup:`e` same by a Pattent, and hath forceably remooved y\ :sup:`e` frame and Timber from of y\ :sup:`e` s\ :sup:`d`: Lott, whereby y\ :sup:`e` p\ :sup:`lt`: is damnifyed y\ :sup:`e`: Vallue of fyve pound etc:—

The def\ :sup:`t`: pleads that hee has bought y\ :sup:`e` s\ :sup:`d`: Land from Peter Alrichs and hath a Pattent for y\ :sup:`e` Same from Govern\ :sup:`r`: francis Lovelace w\ :sup:`ch`: Pattent hee produced; The Co\ :sup:`rt`: thought fitt to Referr y\ :sup:`e` Case to a Jury whoe were Impannelled viz\ :sup:`t`: John Walcker John Smith, hans Miller Oele Thomas, George Moore henry Jones William Geuesse Thomas Woollaston, John Biscus, John hermensen, Isacq Tayne, Thom̃: Gillet— The P\ :sup:`lt`: Produces Sever\ :sup:`ll`: wittnesses to proove that that Ground was none of y\ :sup:`e` Def\ :sup:`ts`: by y\ :sup:`e` Pattent, The s\ :sup:`d`: Pattent bounding y\ :sup:`e` def\ :sup:`ts`: Land on y\ :sup:`e` North w\ :sup:`th`: y\ :sup:`e` Street w\ :sup:`ch`: y\ :sup:`e` p\ :sup:`lt`: Sayes to bee y\ :sup:`e` Mincquaes Street, and not y\ :sup:`e` Bever Street, the s\ :sup:`d`: wittnesses were Vizt:—

Anthony Bryant Sworne before Justice John Moll and Justice William Sempill Sayeth that hee verry well remembers that about 24 Years agoe there was a double Row of houses Standing w\ :sup:`th`:in this Towne of New Castle, w\ :sup:`ch`: Rainged Even w\ :sup:`th`: y\ :sup:`e` house now belonging to Ambroos Bakers and Soe quyte downe to y\ :sup:`e` Cripple; The deponant Sayeth that y\ :sup:`e` s\ :sup:`d`: double Rowe of houses fronted y\ :sup:`e` one towards the Street where Gerrit Smit now Lives in, and the other towards y\ :sup:`e`

River Even wth: y^e s^d: Ambroos Bakers house all w^{ch}: Ground is now att p^{r}sent in fence or fenced in by Reynier Vander Coelen, and further Sayeth nott

Aeltie the wyfe of Ambroos Baker, Sworne Sayeth Verbatim y^e Selfe Same as Anthony Bryant hereaboue and that all y^e s^d: Ground was Laid out in Lotts and built wth: houses, and more that there was a way or Street, w^{ch}: ye people made use of, w^{ch}: Rainged Even wth: hur husbands now dwelling house, downe to y^e: Cripple, and further Sayeth nott:—

John Barentsen Sworne Sayeth the Selfe Same as Anthony Bryant and Aeltie hereabove haue declared, and further Sayeth nott;—

Emilius d' Ring Sworne Sayeth that hee was in those dayes aboves^d: butt young, butt to ye best of his Remembrance hee has Seen where ye Garden & Lotts had ben Laid out, and as hee remembers his father gott a permit from ye then Governo^r: d' hinjossa, for that Land by ye mill and when hee fenced itt hee tooke in all as farr as now itt is fenced by Reynier Vander Coelen and hee also Remembers that his s^d: father than Sayed that if any boddy came & Claymed their Lotts there that then they might haue them out of his fence againe as some afterwards haue done to witt dirk Albertsen whoe had ye same and further Sayeth nott, The depon^t: Em: D' Ringh Sayeth that hee doth not Know whether the permitt of d' hinjossa was for all the Land now in fence by Rynier or noe;—

These aforestanding wittnesses to witt Anthony Bryant Aeltie the wyfe of Ambroos baker John Barentsen and Emilius d' Ringh were Sworne & Examined in New Castle the 16th: day of Septemb^r: 1682. Before us

    John Moll—
    Will: Sempill—

The P^{lt}: allso further produces an old mapp of this Towne of New Castle, wherein hee Shewes that there was another Street then ye Street of Gerritt Smit, w^{ch}: other Street fronts Even wth: ye house of Ambroos Baker and is called in y^e

mapp by ye name of Mincquaes Street and ye Street of Gerritt Smith is called in ye map by ye name of ye Bever Street;—

The Def^t: brings the hereafter mentioned Wittnesses whoe being Sworne in Co^rt: declare as folloewth—

Johannes De haes Sayes that hee knowes nothing of the Bargaine how made betweene M^r: Alrichs and Reynier Vander Coelen, and that hee never Sawe a Street there but a house Stood oppositt to Ambroses

Gerret Smith declares that hee was partner and bought all ye Land w^{th}: Rynier from M^r: Alrichs as far as now ye Street, Excepting the Lott of Giljam d'honeur, and Sayeth further that hee has Lived here 22 Years in ye Street and doth not remember that Ever hee Sawe a Street there;

Dirck huybertsen Sayeth the Same as Gerrit Smith hereabove as to ye particular of Buying ye Land of M^r: Alrichs;

Mathias d' Ring Sworne in Co^rt: Sayeth that ye grant of Allexand^r: d' hinjossa to his father for ye Land in Controversy was for ye Land as farr as now in fence;—

M^r: Peter Alrichs declares that hee remembers that there Stood a house opposit in Ambrooses upon y^e: Corner, but whether there was a Street or more houses hee doth not now remember—

Arent Jansen declares that hee remembers three houses, Standing & fronting South Even with Ambroos's' Lott, and that all of ye Land before itt Lay open—

John hendricks Sayes that hee Knows nothing of ye businesse in Controversy;—

John Boeyar declares that hee Knew a house Right ouer against Ambroos's butt knowes nothing of any Street before now and neither Ever heard of any Street

Jacob Vander Veer declares that hee has been in ye Country 25 or 26 Yeares, and that there was a house or twoo but knowes nothing neither heard of any Street—

Andries Tilly Sayeth that hee has ben 25 or 26 Years herein Towne, and that there were houses on boath Ends of ye Ground in Controversy but knowes nothing of any Street;—

Catherin ye wyfe of Jacob Vander Veer declares that Shee

has ben 25 or 26 Yeares in ye Country and that Shee never heard of any Street there, but Some houses Stood on Gerrit Smiths Syde;—

The debates of boath partees being heard, and all their Evidences papers & proofes Examined; The Charge was given to ye Jury by ye Propriet^{ry}: whoe went out and Returning brougt in their Verdict as followeth Viz^t:—Wee are all agreed and doe find for ye P^{lt}: w^{th}: Cost of Suite: Will: Geuest als Butler foreman

The Court thought fitt to passe Judgem^t: ag^{st}: ye def^t: according to ye Jury Verdict w^{th}: Cost of Suite;—

The def^t: desires an appeale w^{ch}: ye Co^{rt}: Grants proyyded ye s^d: def^t: performes all things according to Lawe

The def^t: before ye Co^{rt}: broake up withdrew his aboves^d: appeale;—

Octob^r: 18th: 1683

C 113. Upon the Peticon of Emilius De Ring administ^r: of ye Estate of Gysbert Dircksen deceased; The Co^{rt}: haue thought fitt to nominate and appoint M^r: John Williams and M^r: hendrick Vanden Burgh appraizers to appraize ye Estate goods and Chattles of s^d: Gysbert dircksen deceased, and to make returne thereof to ye Co^{rt}:—

C 114. Upon the Peticon of William Darvall about the Estate of Ralph hutchinsen deceased The Governo^r: and Court ordered that the Peticon^r: may administ^r: upon ye old Letter of administracon from New Yorke upon ye s^d: Estate of Ralph hutchinson deceased, or haue ye same adminīst: now Renewed or Confirmed;—

C 114. Captn: Cantwell in behalfe of Gabriel Minviell and Peter Alrichs in behalfe of James Mathews desire in Co^{rt}: to bee admitted administrato^{rs}: of the Estate of Ralph hutchinson deceased Joyntly Equall w^{th}: William Darvall, Itt was ordered that if Gabriell Minviell and James Mathews wil & doe by themselves or attorneys Equally act w^{th}: William Darvall in the s^d: Administracon then they to be Equally admitted as desired;—

John Williams, Hendrick Vander Burgh and John Darby C 115.
are appointed by ye Co^rt: for appraizers to appraize the Estate
of Ralph hutchinson deceased, for soe mutch thereof as Shall
bee w^th:in This County of New Castle and to make returne
thereof accordin to Lawe;

Appeared in Co^rt: Andrew Loue whoe produced the Laest C 115.
will and Testament of andrew Andersen deceased, Joseph
holding & James Beswick wittnesses to ye s^d: Laest will and
Testament of Andrew Anderson deceased appearing, did declare that they were p^rsent att ye signing delivering and pronouncing of ye same by ye s^d: Andrew Anderson, Ordered
that the will be allowed and Recorded

Copia Vera:

In the Name of God the father amen, C 116.
being Septemb^r: ye 26th: in ye Yeare 1683
this I: andrew Anderson being of perfect memory praized bee
to God for itt doe make and ordaine this my Laest will and
Testament, first I doe ordaine my boddy to bee burried in
Christian Burriall according to ye discretion of my Executo^rs:
hereafter nominated hopeing throug the merritts of Jesus
Christ to haue free foregivenesse of all my Sins; Ittem I: doe
ordaine and make andrew Loue my Selfe Soale Executo^r:, upon
Condition that he will pay all my debts; Ittem there is due
of my Sea wadges 6 pounds Sterl: of England, Received twoo
Shillings of his wyfe, More Nine pence; Received one p^r: of
broages and one hatt fower Shillings one bottell of Rum, a pair
of Compasses one Shilling, and the Cure of my Legg att St:
George's In wittnesse whereunto I: sett my hand the Day &
Yeare afores^d:

(was Signed)
Andrew Anderson—

In Margine Testo^r:
   wittnesses
  John holding
      his
  James I Beswick
     mark

C 117.   The Governo^r: and Co^{rt}: of New Castle this day did take into Consideracon and Examined the buisnesse of ye Town fly on ye North East Syde of this Towne of New Castle, and also about the foott dyke Lying before ye s^d: fly; and they being Sattisfyed as to ye Right of those as haue Sheares or parts therein, Doe therefore order that all the Inhabitants as now hold parts & Sheares in the s^d: fly Shall take Care to keep their parts in ye foott Dyke in good repair, that through the defect thereof the broad dyke may not bee Spoyled and the Governo^r: & Propriet^{ry}: William Penn doth in open Court promisse, that all those as now haue Sheares in ye s^d: Town fly Shall haue and hold ye same, and that hee will give them further Confirmation thereof by Pattents, upon Condition of keeping ye s^d: foott Dyke repaired as aboves^d: all w^{ch}: was ordered to bee Soe Recorded

The Co^{rt}: adjorned till the first Teusday of ye month of decemb^r: next—

Octob^r: 30th: 1683.

C 123.   Copia Vera

October ye 14th: 1679. Know all men by these p^{r}sents that wee Charles Rumsey and John Wattkins boath of Whyte clay Creeke Plant^{rs}: haueing betweene us one Certaine tract of Land Lying and being by Whyte Clay Creeke w^{ch}: is undivyded, and there being a Convenient place to Sett a Mill and that o^r: neighbors dwelling on Cheese and bread Island doe desire to build a mill there, Wee doe p^r: these p^{r}sents, bind, o^{r}selves o^r: heirs Executo^{rs}: or assignes to grant to these people, hereunder written that Certaine place Lett itt belong to Either of us when that o^r: Land is Sheared, and on Consideracon of ye Conveniencies of soe good a thing for o^r: owne use as well as those, Wee doe by these p^{r}sents give & Grant, to Either or to all of those partees here Setts their hands free Liberty to build a mill to them their heirs for Ever to Cull timber att all tymes for ye use of ye s^d: Mill when wanted to Either build New or mend att or neare ye Mill itt being a boath Sydes of a Little Creeke that Lyeth between Chease & bread Island and s^d: Charles

Rumseys plantation Running into Whyte Clay Creeke, as wittnesse o^r: hands ye date hereof itt being for o^r: use as well as theirs and to remaine a place wth:out any hindrance for a mill and for timber wthout ny molestation by us or any of o^r: heirs or assignes for Ever and hereunto Setts o^r: hands

(: was Signed :)

Wittnesse   Charles Rumsey—
Samuel Barker.   John Wattkins—

More on ye Paper of ye Mill on ye other Syde on folio 153 Recorded Stood these following words and Subscriptions Viz^t:—

Wee that here belong to ye mill is to haue all of us a Lyke, to bee att a Equall Charge to ye makeing of itt and here Setts o^r hands

(: was Signed by :)
John Smith—
Thos: Woollaston—
Abraham Man—
Joseph Barnes—
The mark × of—
Arent Jansen
Oela Thomassen
    marke
The × of
Jacob Jansen
John Nommers—

The mark × of

henry Gerritsen

Copia.

These are to Sattisfy all to whome these may Concerne that this day being y^e: 11th: of Jannuary 1682.— Abram Man, Arent Johnson and Oela Thomassen hath parted and Sheared out ye neck or point of Land Lying North North West from bread & Cheese Island and wee all being Content wth: this parting of o^r: Land and hath marked itt out accordingly as followeth and o^r: hands to

C 125.

itt, that is to Say Oela Thomassen beginneth att a Corner whyte oake att ye mouth of herrins brainch that runneth unto Red Clay Kill and Soe up the s^d: brainch to a Corner whyte oake in a Levell from thence by a Lyne of Marked trees to Red Clay Creeke and by ye Creeke to a Red Small oake bounded and Soe Cros ye s^d: Neck to a whyte oake bounded And from that by a Lyne to a Little whyte oake by ye kings Road, and Soe downe to Red Clay Creeke againe, wich then by that Cros Line beginneth Arent Johnsons Land and bound by Red Clay by a whyte oake in a Swamp, and Soe by ye Creeke to another whyte oake Standing by ye s^d: Creeke on a Levell Soe by a Cros Lyne of marked trees to Red Clay Creeke being the bounds of Abram Mans Land, and ye s^d Abram Man begins att ye s^d: Whyte oake in ye Levell or hill by Red Clay Creeke and by the said Cros Lyne over to ye s^d: Creeke to a bounded beetch by ye said Creeke, and Soe round by ye s^d: Creeke Sever^{ll}: Courses to ye said bounded Whyte oake againe by the said Red Clay Creeke to ye parting Lyne of Arent Johnson, this being the true bounds of o^r: Land and Wee doe bind o^r: Selues and o^r: heirs to performe and keepe ye same in quiet possession to Every one of us to us and o^r heirs for Ever as Wittnesse all o^r: hands the date abouewritten

                                                  (was Signed)

Wittnesse hereunto att ye wryting   Abraham Man
   Benjamin ✕ Goodman   Oela Thomassen
      his marke   The mark ✕ of
   William ☐ Parker   Arent Jansen
      his marke

The fourth day of ye tenth month 1683

Att a Court held in ye Town of New Castle by the Kings authority in ye name of the Honble: Will Penn Proprietory & Governor of Pennsilvania & Terrytorys

The Honble William Penn Propriatory and Governor of Pennsilvania & Territorys therunto belonging

Present
| William Welch
| Arnoldus De la Grange
| James Walliams
| John Williams
| Casparus Harman
| Henry Williams
} Justices

Abraham Man high Sherrif

John White presenting his Comission To Epherim Harman C 128. ye preceeding Clarke to be read the s^d Epherim Harman read it accordingly & resignd his office in ye Court to ye s^d John White who takeing possession of ye s^d: office of Clarke & acted in it

Hendrick Lemans P^lts
Hendrik Andres Def^t

The Pet declares for land unlawfully possest by the Deff^t C 128. as P^r declaration may appear

The Deff^t saith ye Land in Controversy belongeth to ye Church being given by ye first owner

Decembr^r ye 4th 1683

Reneer Van Cooling
John Nomers
Giles barret
Thomas Gillet
Thomas Woolaston
Joseph More
Gerrardus Wessels
Robart Hutchison
Charls Rumsy
Jno Willkinson
Andries Stalcop
Georg More

Laurane Cock being appointed Interpritor was accordingly attested

Samll Peters being attested saith he gave thirty foot of land to ye Church

Epherim Harman being attested saith, y^t Richard Noble he Survayd ye Land in controversy & the inhabitants made no objection

Wrion Wruonsen being attested saith the first donor allowed the Church so much land as it shoud need

The Jury upon ye matter going out bring in their verdict for ye Deff^t with cost of sute

The Court give Judgmen according to ye Verdict of ye Jury

December 6th 1683.
Abraham Mann   P^lt
Thomas Barecroft   Def^t

C 132.   Persuant to former orders of court it was ordered y^t Henry Vandeburg Pn^o Harmanson & William Guest doe apprays ye hous in controversy & make report thereof forth with to the Court

The partys aboue named accordingly under their hands bring in this account

Whereas we under written ware appointed praysers by ye court haue accordingly done our duty

And haue appraysed the house & ground at twenty six pounds country pay & giue it under our hands this Sixt day of ye tenth month 1683

                       Henry Vandeburg
                       William Guest
                       John Harmanson

The Subscribers attested ye appraiment aboue mentioned to be a just & true appraisment according to ye best of their skill & understanding

                       (Subscribed)
                       W̅i̅l̅l̅ Welch Pre^dnt

C 134.   Upon the Petition of John Wootters against Edmond Cantwell concerning a title of Land

Edmond Cantwell appearing desires a declaration according to law wch. ye Court ordered should be done against next Court

This day being ye fift of decembr

C 134.   *John & Christiana Moll &c acknowledg a Deed to Gabriell Rappe*   Appeared in open Court John Moll & Christiana his Wife & acknowledged a deed of Sale of a Plantation to Gabriell Rappe which s^d Deed may more at large appeare in ye office of Registry

This day being the fift of decembr

Robart & Ellinor Moreton & knowldg a deed to Justa Andries
Appeared in open Court Robert Moreton and Ellinor his wife & acknowledged a Deed of sale as ye s^d: deed may more at larg appear in ye office of Registry   C 134.

The Court adjurnd

This instant being the eight day of the 11th month appeared before me John White Clarke of ye County of Newcastle Thomas Bell of newcastle County Planter & did acknowledg a letter of Atturny to Joseph More of Duck Creeke impowring ye s^d Joseph more to receive all ye debts & effects of ye s^d Thomas Bell in anny of ye Kings dominions & by the s^d letter of atturny doth espetially impower the s^d More to acknowledge a deed of sale of two hundred and thirty akres of land scituate in Duck Creeke & Sould to Thomas Harris   C 140.

A List of the Names of all such Persons as Inhabit within ye Constablery of the Town of New castle with ye sums Respectively added to their names what they are to pay towards ye present Tax or Levy for defraying of ye Publicke Charg of the County of Newcastle—   C 141.

	Akres of Land	Town Lotts	Tithebles	Pounds	Shillings	Pence
John Matson for 1/6 of 800 akres	133				1	6
Henry Lemans ye like 133 his Iland 100 in ye back of John Williams	233 445				7	6
Hendrik Andries	133		1		4	2
Eskell Andries	133				1	6
William Jansen	133				1	6
Hendrick Evertson	133				1	6
Jacob Claeson	100				.1	1
John Jaquet	280		1		5	9
Jurian Boatsman	370				4	1
Arnoldus de Legrang	300	4			7	7
Oella Paulson	100				1	1
Paul Laerson	100				1	1
Engelbert Lott	100	2			3	3
Charles Rumsey	100				1	1
William Haigh	400				4	4

	Akres of Land	Town Lotts	Tithebles	Pounds	Shillings	Pence
Charles Rumsey & John Wattkins	640	....	....	....	7	....
John Darby	300	....	....	....	3	3
John Gerretson	200	1	1	....	6	1
Robart Hutchison for his brother	200	0	1	....	4	10
Andries Tilly	150	....	1	....	4	4
John Ogle	400	....	1	....	7	....
Thomas Spry	300	6	1	....	12	5
Samll Land	300	1	1	....	7	....
John Nettleship	170	....	1	....	4	7
Giles Barret	550	2	2	....	10	9
Epharim Harmon	400	2	2	....	9	2
Edward Land	....	....	1	....	2	8
William Welch	....	1	2	....	6	5
Henrick Vandburg	450	4	3	....	17	2
Hans Corderus	100	....	1	....	3	9
John Williams Neering	500	2	6	1	3	7
Peter Allricks	1000	2	4	1	3	8
John Moll	300	6½	2	....	15	7
Capt. Markham	1000	....	....	....	10	10
Mathyas De Ring	....	3	1	....	5	11
Domini Tessemaker	....	6	....	....	6	6
John White	....	1	1	....	3	9
Ambros Baker	80	5	1	....	9	....
Antonous Bryant	....	8	1	....	11	4
Reneer Vandr Cooling	....	12	1	....	15	8
John Cann	....	1	....	....	1	1
James Walliam	....	2	2	....	7	6
Eldeert Egberts	....	1	....	....	1	1
Gerritt Smith	....	3	....	....	3	3
Claes Daniell	....	1	1	....	3	9
Hybert Hendricks	....	2	....	....	2	2
Georg More	....	1	1	....	3	9
John Smith	....	2	1	....	4	10
John ffolk	....	1	1	....	4	10
Sybrant Folk	....	1	1	....	3	9
John Mandy	....	1	1	....	3	9
John Biscus	....	6	1	....	9	2
Lorrain	....	1	....	....	1	1

RECORDS OF THE COURT OF NEW CASTLE. 81

Emelius d Ring	....		5	1	....	8	1
John Bower	....		2	1	....	4	10
Moses d Gam	....		1	....	....	1	1
Adam Hay	....		1	1	....	3	9
Governor Penn	....		1	....	....	1	1
Henricus Williams	....		3	....	....	3	3
Josyn Semple	....		2	....	....	2	2
Johannes de Haes	....		2	1	....	4	10
John Harmansan	....		2	1	....	4	10
Isack Tine	....		1	1	....	3	9
Justa Andries	....		1	1	;....	3	9
John Henrickson	....		1	1	....	3	9
Judah Crawford	....		1	....	....	1	1
Edmond Cantwell	100		2	1	....	5	11
Henry Jones	100		....	2	....	6	5
Mary Block	350		....	....	....	3	10
Joseph More	....		....	1	....	2	8
Willow Marslander	150		....	....	....	1	8
Artman Hyam	40		....	....	....	....	6
John Baretsan	40		....	....	....	....	6
Cornelius Johnson	80		....	....	....	....	11
Peter dewitt	60		....	....	....	....	8
Harman & John Sybranson	150		....	....	....	1	8
William Corseer	150		....	....	....	1	8
John Carter	....		....	1	....	2	8
Vander Cooling	....		....	1	....	2	8
Gerardus Wessells	....		....	2	....	5	4
John Dewson	....		....	1	....	2	8
Isack Slover	....		....	1	....	2	8
Harman Lawree	....		....	1	....	2	8
Eldren Forstbeen	....		....	1	....	2	8
Dierick Hybertson	....		....	1	....	2	8
Claus Daniell	....		....	1	....	2	8
Gerret Jansen	....		....	1	....	2	8
Thomas Langshaw	....		....	1	....	2	8
Hybert Lawrenson	....		....	2	....	5	4
Richard Mattshall	....		....	3	....	8	0
Jan Sybrantson	....		....	2	....	5	4
Tennis deWitt	....		....	1	....	2	8
James Hardy	....		....	1	....	2	8
Harman Johnson	....		....	1	....	2	8
Sybran Jansen	....		....	2	....	5	4
John Screek	....		....	2	....	5	4
Lauranc Andrieson	....		....	1	....	2	8

	Acres of Land	Tithebles	Pounds	Shillings	Pence
Mathyas Lawson			1		2	8
Hendrick Leman			2		5	4
Jacob Clasan			1		2	8
Peiter Jaquet			1		2	8
Vrion Boreson			2		5	4
Oella Paulson			1		2	8
Edward Harry			1		2	8
Paul Lawson			2		5	4
Humphry Nicolls			1		2	8
John Brisco			1		2	8
The Summ totall of ye Constablery of Newcastle town amounts to.........				℔ 25	:9	7

The List of the Constablery of North Christina Creeke

		Acres of Land	Tithebles	Pounds	Shillings	Pence
C 143.	Valentine Hollingsworth	1000	4	1	1	6
	Morgan Drewet	500	2		8	11
	John Jerson		1		2	8
	Thomas Gulping		1		2	8
	Michall Woollson	230	1		5	2
	Siek Woollson		1		2	8
	Wolla Woollson	250	2		8	
	Christopher Myars	230	1		5	2
	Lauranc Oalson	150	2		7	
	John Monson	150	2		7	
	Giesbert de Voos		1		2	8
	Oalla Thomas	200	2		7	6
	Hans Peters	600	2		11	10
	Justa Paulson	125	1		4	
	Lullof Stidden	250	2		8	
	Asman Stidden	100	3		9	1
	Charles Stalcop		3		8	1
	Thomas Woollaston	370	2		9	6
	Conrade Constantine	560	2		11	5
	Jacob Vandr veer	500	1		10	9
	John Nomers	240	2		8	
	Will: Vanderveer		1		2	8

RECORDS OF THE COURT OF NEW CASTLE.

Jacob Clements	150	1	....	4	4
Andrew Stalcop	117	3	....	9	4
Samuell Peterson	117	1	....	4	....
Charles Peterson	250	1	....	5	3
Henry Lantson	150	1	....	4	4
Henry Gerritson ⎱ Paul Gerritson ⎰	200	1	....	10	2
Moses de Gam	....	1	....	2	8
Paul Monson	80	1	....	3	8
Jonas Arskue	400	1	....	7	0
James Clarke	....	1	....	2	8
Arnoldus delaGrang	1150	2	....	17	9
Brewer Senecar	770	3	....	16	6
John Cann	500	2	....	10	9
Jan Vanderveer	....	2	....	5	4
Giles Barret	550	1	....	8	8
Mathyas Smith	50	1	....	3	3
Abraham Man	570	3	....	14	4
John Moll	210	2	....	7	6
Robart & John Vance	....	2	....	5	4
Gisbert Janson	300	1	....	5	11
Joseph Barns	350	1	....	6	6
Joseph Cookson	200	1	....	4	10
Henry Dull	100	1	....	3	9
Joseph Bowles	300	1	....	5	11
Thomas Gillet	300	2	....	8	11
William Guest	700	4	....	18	3
John Smith	800	1	....	11	4
Samll Barker	200	1	....	4	10
Robart Winson	200	2	....	7	10
Adam Sharply	300	1	....	5	11
Will Lesser	....	1	....	2	8
Nicholas Nelson	230	2	....	8	8
Jacob Clementson	....	1	....	2	8
Jonas Cauging	150	1	....	4	4
Jacob Henrickson	300	....	....	3	3
Jan Stalcop	717	....	....	17	9
Aaron Johnson	212	....	....	2	4
John Oagle	1000	....	....	10	10
Andrew Stilly	100	....	....	1	1
Lucas Steddam	200	....	....	2	2
Samll Land	400	....	....	4	4
John White	200	....	....	2	2

A List of ye Constablery of ye North side of Duck Creeke	Akres of Land	Tithebles	Pounds	Shillings	Pence
4. Morris Liston	750	5	1	1	6
Joseph Alman	200	2	....	7	6
Ralph Horsly	....	1	....	2	8
William Sharwood	150	2	....	7	....
Christopher Ellet	....	2	....	5	4
John Taylor	215	1	....	....	....
Michall Offly	312	2	....	8	9
Edward Owen	117	3	....	10	....
Joseph More	1100	1	....	14	7
Thomas Harrison	800	1	....	11	4
Andren Loue	200	1	....	4	10
Benjamen Gumly	280	1	....	5	8
Thomas Snelling	666	2	....	12	6
John Wallker Senior	500	2	....	8	1
Timothy Pead	....	2	....	5	8
Henricus Williams	400	5	....	17	8
Will: Grant	765	2	....	13	9
Robart Moreton	....	2	....	5	4
Joseph Holding	....	1	....	2	8
Dierick Johnson	100	3	....	9	1
Justa Anderson	200	....	....	2	2
Epharim Harman	1200	....	....	13	0
Peter Bayard	600	....	....	6	6
Fabee	70	....	....	....	10
Mall francis	60	....	....	....	9
Christopher Ellit	600	....	....	6	6
Edward Cantwell	4285	17	4	11	10
Ann Wertherdale	480	....	....	5	3
Thomas Gelping	480	....	....	5	3
John Barker	240	....	....	2	7
Joseph Harris	214	....	....	2	4
Isack Weelden	220	....	....	2	4
Ould Johnson	100	....	....	1	1
Claes Johnson	100	....	....	1	1
Francis Wallker	100	....	....	1	1
Mary Francis	50	....	....	....	7
Thomas Bell	200	....	....	2	2
Will Scarf	200	....	....	2	2

RECORDS OF THE COURT OF NEW CASTLE. 85

John Peirson	190	....	....	2	1
Christian	200	....	....	2	2
Sybrant ffolk	200	....	....	2	2
Widdow Moretons Children	850	....	....	9	3
Widdow Moreton	470	....	....	5	2
Robart money alien	400	....	....	6	6
Basilia Osborn Alien	400	....	....	6	6
John Jervice	200	....	....	2	2
Joseph Holding	466	....	....	5	2

A List of ye Inhabitants of ye Constablery form Georgs Creek to ye north side Apaquemene	Akres of Land	Titheables	Pounds	Shillings	Pence
Casparus Harman	400	5	....	17	8
Danell Smith	....	1	....	2	8
Henry Williams	250	4	....	13	5
Cobus Andries	165	3	....	9	10
Henry Wallraven	225	1	....	5	2
John Foster	250	1	....	5	5
John Taaylor	200	2	....	7	6
Thomas Snoding	350	2	....	9	6
William Phillips	450	1	....	7	7
Isack Killingworth	....	1	....	2	8
John Peterson	684	3	....	15	6
Gerrett Otto	452	9	1	8	11
John Wallker	950	3	....	18	4
Roelofe Anderson	350	3	....	11	10
Hans Hanson	500	1	....	8	1
Adam Peterson	390	2	....	9	8
Peter Absinck	109	1	....	3	11
Abraham Enloos	....	2	....	5	4
John Parry	....	3	....	8	....
Ellis Humpheris	200	2	....	7	6
Judeth Crawford	600	2	....	11	10
John Macklin	150	1	....	4	4
John Choes	....	1	....	2	8
John on grants Land	....	1	....	2	8
Peter Allricks	400	1	....	7	0
Oalla Toolsen	200	2	....	7	6
John Darby	400	2	....	9	8
John Darby for Robart Parks	400	....	....	6	6

C 145.

Jnº: Willkinson & Benit Stayes	400	2	....	9	8
Gabriell Rappe	1000	6	1	6	10
Jacob Young	1000	3	....	18	10
John Elderkin	....	1	....	2	8
Jacob Archer	150	....	....	1	8
William Cheeke	300	....	....	3	3
Huybert Laurance	330	....	....	3	4
Robart Hutchison	400	....	....	4	4
Augustin Dicks	150	....	....	1	8
John Scot	400	....	....	4	4
Edward Green	470	....	....	5	4
Antony Wallice	250	....	....	2	9
Richard Hudding	200	....	....	2	2
Ephrim Harman & Johannes de Haes	400	....	....	4	4
Magnus White	170	....	....	2	....
Richard Noble	200	....	....	3	3
Richard Ingelo	256	....	....	4	0
Bryan Omely	400	....	....	6	6
Henry Vandburg	1000	....	....	10	10
Henry Vandburg	200	....	....	2	2
Capt Ward	600	1	....	9	4

The foregoing List of all the Land and Titheble̲s was presented by the severall Constables of this County according to their distinct bounds to the Justices who hauing adjusted every mans proportion comanded coppys to be taken & warrants to be issued out to the fores^d. Constables for the Spedy Levying the severall Sums annexed which was accordingly done.

Fabruary y^e 19. 168$\frac{3}{4}$

C 146.   Att a Court held att Newcastle by the Kings Authority in y^e name of the Propriatary & the 19^{nth} of y^e 11th month called Fabruary 168$\frac{3}{4}$

	William Welch Pres^{dnt}	
	James Walliam	
Pres^{nt}	John Williams	Justices
	Henry Williams	

C 147.   Richard Smith acknowledged a Deed of four hundred Akres of Land to Samll Land

C 148.   Valantine Hollingsworth presents a petition about y^e estate of James Scot deceased the Court Referr him to ye Pres^{dnt} for letters of administration

Bryan Omely acknowledged a Deed of two hundred akres of Land to John Wallker Junior

The Court adjurned untill ye next County Court in Aprill next   C 149

April 15 1684

Att a Court held at Newcastle for our Lord the King & ye C 154. Honble William Penn Propriat^y ye 15th of Aprill 1684—

The Honobl^e Proprietor

Being Pres^{nt}
William Welch Pres^{dnt}
John Cann—
James Walliam
John Williams
Casparus Harman
Justices

Samuell Land High Sherrif

George Forman P^{lt}:
atturny of Jaruis Marshall
Oalla Toolson   Def^t

The P^{lt} pleads for land now in ye possession of ye Def^t pretending a purchase from Patrick Carr the former owner

The Def^t pleads a deed and brings evidence y^t ye P^l renounct his bargain of ye s^d Land Vizt

Samll Land Casparus Harman Jacob Young, Wittness for ye Def^t

Patrick Carr deposeth ye s^d Land was never Sold to ye Def^t to ye best of his knowledg

Judgment
Jarvice Marshall deposeth he never renounct his Bargain

Robart Hutchison attested saith ye P^{lt}: paid 500 ℔ for tobacco for a Sute of cloths in part of pay for the s^d land

The Court demanding if ye Plt had ever a deed for the s^d Land which not appearing & ye Def^t produceing a good Deed from ye s^d Carr the Jury going out at their return find for the Def^t with costs of Sute the Court approve ye Verdict

88 RECORDS OF THE COURT OF NEW CASTLE.

C 157. Acknowledgments of Deeds
A Deed from Helena Moreton to Joseph Holding for two hundred Akres of Land baring date ye 15 day of ye 11th month 1683 was acknowledged in Court

C 157. A Deed from Helena Moreton to Edmond Cantwell for two Hundred Sixty one akres of land baring date ye 14 day of ye 11th month was acknowledged in Court 1683

C 157. A Deed from Thomas Snelling to Edmond Cantwell for 550 akres of land baring date ye 14 of ye 11th month 1683 was acknowledged in Court

Aprill 16: 1684

C 158. Robart Darby presenting a petition for a town Lott the Governor was pleasd to grant it

C 158. The Court adjurned to ye usuall time

C 161. Att a Court held at New Castle for our Lord ye King & ye Honble Propriatary and Governor June ye 17th 1684:

Pres^{nt}
William Welch Pres^{dnt}
John Cann
James Walliams
John Williams

Samll Land High Sherrif

C 166. A Morgage formerly made to John Moll from Daniell Lindsay was by the s^d Moll assignd ouer to Robart Hutchison

C 166. The Court order the Inhabitants be deuided in severall proportions & y^t the Town flys shall be deuided in the like number of proportions & every proportion to cast lotts for their parts y^t none shall presume to cutt the grass untill ye 20th of July next

The Court Adjurned

July 15: 1684

Att A Court held for our Lord ye King and the Honble Propriatary & Governor at Newcastle on ye 15^{nth} of ye 5th month 1684

Present
William Welch Pres^dnt
James Walliam
Henry Williams
Valantine Hollingsworth
} Justices

Barbara Marslander P^lt
Artman Haym Def^t   C 168.

The Def^t and his wife promis in ye open Court to make &
acknowledg a firm Deed for the land in controversy upon Saturday next before two Justices by ye Court impowred for y^t
purpose for ye use of Barbara Marslander ye P^lt who upon
y^t condition agrees to suspend farder proceedings in law

Jacob Vander Veer P^lt
Artman Haym Def^t   C 168.

The P^lt being bound in a 100 ^lb bound y^t ye Def^t shall perform certain conditions to ye above s^d Barbara Marslander
upon ye Deft promis in Court to perform ye conditions the
tryall is suspended

Adjurnd untill ye 19^nth of this Instant

Att A Court Held at Newcastle for our Lord ye King & y^e
Honble Propriatary & Governor August ye 19^nth 1684—   C 171.

Pres^nt
William Welch Pres^dt
John Cann
James Walliam
Casparus Harman
} Justices

Samll Land high Sherrife

Georg More Acknowledged a deed of Sale for his right to   C 175.
a hundred eighty five Akres of Land Surua'd ye 15 of August
1682 to Job Nettleship & Edward Boulton

Agust 20th 1684—

Derick ffransen acknowledged a Deed of Sale for assigna-   C 176.
tion for a Plantation Lying in Swanwick q^t 40 Rod before
and behind and in length four hundred Rod and bearing
date this Instant to Ambrose Baker

C 176. A Deed from Artman Haym to Barbara Mars Lander baring date ye 12th of August 1684 was acknowledged in Court

The Court Adjurnd untill ye third teusday in September next

September 16 1684

C 177. At A Court held at Newcastle for our Lord the King & the Honble Propriatary & Governor the 16^{nth} of September 1684

Pres^{nt}
John Cann
James Walliam
John Williams
Henry Williams
} Justices

Samll Land high Sherrife

C 179. John White Petitioning to haue an Attachment Allowed ags^t ye estate of John Carter and that what Effects the s^d John White can find of the s^d John Carters in this County may be likewise Attached for the s^d Whites use he hauing made it Appear y^t the s^d Carters estate is indebted in seuerall considerable sumes of money whereupon the Court grants his Petition

C 179. A Voluntary Conditionall Deed was acknowledged in Court by Gabriell Rappe & John Moll for the use of Mr Daniell Duthay Merchant at London baring date this Instant as p^r the s^d Deed may Appear

C 180. A Deed from Arnoldus D Legrang baring date ye 19th of August 1684 was acknowledged to Robart Robinson

C 180. Robart Robinson acknowledged a bond & Morgage for payment of forty pounds money of Pensiluania to Arnoldus D Legrang for wch 200 Akres of Land is Morgaged the bond is Since Paid & the Mortgage discharged in open Court March 16^{nth} 1685

C 180. Arnoldus D Legrang acknowledged a Deed of 200 akres of Land baring date this Instant to Lucas Stiddum

C 180. Lucas Stiddum Acknowledged a Deed of 230 Akres of Land baring date this day to Arnold Legrang

Arnold D Legrang Acknowledged a Deed of 200 akres of Land baring date ye 15th of this instant to Oalla Paulson C 180.

Edmund Cantwell Transports a pattent for 200 akres of Land & baring date this Instant to Hans Miller— C 180.

Engelty Barns Acknowledged a Deed of Morgage of hir plantation at Swanwick baring date ye 1st of September 1684 to ye Presdnt & Court of Orphans of the town & County of newcastle for payment of thirty two pounds & ten Shillings to hir Daughter Branchee Barns when s^d Daughter Shall arriue at ye age of twenty one years or at hir day of marryage wch shall first happen C 180.

An Indenture betwixt James Hallyday & Engel^ty Barns for Settlement of ye Land of the s^d Engel^ty upon a consideration of Marryage & for other uses therein mentioned baring date ye 1st of Septembr 1684 was acknowledged in Court C 180.

John Cann by order of the Provinciall Counsell is Appointed Register of the town & County of Newcastle wch order was read in Court C 181.

The Court Adjurns untill the 3rd Tuesday in October next

Octobr 21 1684
Att A Court Held at Newcastle the 21 of October 1684 for our Lord the King & the Propriatary & Governor

Pre^snt: John Cann
James Walliam
Henricus Williams } Justices
Valantine Hollingsworth
Samll Land High Sherrife

Magnus White Petitions to haue his writings concerning his Land now in ye hands of Mrs Welch the Court sends a messenger for ye s^d papers C 183.

John Peterson & Derick Williams Petition this Court concerning the Estate of Garret Otto the Court order the widdow to make application for Letters of Administration & if she Refuse y^t some other p^rson be appointed to Administer C 183.

C 183. John Peterson & Derick Williams appointed Appraysers of Estate of Garret Otto—

C 184. John Peterson Exhibiting a Petition and an Account concerning the Estate of Thomas Sadler Deceased the Co^{rt} think fitt to consider of it whilst the next County Co^{rt}:

C 184. Justus & Alchy Anderson acknowledge a Deed of one hundred & seventy Acres of Land to Magnus White

C 184. John Pearson Acknowledged a Deed to Christopher Ellit for a psell of Land called Pearsons Lodge

The Co^{rt} Adjurns

1684 Novem 19

C 185. Att a Court Held at Newcastle the 19th of November 1684 for our Lord the King & the Honble Propriatary & Governor:

Pre^{snt}:
John Cann
James Walliam
Casparus Harman
Valantine Hollingsworth
} Justices

Samll Land High Sherrife

C 192. Casparus Harman acknowledged a Deed in Open Court of a Pattent for a psell of land called the good Naibourhood to Jno Biscus Roalof Andrews & Mathyas Defoss who again in open Court Assigned ouer all their Seuerall Rights & Interest to Hybert Lauranson

C 192. Hans Corderus Acknowledged a Deed for a Lott of land in the town of Newcastle betwixt ye Minquas Street & the Beaver Street to John Harmanson.—

C 194. Know all men by thes p^{r}sents that I Gerardus Wessels of the town of Newcastle & Territorys of Pensilvania doe acquit Release & Discharge Reneer Van Coolen of the same town & place of & from a Contract of Partnership Contracted at ye town of Lewis in ye County of Sussex dated ye 5th day of the third month 1682: and allso doe Resign over unto ye s^d Coolen all ye land and part of the two houses that I was to haue of ye s^d Reneer Van Coolen in ye town of Newcastle hauing Re-

A true coppy of ye Originall

ceived a Consideration for ye same as Wittnes my hand and Seal this 9th day of the 5th month 1684

Testis
John Hillyard
Robart Hutchinson

Gerardus Wesselle (sele)

Att a Court held at Newcastle for our Lord ye King & ye Honble Propriatary December ye 16^nth 1684—

Present

John Cann
James Walliams
John Williams
Henricus Williams
Valantine Hollingsworth
Casparus Herman
} Justices

At ye Request of James Reed Abraham Man & John Smith Junior ware Attested who declare they heard John Smith senior deceased say in his life time y^t his deeds concerning his Land in new jarsey ware burnt C 196.

The Court order ye Estate of Eldred fforsbeen be Exposed to Sale betwixt this Court & the last day of ye next Court for payment of his debts. C 196.

Peter Andries Hallman ordered to make Return of ye Appraysment of Laurance Toorsons Estate to ye next Court C 196.

Ordrd that the Swamp lately belonging to Peter allricks by his house be recorded to be fforfaited to ye Town of newcastle according to his own promise C 196.

Ordrd y^t if the owners of ye land on this side Christina Creek doe not speedily keep a fferry that upon their Refusall anny other person may have ye benefitt C 196.

Elisabeth Ogle brings in an account in Court that She hath paid many pounds more to hir husbands Crds then the whole Estate of hir s^d late husband did amount to by ye Appraysment C 196.

Georg More Resigns in open Court his Right to a Warrant C 197.

for a hundred and six Acres of Land Survayd ye 17^nth of Decembr 1683: called Thick Wood

The Court Adjurned

At a Court held at newcastle for our Lord ye King & ye Honble Propriatary ye 20th of January 1684 it being a quarter Sessions—

Present — Justices Present:
- John Cann
- James Walliam
- John Williams
- Henry Williams
- Valantine Hollingsworth
- Edward Green
- Casparus Herman
- Henry Lemmans

Samuell Land high sherrif

C 197. Otto Otto Presenting a Petition concerning his ffathers Estate The Court order ye Constable of that Precinct with thos persons formerly appointed by ye Court to take a true Inventory & Appraysment of ye s^d Etate & to make Report at ye Court & if ye s^d Widdow refuse to Administer some other p^rson be appointed thereto without delay: Casparus Harman John Wallker & Adam Peterson are appointed Guardians of ye Children of Garrat Otto deceased

C 198. Upon ye Petition of Jan Paul Jaquet to be discharged from ye trouble of keeping a fferry The Court order that Charles Pickering & Georg more consider of ye most convenient Place with ye least damage to ye owners of ye Land for ye keeping a fferry over Christina Creek & to make Report at ye next Court:

C 201. John Wodkings by his Atturny John Nomers Acknowledged a Deed for a parcell of Land called non such wch Deed bare date ye 9th day of January 1684 to Charls Rumsey

C 201. Jacob Clausan acknowledged a Deed to Claus Andrews for a parcell of Land at Pert Hooke & did acknowledge the Receipt of ten pounds in part of payment

The Court Ajurns

Fabruary 17^nth : 168¾
At a Court held at Newcastle for our Lord ye King & ye C 202.
Honble Propriatary & Governor ye 17^nth day of ffabruary 1685/5

Present
- John Cann
- James Williams
- Henricus Williams
- Valant: Hollingsworth
- Henry Lemmans
- William Guest
} Justices

Samll Land High Sherrif

Edmund Cantwell in open Court did acknowledge y^t he did   C 206.
allow of ye Sale of his house & ground taken upon Execution
for Evert Henricks & y^t he hath no Pattent but y^t ye s^d
house & ground was his own before it was Executed

Upon ye motion of Casparus Harman concerning ye Estate   C 207.
of Will Maruill Deceased ye Court order ye s^d s^d Casparus
Harman to take ye Effects of ye Deceased into his custody to
pay ye debts of ye s^d Maruill therewith & to make Report of
his proceedings therein at ye next Court

Lewis Dauis Administrator of ye Estate of Evan Salisbury   C 207.
Petitions ye Court for his quietus est: he haue proud by y^e
Records that he had allready payd more then ye Effects did
amount to & no Crdr coming in according to ye direction of y^e
Law:
The Court grant him his quietus est:

Upon ye Petition of Mathyas Toreson for Lett^rs: of Adminis- C 207.
tracon on his ffathers Estate ye Court ord^r y^t ye Administrator
to whom ye Letters of Administracon are allready graned shall
pay no debts out of ye s^d Estate but what are first allowed in
Court

James Becwick acknowledges a deed of all his Right to 400   C 208.
acres of Land (in pnership betwixt him ye s^d James & ffrancis
Hutchins) to Andrew Loue:

Jonas Arskin acknowledges a deed of sale of a Pattent for   C 208.
200 acres of Land callend ye Barron Point to John White of
newcastle.

C 208.   I doe by thes Presents assign & make ouer unto Samuell Land high sherrif of y[e] Town & County of Newcastle one certain house & ground lying & being in y[e] 2nd Street next adjoyning to y[e] house & ground of y[e] s[d] Land it being for his Security of a certain Execution obtained by Euert Henricks against me giuing him full power to Expose to Sale at his will & pleasure y[e] s[d] house & ground for y[e] satisfying of y[e] s[d] Execution in wittnes whereof I haue hereunto sett my hand y[e] 20th of october 1684

  Testis   Ed Cantwell
 John Cann
 John Mandy

y[e] aboue s[d] is a true coppy of y[e] originall paper

C 209.   Charles Pickering & Georg more conform to a former order of Court make Report y[t] y[e] ffittest place to Keep a fferry on Christina Creek is on the south side

C 209.   Samuell Land acknowledged y[e] Assignment of his Pattent of 400 acres of Land in White Clay Creek to John Cann

A List of y[e] Land & Tithebles of y[e] County of necastle Returned by[e] Constables 1684/5	Acres	Tithebles	Lotts	Pounds	Shill.	pence
Mathyas De Ring	0000	01	03	000	05	11
Dominy Tesmaker	0000	00	06	000	06	6:5
Anthony Bryan	0000	00	03	000	05	11
Peter Allricks	1475	03	02	001	06	1
Capt Markum	1000	00	00	000	10	10
Isack Slouer	0000	01	01	000	03	9
Thomas Langshaw	0200	01	01	000	05	11
Abraham Man	0000	00	02	000	02	2
ffrancis Scot	0000	07	00	000	18	8
John Henricks	0000	01	01	000	03	9:5
Justa Anderson	0000	01	01	000	03	9
William Kemmell	000	01	00	000	02	8
Robart Hutchinson	0400	01	00	000	07	0
Emelius de Ring	0000	01	05	000	08	1
Reneer Vand[r] Coolen	0000	02	04	000	09	8
Gerardus Wessells	0000	01	00	000	02	8
Anthony Tomkings	0000	01	00	000	02	8

C 210.

RECORDS OF THE COURT OF NEW CASTLE.

Name	Acres	Town Lotts	Tithebbles	lb	s	d
John Harmsen	0000	02	02	000	07	6
John Boyer	0000	01	01	000	03	9
Hendrick Vandrburg	0650	02	05	000	17	10:5
John Dehaes	0050	01	01	000	04	3½
Edmond Cantwell	0050	00	01	000	01	1
John Williams	0550	02	02	000	13	6
Joslyn Semple	0400	00	01	000	05	5
John Biscus	0000	01	03	000	05	11
James Walliam	0000	02	01	000	06	5
John Cann	0000	00	02	000	02	2
James Walliam	0000	00	01	000	01	1
Mathyas Vand^r Heyden	0000	02	00	000	05	4
Susannah Welch	0000	00	02	000	02	2
Hendrick Williams	0000	01	02	000	04	10
				010	07	3

Name	Acres	Town Lotts	Tithebbles	lb	s	d
John Valke	0000	01	01	00	03	9
William Bandfall	0000	00	01	00	02	8
Ergelbert Lott	0150	03	00	00	04	10
William Crosee	0000	01	01	00	03	9
William Hauge	0436	00	00	00	04	9
John fforeat	0000	00	01	00	02	8
Henry massyan	0000	00	01	00	02	8
Moses Dejam	0000	00	01	00	02	8
Samuell Land	0200	01	01	00	05	11:5
John Smith	0000	02	01	00	03	10
Joseph Burnham	0000	01	00	00	01	1
Sybran Valk	0000	01	00	00	01	1
Widdow Hiberts	0000	03	00	00	03	3
John Hulk	0000	00	01	00	02	8
Jacob Gerret	0000	00	01	00	02	8
Claes Daniell	0000	01	01	00	03	9
Thomas Spry	0300	04	01	00	10	3
William Little	0000	00	01	00	02	8:5
John mandy	0000	01	01	00	03	9
John Moll	0300	05	01	00	11	4
Epharim Herman	0400	02	01	00	09	2
Arnoldus Legrang	0400	03	00	00	07	7

Name	Acres	Town Lotts	Tithebls	lb	s	d
Garret Smith	0000	03	01	00	05	11
Mathyas Devoos	0000	01	00	00	01	1
John White	0600	0½	03	00	15	0
Joseph More	0000	01	01	00	03	9
Ambros Baker	0000	05	01	00	08	1
Henry Jones	0100	00	01	00	03	9
Mary Block	0400	00	00	00	04	4
Hybert Laurence	0300	00	01	00	05	11:5
Peter Valkerson	0000	00	01	00	02	8
Barbara Marslander	0097	00	00	00	01	1
Edward Boulton	0100	00	01	00	03	9
Artman Haym	0097	00	01	00	03	9
John Jaquet	0080	00	01	00	03	6
Tunis De Witt	0060	00	01	00	03	4½
John Doedus	0050	00	01	00	03	3
James Halliday	0050	00	01	00	03	3
Humphery Nicholls	0000	00	01	00	02	8
			03	08	11	10

A Continuacon of newcastle Constably

Name	Acres	Town Lotts	Tithebls	lb	s	d
William Sute	000	000	01	00	02	8
Thomas Peirson Survayor	000	000	01	00	02	8
Lewis Dauis	0200	000	01	00	04	10
Elisabeth Johnson	0100	000	00	00	01	1
John Pristner	0000	000	01	00	02	8
Sybran Johnson	0050	000	01	00	03	6.5
John Sybrance	0050	000	01	00	03	6
Clas Andrews	0030	000	01	00	03	0
Widdow of Harman Johnson	0050	000	00	00	00	6
Henrick Euertson	0240	000	01	00	05	4
John mathyasan	0120	000	02	00	06	2
Lace Anderson	0000	000	01	00	02	8
Lasse Larson	0000	000	01	00	02	8
Mathyas Lareson	0120	000	01	00	03	11
Henrick Anderson	0180	000	01	00	03	6
Henrick Lemmans	0830	000	02	00	14	4
Jacob Clasan	0300	000	01	00	05	11.5
William Willix	0000	000	01	00	02	8

RECORDS OF THE COURT OF NEW CASTLE. 99

John Jaquet & 2 sons	0290	000	02	00	08	6
Jurian Boreson	0370	000	01	00	06	8
Oalla Paulson	0200	000	01	00	03	10
Paul Aersen	0200	000	02	00	07	6
Charles Rumsey	0640	000	01	00	07	5
John Garetson	0400	001	01	00	08	1
John Pennington	0200	000	02	00	07	6
William Green: The Peirson: pays.	0200	000	00	00	02	2.5
Andrew Stilly	0500	000	01	00	08	1
Jonas Arskin	0200	000	01	00	04	10
Edward Land	0100	000	01	00	03	9
Job nettleship	0100	000	01	00	03	9
Walter Powell	0000	000	01	00	02	8
Hans Hansen	0200	000	02	00	07	6
Jacob Cornelison	0000	000	01	00	02	8
William Woodhouse	0000	000	01	00	02	8
				07	19	2

a List of ye north of Duck Creeke	Acres	Tithebles	lotts	£	s	d	
John Taylor	0250	01	00	00	05	4	C 213.
Widdow Ellit	0400	00	00	00	04	4	
Andrew Loue	0200	00	00	00	02	2	
Joseph ormond	0200	03	00	00	10	2	
Epharim Harman	1600	00	00	00	17	4	
Peter Bayard	1000	00	00	00	10	10	
Francis Latts	0050	01	00	00	03	2½	
Ralph Horsly	0050	01	00	00	03	2½	
Morris Liston	0750	05	00	01	01	9	
Will Sherrer	0150	00	00	00	01	8	
Edward Owen	0175	05	00	00	15	2	
Antony Tomkings	0500	02	00	00	10	8	
Thomas Harris	1200	04	00	01	03	8	
Thomas ffurby	0200	00	00	00	02	2	
Gisbert Wolluerson	0200	00	00	00	02	2	
Joseph more	0600	00	00	00	06	6	
William Scarf	0200	00	00	00	02	2	
William Hatten	0600	00	00	00	06	6	
Michall offly	0312	01	00	00	07	0	
Daniell mackarty	0200	01	00	00	03	9	

Derick & Claus Johnson	0200	00	00	00	02	2
Francis Wallker	0100	00	00	00	01	1
Richard Michall	0200	00	00	00	02	2
Thomas Gelping	0480	00	00	00	05	4
Ann neeterdale	0480	00	00	00	05	4
John Barker	0240	01	00	00	05	4
Joseph Harris	0214	00	00	00	02	4
Isack Weelden	0220	00	00	00	02	4:5
Thomas Snelling	0866	00	00	00	17	3
Benjamen Gumley	0280	01	00	00	05	5
Elenor Moreton	1300	01	00	00	16	9
John Wallkersen	0500	01	00	00	08	1
Robart money	0400	00	00	00	04	4
Basilia osborn	0400	00	00	00	04	4
Justus Anderson	0200	00	00	00	02	2
Henricus Williams	0450	04	00	00	15	8
Richard Quinch	0200	00	00	00	02	2
Joseph Holding	0486	03	00	00	13	3
Edmond Cantwell	4396	011	00	03	06	0
William Grant	0250	01	00	00	05	4
Widdow Persivall	0000	01	00	00	02	8
John ffeild & John Seaton	0000	02	00	00	05	4
				17	15	0

a List of ye Southside of Apoquenimy	Acres	Tithbles	lb	s	d
John Wallker	0400	02	00	09	8
Roalof Anderson	0500	02	00	10	9:5
Georg Baker	0200	01	00	02	9
John Taylor	0300	02	00	08	7
William Padeson	0400	02	00	09	8
Robart Courtney	0000	01	00	02	8
John De haes	0400	00	00	04	04
Elixander Cambell	0300	00	00	03	03
Richard Noble	0280	02	00	08	01
Richard Ingelo	0256	00	00	02	09
Jacob Anderson	0150	03	00	09	07
Henry Wallrauen	0200	01	00	04	10
Derick Williams	0250	02	00	08	01
Casparus Harman	1200	03	01	01	00

Daniell Smith	0200	02	00	07	06
Hans Hansen	0500	00	00	05	05
Adam Peterson	0390	01	00	06	11
Peter Absinck	0109	01	00	03	09
John Perce	0000	02	00	05	04
Ellis Humphries	0200	02	00	07	06
Judah Crawford	0600	02	00	11	10
John Macklin	0150	00	00	01	07
John on grants land	0000	01	00	02	08
Peter Allricks	0400	01	00	07	00
Jacob Archer	0450	01	00	07	06
Oalla Torson	0200	00	00	02	02
Jacob Young	1000	00	00	10	10
Roalof Anderson	0300	00	00	03	03
Hybert Laurane	0300	00	00	03	03
Robart Hutchinson	0400	00	00	04	04
Austin Dickes	0150	00	00	01	07
Widdow Scot	0400	00	00	04	04
Richard Huddy	0200	01	00	04	10
Magnus White	0170	02	00	07	01
Bryan Omely	0600	00	00	06	06
Will Grant	0800	00	00	08	08
Thomas Laws	0600	02	00	11	10
Joseph more	0100	01	00	03	09
Widdow Snoding	0200	00	00	02	02
Eward Green	0450	12	01	16	11
John ffoster	0000	00	00	05	04
John Hayly	0200	01	00	04	10
Philip chandler	0000	02	00	05	04
Erasmus milkes	0400	00	00	04	04
			13	03	04

The Southside of Apoquenimy	acres	Tithebles	℔	s	d
Peter Hanslo	0100	01	00	03	9
Gerret Otto	0452	02	00	10	3
John Darby	0400	02	00	09	8
To Darby for Sparks	0400	00	00	04	4
John Willkinson	0400	02	00	09	8
Gabreell Rappe	1000	06	01	06	10

	Acres of Land	Tithebles	lb	s	d
John Peterson	0680	03	00	15	6
Antony Wallis	0250	00	00	02	9
Henry Vandburg	1200	00	00	12	12
Willow ward	0600	01	00	09	2
			05	04	11

A List of ye north side of Christina Creeke

	Acres of Land	Tithebles	lb	s	d
Timan Stidum	0250	01	00	05	5
Thomas Gulping	0100	02	00	06	5
Thom: Langshaw	0100	02	00	06	5
Thomas Gillet	0300	03	00	11	3
Thom: Woolaston	0400	01	00	07	0
Will: Lester	0100	01	00	03	9
Willi Guest	1000	06	01	06	10
Will Jessop	0200	00	00	02	2
Widdow ogle	1000	00	00	10	10
Widdow Stalcop	0770	00	00	08	4
Vall Hollingsworth	1000	03	00	18	10
Justa Paulson	0125	01	00	04	0
Aron Johnson	0230	01	00	05	2
Gisbert Wallrausen	0300	00	00	05	11
Henry Dull	0100	01	00	03	9
Andrew Stilly	0100	00	00	01	1
Andrew Stalcop	0136	00	00	01	1
			05	03	6

A List of ye North side of Christina Creeke

	Acres of Land	Tithebles	lb	s	d
Adam Sharply	0300	01	00	05	11
Adam Stidum	0100	01	00	03	09
Arnold Legrang	0600	03	00	14	06
Abraham man	0500	03	00	13	05
Brewer Senex	0780	03	00	15	07
Corneluis Van Herre	0000	01	00	02	08
Charles Peterson	0350	01	00	06	03

C 215.

Christ: Miers	0100	01	00	03	09
Charles Bayly	0000	01	00	02	08:5
Conrad Constantine	0570	01	00	08	10
Henry Renolds	0250	00	00	03	06
Hans Peterson	0600	02	00	11	10
Henry Garetson	0200	03	00	10	02
Jacob Clementson	0150	01	00	04	04
Jonas Scogging	0150	00	00	01	08
John Mounson	0150	02	00	07	00
James Brown	0130	00	00	01	06
John Grub	0200	01	00	04	10
John Buckley	0100	01	00	03	09
John Prue	0100	01	00	03	09
Isack warner Edr: Eglington	0400	00	00	04	04
John Vance	0200	01	00	04	10
Jacob Vanderueer	0500	03	00	13	05
James Clark	0016	02	00	05	06:5
John Can	0500	03	00	13	05
John Moll	0200	00	00	02	02
John Nomers	0240	03	00	10	08
James Clay Pole	0320	01	00	06	01
Giles Barret	0550	02	00	11	00
John White	0200	00	00	02	02
John Smith	0200	00	00	02	02
Jonas Arskin	0200	00	00	02	02
John Iris	0100	01	00	03	09
James Reed	0800	03	00	16	08
Joseph Barnes	0315	01	00	06	00
Mathyas Denoos	0470	01	00	07	09
Lucas Stidum	0200	02	00	07	02
Niels Nealson	0233	00	00	02	08:5
michal Oalson	0100	00	00	01	01
Oalla Toarson	0250	03	00	10	08
Oalla Roason	0250	00	00	02	09
Oliver Coop	0100	01	00	03	09
Oalla Tomson	0200	03	00	10	02
Peter Hallman	0150	02	00	06	09
Peter Oalson	0100	00	00	01	01
Paul mounsen	0016	01	00	02	10
Robart Robinson	0200	02	00	07	02
Samll Peterson	0437	01	00	07	06
Sick oalson	0000	01	00	02	08
Samll Barker	0200	01	00	04	10

Samll Land	0100	00	00	01	01
John Cann	0300	00	00	03	03
			15	12	02

March ye 18^nth: 1684

At an orphans Court held at Newcastle for our Lord ye King & ye Honble Propriatary & Governor the 18^nth of ye 1st mo^t: 1684

Present
  John Cann
  James Walliam
  John Williams
  Casparus Herman
    Justices

C 217. discharged in Court March 21th 1692—   John Wallker Peticons to haue ye mortgage taken off from ye Plantacon he now liues on wch s^d Plantacon was bound by a former order of ye Court of newcastle for ye Payment of the childrens Potions being ffowr thousand seuen hundred guild^r & the one half being allready paid the s^d John Wallker in leiue of the Plantacon he now liues on tendereth a tract of Land called ye mill neck being 110 acres & the moyety or on half of ye mill Scituat in Drawers Creeke being in joynt Partership betwixt s^d. Jno Wallker and Joseph more ye court accept of ye Security on condicon ye s^d John Wallker & Joseph more keep the s^d mill in good Rapair wch s^d John Wallker & Joseph More doe by thes Presents engage to doe & in ye court oblige themselfs to keep s^d mill in good Repair for ye better securing ye Potion of his Predecessors children & John Wallker doth bind himself in ye Penalty of one hundred pounds to procure a good title to ye Land cald ye mill neck

C 217. John Taylor an orphan Peticons about his ffathers estate y^t ther may be an administrator appointed to take ye care of it & that he may To choose his Gardians The court order the Widdow & Relict to administer by next court The Peticoner John Taylor chosing John Walker Joseph more & Will Phillips his guardians ye Court allof of his choyce

Edmund Cantwell Delivers in Court the books bills & ac- C 218.
counts of ye Estate of Wallter Wharton to Georg more ye s^d
George more being to giue an account of what he receives of
ye s^d estate to ye county Court

October ye 16 1684
   (Att a Court of Assizes)
A Complaint was Exhibited in Court for want of a fferry   C 224.
ouer Christina & Brandywine Creek ye Judges order the
County Court to speedy care about it y^t it may be forthwith
done

At a County Court held at necastle for our Lord ye King &   C 225.
ye Hon'ble Propriatary and Governo^r ye 21st of April 1685

   a quarter Sessions

Pres^{nt}	John Cann Peter Allricks Edward Green James Walliam Valantine Hollingsworth Henricus Williams	} Justices

    Samuell Land High Sherrif

The Court being Adjurnd from the 21st to ye 23rd Instant

Upon ye Peticon of Daniell Smith to Erect a fferre at   C 231.
Christina Creek: ye Court having tendred the first offer to
John Jaquet Senior ye owner of ye Land according to law &
he Refuseing ye Court order ye Petitioner to Erect a fferre at y^e
s^d Creek & order ye Land Limited by ye law for ye accomodacon of a fferre to be Layd out by ye Survayor at ye apoint-
ment of James Wallaims and Peter Allricks to ye Least dam-
age to ye owner of ye Land & best accomodacon of ye fferre y^t
possibly may be ye s^d: Daniell Smith being ordered to Pay
one busshell of wheat ℔ year for euer as a Rent to ye owner of
ye s^d Land—

Aprill 23: 1685

C 232. John Barker by his Attorney Daniell Smith doth acknowledge a Deed of Sale to Isack Weeldon for a Plantacon in Black Bird Creek containing Two Hundred & ffowrteen Acres of Land as ⅌: yᵉ Deed may appear

C 232. Henrick Vand Burgh Acknowledgeth a Deed of Enfeofment to William Hauge for a tract of Land Scituat in Christina Creeke called Buswick containing ffowr Hundred & Thirty six acres of Land:

C 232. Broer Sinexen Acknowledgeth a Deed of Enfeofment for yᵉ one moyety or half Part of a Tract of Land Scituat on White Clay Creek the whole Two Parts containing Two hundred & Twenty Acres of Land to Humphry Best & Edward Green:

C 232. Humphry Best & Edward Green acknowledg a Deed of Morgage of yᵉ aboue sᵈ Land for yᵉ Payment of Sixty Pounds with three in yeers to yᵉ sᵈ Groer Sinexen

C 232. Artman Haym Acknowledgeth a Deed of Sale to John Jaquet for a Tract of Land as ⅌ yᵉ Deed bearing date yᵉ 30ᵗʰ day of March 1685 wᶜʰ sᵈ Land is Scituat on yᵉ Pert Hooke in yᵉ County of necastle

C 232. John Moll Senior & Christian His Wife & John Moll Junior all acknowledge a Deed of Enfeofment to William Rakestraw a Plantacon containing Two hundred & Ten acres of Land Scituat on yᵉ north side of white Clay Creeke as ⅌ yᵉ Deed baring date yᵉ 20ᵗʰ of Aprill 1685 may appear

C 232. William Rakestraw doth Acknowledge a morgage of yᵉ aboue sᵈ 210 acres of Land to John Moll for yᵉ Payment of Eeigty Seuen Pounds & ten Shillings included in three seuerall Bonds

C 233. William Rakestraw acknowledgeth Three seuerall Bonds for the neat Payment of Twenty nine Pounds Three Shillings & ffowr Pence in each Bond in yᵉ whole to the sum of Eighty seuen Pounds & ten Shillings To be Paid to John Moll in 3 seuerall Payments

C 233. Christian Juriansan Acknowledgeth to be Satisfyed with yᵉ Particon of his Deceased ffathers Estate & to haue Received ffiue hundred Guild{r} of his ffather in Law Broer Sinexen in full of his Portion:

Broer Sinexen Acknowledgeth a Deed of one hundred acres of Land being Part of a Truct of three hundred acres Lying on both sides of White Clay Creeke cald Water Land as ⅌ ye Deed baring date ye 13{nth} Day of Aprill 1685 to Christian Jurianson

C 233.

At a Speciall Court held at Newcastle ffor our Lord ye King & ye Honble Propriatary ye 23d of May 1685

C 234.

Present
- John Cann
- James Walliam
- Edward Green
- Will Guest
- Henry Lemman

} Justices

Thomas Spry his Last Will & Testament being Proued in Court it is ordered yt James Walliam and John mandy be Administrators & John De Haes & Gerardus Wessells to Apprays ye Estate & to make Report by ye Last of June next

C 235.

At A Court held at Newcastle for our Souaraign Lord ye King & ye Honble Propriatary & Gouerno{r} the 2nd & 3rd of ye 4th month 1685

Pres{nt}:
- John Cann
- James Walliam
- Valentine Hollingsworth
- William Guest
- Henry Lemman

} Justices

Samll Land h: Sherrife

June ye 3rd: 1685

Mrs Mary Block Exhibiting an account of the Estate Peter ffolchr whereby it appears by ye Appraysment of Henrick Vandenburgh and John Hulk yt ye Estate is

C{rd} by 150 guild{r} & yt sd Estate is

Dr to 167 guild{r} as ye account

C 242.

The Court order Mrs Block to take ye s^d Estate into his Possession & Pay the debts by Proportion as far as it will goe

C 243. Upon the Peticon of John Hayly in behalf of his Late wife for a Part of Barent Egberts Estate. The Court order ye Peticoner to make applicacon to ye next Court of orphans

C 243. Peter Johnsoe Exhibiting an account agst ye Estate of John Taylor deceased John Quartermus being Attested saith y^t all accounts were discharged betwixt ye s^d: Johnsoe & John Taylor upon ye consideracon of ye s^d Taylors giving ye s^d Johnso a tract of Land

C 244. Jane Taylor Administratrix of John Taylor Deceased acknowledged a Deed of Gift for one hundred Acres of Land being Part of two hundred & ffiuety Acres Lying on ye head of ye second Drawers Creeke w^ch: s^d. Land was Given by John Taylor deceased during his life time

C 244. Hans Peterson acknowledged A Deed of Enfoeffment to Cornelius Empson ffor six hundred Acres of Land more or Less Lying in Skilpads Kill: wch s^d Deed was conditionall & mortgaged Back to ye s^d Hans Peterson for the Payment of ffiue hundred Pound of currant money to ye s^d Hans Peterson by Cornelius Emsen as p^r ye Deed baring date ye 28th of march 1685 may appear

C 244. Mary Block Barbara Marsland & Christian Stalcop acknowledge a Deed of Sale to Cornelius Empson of all their Right & Title to a dutch Pattent for a tract of Land Scituat & lying on ye mill creek y^t runs into Scilpads Creeke in ye County of newcastle as p^r ye Deed baring date ye 2nd of June 1685.

C 244. Cornelius Empson Acknowledges a bond to Saue and Keep harmles ye s^d mary Block Barbara marshland & christian Stalcop agst all Persons y^t may molest ye afores^d Persons for delivering ye Pattent of ye s^d Mill creek land to ye s^d Empson as p^r ye Bond bearing date l^e 2nd of June 1685

C 245. Peter Andries Hallman Administrator of ye Estate of Lasse Oalson acknowledged a Deed of Enfeoffment to Hans Peters ffor ffiuety Acres of Land Scituate on Verdredee Hooke as p^r ye Deed bareing date ye 28th of march 1685 may appear

John Wallker Acknowledged a Deed of Enffeofment to An- C 245.
drew Peterson of a Tract of Land called new Saxony Scituat
on Drawers Creek in ye County of newcastle—containing one
hundred & ffiuety Acres of Land as p^r ye Deed beareing date
ye 2nd of June 1685 may appeare

Justice James Walliam mouing ye Court to appoint another C 246.
Person in ye Steed of Dr Wessells who is now sick to apprayse
ye Estate of Thomas Spry ye Court order John Harmanson

The Court order Richard Hudden to Administer upon ye C 248.
Estate of ye Widdow otto his mother late Administratrix of
ye Estate of Gerret Otto & to give good security for due administracon ye Richard Hudden desireing to haue Joseph more
Joynd with him ye Court allow it—

July 20th: 1685

Att a Court held at Newcastle for our Lord ye King & y^e
Honble Propriatary & Gouvernor this 20th of ye 5th month
1685

Pres^{nt}: John Cann
Peter Allricks
Edward Greene } Justices
James Walliam
Henry Lemman

Samuell Land High Sherrif

The Court called for the Return of their order concerning C 250.
a fferry at Christina past at a Court held at Newcastle Aprill
ye 23rd last past

Peter Allricks & James Walliam being ye persons appointed C 250.
to take the care & charg of that bussines according to y^e
Courts order they make a Report of their doings & Produce
ye suruayers Certificate wch being Read ye Co^{rt} allow of y^e
Suruay & the Sherrif Reports he gave Daniell Smith Posses-
sion which ye Court Confirms

Upon ye Peticon of ye Sons of Jean Paul Jaquet Deceased C 259.
that no other Person might Keep a fferry on their Land but
themseleus the Court doe inform ye Peticoners they haue allready disposed of the s^d fferry according to law

July 22 1685

C 260. Peter abrink acknowledged a Deed in open Court to Adam Peterson a certain tract of Land called New Tiell Scituate on ye North side of apoquenimy Creeke and containg one hundred & ninety acres of Land as per ye Deed bearing date the 21th day of July 1685

C 260. Oalla Paulson acknowledged a Deed of two hundred acres of Land twenty ffiue acres of marsh called Poplar neck & bounding on John Williams Land: to Henry Lemman as per ye Deed bearing date ye 26th day of June 1685 may appear

C 262. Samuel Land being impowred by a Letter of Attorny produced in ye Court under ye hand & seal of Lucas Peterson did in open Court acknowledg a Deed from ye sd Luces Peterson to Hans Peterson for all ye Right & title of ye s^d Lucas to a Watermill & Land thereunto belonging according to ye Pattent ye Deed baring date ye 10th of June 1685

C 262. Cornelius Empson in open Court enters a Caueat against ye s^d sale of ye aboue s^d water mill & Land affirming he ye s^d Empson hath allready bought ye premis

C 262. Sarah Lindsey in open Court doth acknowledg an old Morgage of a Plantacon containing ffour hundrd acres of Land being near ye head of Apoquenimy the ye s^d Lindsey doth acknowledg ye Alination in open Court

C 262. Judah Crawford acknowledged a Deed for 400 acres of Land scituat near duck Creek to Samuell Rowland Marriner as per ye Deed baring date ye 21st of July 1685

C 262. Oalla Toarson acknowledged a Deed for a certain Plantacon in Swanwick to Barbara Marslander as P^r ye deed bearing date ye 1st day of July 1685 may appear

At a Court held at Newcastle for our Souaraign Lord ye King & the Honble Proprietary & Gouernor on ye 20th of October untill ye 23^d of the same instant 1685

Present
John Cann
Peter Allricks
James Walliam } Justices
Vallantine Hollingworth
Henry Lemman

James Brown P^lt	Benjamin Chambers P^lt	C 267.
John Mattland Def^t	John Mattland Def^t	
The P^lt declares for twelue Pounds & nine shillings as pr ye declaracon may appear	The P^lt declares for nine pounds thirteen Shillings as by ye Declaracon may more at larg appear	

both ye above s^d accons hauing been continued against ye Def^t John Mattland three Courts & debts proved The Court give Judgement for both ye s^d Sums

The Court order ye Def^ts Land to be Sould according to law & y^t John DeHaes & John Harmson be appointed to apprays ye land and Effects of ye Def^t & y^t ye s^d land be after Sould at a Publick outcry to ye highest bidder all persans hauing liberty within one month to exhibit their lawfull claim to anny of ye Def^ts effects within one month after ye Publick outcry in order to haue a Share according to ye rule of proportion it being ye Defts own Request as by a Lett produced in Court

The Partys laying their claim Paying their Proportion of charges it is ordered ye land be appearsed betwixt this & ye 5th day of ye next month & to be sould at ye town of newcastle ye 10th day of ye next month

John Wootters Plt   C 269.
Edmund Cantwell Deft

The Plt declares for a Plantacon detained contrary to law & one hundred pounds damage

The Deft Pleads he is not Prouided by reason he had not his Sommons according to law

a question arrising whether ye cause should be left to ye Jury it was carryed in ye negatiue by ye major Votes of ye Justices—

Edmund Cantwell being Attested y^t his house in town was Lett & not in his possession when ye Declaracon was Delivered & y^t at this time he hath no Possession thereof but by Permission

Edmund Cantwell ye Deft Promises to come to a tryall by consent ye next County Court

John Wootters desireing his euidence may be attested

Thomas Snelling Attested saith y^t he Knew y^t about twelue years since ye Plt did settle a Piece of land on ye south side of black bird Creeke called Wotters his Land & y^t he did build a dwelling house and planted trees & y^t he made a crop thereon with his seruants & that ye s^d Land is ye same now in dispte with ye Deft and a ffier hapning y^t burnt ye house and improuements & corn & tobacco & there was a man upon it when it was burnd

Elinor morton Attested saith y^t ye P^{lt} settled a piece of land on ye south side of black bird creeke being the land now in controversy with three seruants and ye P^{lt} John Wootters left a ffreemen on ye s^d Land who dyeted at ye Attestants house which flreeman was to Pay 100 ^{lb} of tobacco for Rent & y^t a ffier hapning did burn ye corn and tobacco on ye s^d Land

Casparus Herman Attested saith y^t he cald once at ye house of J^{no} Wootters on ye south side of black bird Creek about nine or ten years since

Octobr 24 1685

C 276. Jane Taylor administratrix & Relict of John Taylor acknowledged a Deed of 620 acres of Land in Drawers Creek called Lackford Hall: to Edward Green Merch

C 277. Edward Greene doth in open court bind himself in the sum of ffiuety Pounds to Keep harmles Jane Taylor administratrix of John Taylor deceased in relacon to twenty ffi̅e pounds more pretended to be dew for ye Payment of ye Plantac̅on from anny Person y^t may molest ye s^d administratrix wch s^d moneys of 25 ^{lb} arises upon ye Differance of moneys of old england & this country

C 277. The Will of Jan Paul Jaquet was Proued in Court

C 278. Paul Laerson acknowledged a Deed of 200: acres of Land at ffirne Hooke to Justus Anderson

Stoffell Myers acknowledged a Deed of one hundred thirty & three acres of Land Scituat in ye Bowght near Verdretye Hooke to Thomas Clifton C 278.

John White Acknowledged a Deed for a house & Lott of ground scituat in newcastle as ℏ ye Deed C 278.

Marcus Lawranson acknowledged all his Right to 700 acres of Land scituat in ye Bonght near to Verdretys Hooke to Stoffel myers C 279.

Adam Hay acknowledged a Deed for a Lott of Land in newcastle to Isack Slouer— C 279.

Upon ye Peticon of Peter DeWitts Administrator Henricus Williams, y^t ye orphans of Jurian Janson might be ordered to receive certain money dew ffor Land bought at an out cry C 279.

The Court Refer ye matter to next Court & in ye mean time y^t notice be given to ye guardians of s^d orphans

The Court Ajurnd untill ye 15^nth of December next

At a Court held at Newcastle for or Lord the King & ye Honble Propriatary & Gouern^r on ye 15^nth of ye 10th mo^th 1685

Pre^snt

John Cann
James Walliam
Vall^t. Hollingsworth
Henry Williams
William Stockdale
Henry Lemmen
Peter Allricks

} Justices

Cornelius Empson P^lt
Jacob Vanderveer Deft C 281.

The Plt declares y^t ye Deft hath contrary to Law inuaded his Land & drawn new lines thereon & cutt down diuers trees molesting ye P^lt in his Right full Possession as p^r ye Declaracon may more at larg appear

The Deft comes & saith ye Land in controuersy is ye Defts own Land & for Proof brings diuers Papers & Pattent wch ware read in Court

The Plt produced in Court a Pattent from ye Gouverment

of New york of an elder date then ye Defts Pattent

Thomas Peirson attested saith y^t by Virtue of a warr^t from ye Gouerno^r he resurvayed ye Defts Land & Saw & compared ye Pattents of ye Plt & Deft & then resurvayed to ye best of his Judgment

Loalof Stiddum Attested saith y^t on ye West side of Hans Petersons Land wch is now ye Plts there is a Line of Markt trees made by Wharton and y^t a Corner White oake now standing by ye mars side by ye Tobacco ffeild is ye corner tree

Jury men
Humphry Ellis
Jonas Arskin
Reneer Van Coolen
Emelius De Ring
Wliliam Alloway
John Penington
Thomas Gillet
John Prestner
Georg More
Hugh Marsland
James Halliday
Thomas Woolaston

Justa Paulson Attested saith y^t ye White oake corner tree Standeth on ye west side of ye branch by ye marsh

Charles Pickering Attested saith Hans Peterson shewed him a tree wch he s^d was his corner tree & saith he saw ye place wch ye Deft cald a Run but no water ebd or fflowed there

Benjamin Stiddum Attested saith y^t ye old Line Runs up by ye West side of ye Plts tobocco ffeild

The Attestacon of Lucas Peterson was read wch is as followeth ye 31st of ye 1th mo 1685

Lucas Peterson deposeth before me Henrick Lemmens that he did remember uery wll y^t ye small Creeke in ye Meddow he being upon ye place & Shewed to Henrick & ye White oake marked there by Capt Cantwell is ye same he sett out at ye ffirst grant from Govern^r Louelace to Hans Peterson I had order from ye Gouerno^r for laying out ye same

    Hend: Lemmen   mark
                                      Lucas × Peterson

The Jury after ye heareing ye whole matter went out & at their Return brought in their Verdict Viz^t

We ffind for ye Plt with costs of sute
                                Thom: Woolaston fforeman

The Court give Judgment according to Verdict

Decembr 16 1685

The Deft appeales ye Court grant an appeal he Paying ye Present Charges & giuing Security according to Law ye Plt in Court became his security

Decembr 17 1685.

Sicca desired to haue some Wittnesses Attested

Woolla Toarson Attested saith y^t Lacy Toreson gaue to his daughter Margrett ye wife of sicca Woolson flfuety Acres of land lying on ye west side of s^d Lacy Toresons Land it being ye same wch sicca formerly liued on & he ye Attestant heard said lacy Toreson giue it his daughter on his death bed C 288.

Hendrick andryson being attested saith he heard Lacy Toreson say to him he had given 50 acres of land to his daughter for a portion lying on ye west side of his Land & y^t he gaue on his death bed

Anniky Toreson Attested saith she heard Lacy Toreson say he gaue 50 acres of land to his daughter margrett

Lacy Toreson Attested saith he heard his ffather upon his death bed say y^t he gaue Sicca Oalsons wife 50 acres of Land lying on ye west side of ye Point & y^t he heard say his ffathers wife that she must take care to deliuer a Letter from ye s^d 50 acres of Land to sicca oalsons wife

Henricus Williams both at ye beginning of this Court & at ye latter end also tenders ye Pay dew to ye orphans of Urian Johnson dew for Land C 288.

December 17 1685

Mathyas Toreson acknowledged a Deed for a Plantacon in Crane Hooke to Hance Peterson C 289.

Justa Paulson acknowledged a Deed of one hundred & twenty nine acres of land in ye mill Hooke to Hans Petersen Vall^t Hollingsworth enters a Caueat agst ye s^d Deed in behalfe of Wm Lesster C 289.

Hans Petersen acknowledged a Deed for a Lott in Crane Hooke formerly ye Land of Wm Johnson alias Scott to Justa Paulson C 289.

C 289.   Sicca Woollson acknowledged a Deed of 50 Acres of Land and Proportion of meddow lying at Verdreytyes Hook to Hans Peterson

C 289.   Andrew Stilly acknowledged a Deed of one hundred twenty & three acres of land lying on ye North side of Christiana Creeke to Robart Hutchinson

C 289.   Mathyas Devoos by Thomas Peirson his Attorney doth acknowledg a Deed of Enfeoffment to Charles Pickering for all his Plantacon with all ye Proportion of Land thereunto belonging wth all ye housing & improuments of his Plantacon upon Christana Creeke

C 289.   Charles Pickering acklowledged a Deed for nine hund^r & Sixty acres of land & marsh Scituat on ye north side of Christina Creeke to Richard Bridgman

C 290.   John Darby by his Attorney John White acknowledged a Deed for Swarten nutten Island & an out Lett in all 400 acres of Land to Robart Dyer and Edward Blake

C 290.   A true coppy of ye aboues^d originall Deed from John Darby to ye s^d Robart Dyer & Edward Blake was examined in court & Attested by John Cann Pres^{dnt} & William Stockdale

C 290.   The Letter of Attorney from Jno Darby to John White to acknowledged ye s^d Deed was proued in Court by Gerardus Wessells & James Walliam

C 290.   Jonas Arskin acknowledged a Pattent ffor a Tract of Land called Westminster to John White q^t 140 acres of Land & Scituat in white Clay creeke

C 290.   Anthony Bryant acknowledged a Deed for tract of Land Scituat in ye Town of newcastle & containing about 3 acres of Land to John White bounding to ye Street of Garrit Smith to ye N: W: and to ye Street y^t Parts ye Domines Land to ye S: W: & swamp N E

C 291.   Upon ye Peticon of Edmund Perkus concerning the estate of John How Deceased the Court order Richard noble & John Peterson to apprays ye estate

C 292.   Johanes DeHaes & Gerardus Wessells being appointed appraysers of ye estate of John mattland doe apprays ye land at twenty Pounds wch they testefye under their hands

The Court adjurns until ye 3rd tuesday in march next

At a Speciall Court held at Newcastle on ye 29th day of C 293. December 1685:

John Cann
James Walliam
William Gueste
Cornelius Empson
} Justices Pres^nt

At an Orphans Court held at Newcastle for our Souaraign Lord ye King & ye Honble Propriatary & Gouernor ye 2nd of ye 1st mo^th 1685-6

John Cann
James Walliam
William Guest
Vallantine Hollingsworth
Henry Lemman
} Justices Pres^nt

John Peterson of apoquenimy doth in open Court Promise C 295. & engage to allow & giue his mother Catalinta Debrina twelue Pounds & ten shillings this year to be at his house in Apoquenimy upon Demand & ten Pounds p^r year yearly for every year during his s^d mothers naturall life on ye 2nd day of march at his house afores^d

Catalinta De brina in consideracon of ye aboues^d Engag- C 295. ment of hir son John Peterson doth for euer Renounce all claim title Interest & Demand of all & euery part of ye Estate of hir s^d son either Reall or Personall that did or euer formerly might to ye s^d Catalinta or hir late husbands Estate belong

John Jaquet in open Court tendered his Pay dew to ye C 296. orphans of Jurian Jansen but noe one appeared to Receive it.

The Court Adjurns

Att a Court held at Newcastle for o^r Lord ye King & ye C 299. Honble Propriatary & Gouern^r on ye 16 17 18^nth days of ye first mo^th 1685-6

John Cann
James Walliam
Vall^t Hollingsworth   } Justices Pres^{nt}
William Guest
Henry Lemmens

March 18: 1685

C 310.   John Can acknowledged a Deed of Enfeofment for his house in ye thawrt street to John White

C 310.   John White acknowledged a Deed of Enfeofment for his house he bought of John Cann to Susanah Welch

C 310.   Susannah Welch acknowledged a mortgage of hir house bought of John White to ye s^d John White for ye Payment of one hundred Pounds

C 311.   William Rakestraw acknowledged a Deed of Enfeofment to Charles Pickering for two thousand fiue hundred acres of Land & Premises being ye same wth all its appurtenances y^t William Rakestraw bought of ye Propriatary in England

C 311.   Reneer Vander Coolen acknowledged a Deed of Enfeofment for a house & Lott in ye town of newcastle to Gerardus Wessels as p^r ye Deed bearing date ye 4th day of January 1685

C 311.   John Sybrane acknowledged a Deed of Enfeofment for a tract of marsland betwixt ye land of James Hallyday & Bilchy Johnson to John Priestner as by ye Deed bearing date ye 17th of march 1685

C 311.   Gabriell Rappe by John White his Attorney Renounces all claim & Pretentions to a Plantacon called ye Exchange formerly bought of M^r. John Moll: again to Return to ye s^d John Moll & his heirs forever

A Receipt from ye s^d Gabriell Rappe & ye delivery of ye aboues^d: Plantacon to ye s^d. John Moll from ye s^d Gabriell Rappe was day read in court under ye hand & seal of ye s^d Rappe bearing date of 14^{nth} of January 1685-6:

C 311.   Samuell Peterson Justus Paulson and Asman Stiddem acknowledg a Deed of sale for their Part in a mill Run in Skilpads Creek to Hans Peterson as p^r ye Deed bearing date march ye 8th 1685-6

RECORDS OF THE COURT OF NEW CASTLE.

William Scarf acknowledged a Deed of 200 acres of Land C 312.
to Epharim Herman

Upon the Peticon of Christian Stiddem ye Widdow of C 312.
Doctor Stiddem concerning her late husbands estate

The Court doe order y^t after ye Palment of ye Deceased
husbands just debts ye Peticoner shall haue on third part of
her husbands estate both Reall & Personall ye reall estate only
to Reuert back to ye Heyers of Timmen Stiddem after y^e
Peticoners decease it being according to ye Laws of this
Government

A List of ye Land & Tithebles brought in by ye Constable of Newcastle for ye year 1685/6.	Ackres of Land	Town Lotts	Tithebles	℔	s	d	
John Garetson	0400	01	01	00	07	06	C 314.
Robert Hutchinson	0500	00	01	00	07	6	
John White	0635	01	03	00	14	6	
Wallter Powell	0000	00	01	00	02	6	
Job nettleship	0100	00	01	00	03	6	
Edward Land	0100	00	01	00	03	6	
William Little	0200	00	01	00	04	6	
John Penington	0200	00	02	00	07	0	
Samll Land	0200	03	01	00	07	6	
Charles Rumsey	0640	00	02	00	11	5	
Pauell Lawson	0200	00	02	00	07	0	
Paul Paulson	0200	00	01	00	04	6	
one Lott to matheys ☞ Arnoldus Legrang.	0400	03	00	00	07	0	
Urian Borsman	0354	00	02	00	08	0	
Jacob Clason	0250	00	02	00	07	6	
Peter Jaquet	0300	00	02	00	08	0	
Hendrick Lemmens	0800	00	02	00	13	0	
Mathyas Lawson	0120	00	02	00	06	02	
Erick Paulson	0	00	02	00	05	0	
Daniell Smith	0012	00	02	00	05	01½	
Hendrick Anderson	0150	00	01	00	04	0	
John Scrike	0120	00	02	00	06	3	
John ffaulkenburg	0000	00	01	00	02	6	
Hendrick Euertson	0260	00	01	00	05	0	
Sybran Johnson	0050	00	01	00	03	0	
John Sybrance	0050	00	01	00	03	0	

John Prestner	0100	00	03	00	08	6
☞ James Hallyday	0200	00	02	00	07	0
John Jaquet	0200	00	02	00	07	0
Artman Hyam	0100	00	01	00	03	6
Barbara Marslander	0100	00	03	00	08	6
Mary Block	0400	00	02	00	09	6
Henry Jones	0200	00	02	00	07	0
John De does	0000	00	01	00	02	6
Isack Slouer	0000	00	01	00	02	6
				11	03	05

Newcastle Constablery continued	Acres of Land	Town Lotts	Tithebles	£	s	D
Henrick Williams	0000	02	00	00	02	00
James Walliam	0000	02	02	00	07	00
John Biskus	0000	02	01	00	04	06
Joslyn Semple	0400	01	00	00	05	00
John Wallker	0000	01	01	00	03	06
Edmund Cantwell	0050	01	00			
Jacob Cornelison	0550	00	01	00	08	00
☞ Johanes De Haes	0050	01	01	00	14	00
Henrick Vandburg	2000	05	02	01	10	00
John Boyer	0000	02	01	00	04	06
John Harmanson	0400	02	02	00	07	00
Epharim Herman	0400	02	01	00	08	06
Emeluis De Ring	0000	03	01	00	05	06
Isack tyne	0000	04	01	00	06	06
Edward Boulton	0070	00	01	00	03	00
Justa Anderson	0000	01	01	00	03	06
John Henrickson	0000	01	01	00	03	06
ffrancis Scott	0000	00	02	00	05	00
Peter Allricks	1475	02	05	01	09	03
Antony Bryant	0000	01	00	00	01	00
Mathyas De Ring	0000	02	01	00	04	06
Dom testmaker	0000	02	00	00	03	00
Engelbert Lott	0150	03	00	00	04	00
Sarah Welch	1000	02	00	00	12	00
John Cann	0000	02	00	00	02	00
Garret Johnson	0000	03	01	00	05	06
John mandy	0000	03	01	00	05	06

RECORDS OF THE COURT OF NEW CASTLE. 121

John Smith	0000	02	01	00	04	06
Claes Daniell	0000	01	01	00	03	06
Moses DeGame	0000	01	01	00	08	06
John fforeat	0000	01	01	00	03	06
William Crosee	0000	01	01	00	03	06
Georg more	0000	01	01	00	03	06
John Moll	0300	04	01			
Reneer Vander Coolen	0000	04	01	00	06	06
Gerardus Wessells	0000	01	01	00	03	06
Edmund Cantwell	4398	01	10	03	10	00
John Moll	1000	00	01	00	19	06
				14	19	03
				14	19	09

Land & Tithebles on ye northside of Christian Creeke	Acres of Land	Tithebles				
William Guest	1250	06	01	07	06	C 316
Thomas Graues	0200	00	00	02	00	
William Jessop	0200	01	00	04	06	
Ola Thomason	0200	03	00	09	06	
Aron Johnson	0200	02	00	07	06	
Broer senexen w^t clay Creeke	0200	00	00	02	00	
Gisbert Wallrauen	0235	01	00	05	00	
Broer senexon	0460	02	00	09	06	
Christian Bro^r: son in law	0100	01	00	07	06	
Arnold Legrange	0600	03	00	13	06	
Isarell Helm	0474	00	00	04	09	
Charles Pickering	0776	02	00	12	09	
Benjamen Stiddem	0150	01	00	04	00	
Adam Stiddem	0100	01	00	03	06	
Jacob Henrickson	0300	00	00	03	00	
mathyas Deuoos	0400	01	00	06	06	
Samll Peterson	0750	02	00	10	00	
Christian Stalcop	1050	04	01	00	06	
Robart Robinson	0500	04	00	15	00	
Georg Reed	0100	00	00	01	00	
Richard Robinson	0200	00	00	02	00	
Docter timan	0366	01	00	06	02	
Lucas Stiddem	0265	02	00	07	07	

William Gregs	0400	02	00	06	06
John Gregs	0200	01	00	04	06
Henry flournis	0260	00	00	02	08
Joseph Cookson	0200	00	00	02	00
Jonas Arskin: J: White	0400	02	00	09	00
Andries Tilly	0250	01	00	05	00
Elisabeth Ogle	1000	00	00	10	00
Joseph bond	0300	00	00	03	00
Hugh Marsland	0200	01	00	04	06
James Claypole	0500	00	00	05	00
Humbry best Ed: Greene	0300	03	00	10	06
John Bristoll	0300	01	00	05	06
John nomerson	0240	04	00	12	06
James Reed	0800	02	00	13	00
Henry Dull	0100	01	00	03	06
			12	18	05
John Alloway	0200	03	00	09	6
Thomas Langshaw	0250	00	00	12	6
Giles Barret	0600	01	00	08	6
Thomas Peirson	0600	01	00	08	6
John Smith	0200	00	00	02	0
Thomas Woolaston	0400	01	00	06	6
Joseph Barnes	0350	02	00	08	6
Henry Jacobson: Jn⁰ Powell	0400	03	00	11	6
William Rakestraw	0750	02	00	12	6
John Cann	0900	02	00	14	0
Abraham man & Will man	0	03			
Isack Slouer	0000	00	00	00	0
Andrew Stalcop	0450	02	00	09	6
Samuell Barker	0400	02	00	09	0
Thomas Gillet	0300	02	00	08	0
Neels Lawson at upland	0700	00	00	07	0
			5	17	6
Land & Tithebles of ye north side of Duck Creeke					
Peter Byard	0600	01	00	08	6
ffrancis Letts	0050	01	00	03	0
Ralf Horsly	0070	00	00	00	9
Joseph Hallman	0100	02	00	06	0
Derick Johnson Clare Jonson ffrancis Wallker	0300	00	00	03	0
ffrancis Hutchison	0390	01	00	06	6

RECORDS OF THE COURT OF NEW CASTLE. 123

John Taylor	0200	02	00	07	0
Antony tomkings	0500	03	00	12	6
William Hatton	0600	03	00	13	6
michall Offly	0300	01	00	05	0
Georg Taylor	0100	01	00	03	6
Judith Crawford	0400	00	00	04	0
Tho Harris W^m osborn	1200	03	00	19	6
Edward Owen	0370	02	00	08	9
Sybrant	0200	00	00	02	0
Samson Atkingson	0200	00	00	02	0
Richard Quince	0100	01	00	03	6
Benjamin Gumly	0280	02	00	08	0
Joseph houlding	0480	02	00	09	10
Joseph Harris	0200	00	00	02	0
Morris Liston	0650	03	00	14	0
				07	5	4

A continuacon of ye north of Duck Creek

Daniell mackarty	0200	01	00	05	6
Epharim Herman					
John Hartops Child	0850	01	00	11	0
Widdow moreton	0470	01	00	07	3
Gustauus Anderson	0200	00	00	02	0
Thomas Snelling	0860	02	00	11	0
Jsack Weeldon	0460	01	00	07	1
An Westingdale	0480	00	00	04	10
Thomas Gelping	0480	00	00	04	10
Joseph more	0700	00	00	07	0
John Wallker	0500	02	00	10	0
Robart money	0400	00	00	04	0
Bazilla osborn	0400	00	00	04	0
Hericus Williams	0450	04	00	14	6
William Grant	0250	03	00	10	0
William Scarf	0200	00	00	02	0
ffrancis Johnson	0000	01	00	02	6
Hugh mash		02	00	05	0
Andrew Loue ...16-	0200	01	00	04	6

C 317.

Land Tithebles of yᵉ
northside Appoquenimy

	Acres		£	s	d
Adam Peterson	0390	02	00	08	10
Robart Hutcheson	0400	00	00	04	00
Johanes De Haes	0400	00	00	04	00
Alixander Cambell	0350	00	00	03	06
Georg Baker	0200	01	00	04	06
Roalof Anderson	0350	03	00	11	00
Joseph More	0200	02	00	07	00
Gabriell Rappe	0200	03	00	09	00
Wallrauen Otto	0200	03	00	09	00
John Peters	0450	06	00	19	06
Andrew Peterson	0150	00	00	01	06
Richard Ingelo	0300	00	00	03	00
John Wallker	0400	00	00	04	00
Richard Hudden	0400	01	00	06	06
John Pash	0200	00	00	02	00
Amos Nicholls	0500	00	00	05	00
Thomas Laws	0400	01	00	06	06
John Scott	0400	00	00	04	00
			11	07	10

A continuacon of yᵉ north side
of Apoquenimy

	Acres of Land	Tithebles	£	s	d
Jane Taylor	0150	00	00	01	06
Edmund Lindsy	0200	00	00	02	00
William Grant	0400	00	00	04	00
John jaruice	0400	01	00	06	06
John ffoster	0200	01	00	04	06
Robart Darby	0200	01	00	04	06
Hans Marcus	0200	01	00	04	06
John Wright	0400	00	00	04	00
Peter Johnsoes	0100	01	00	03	06
Edward Green	0800	01	00	10	06
Edmund Perkus	0170	01	10	04	03
Bryan Omella	0600	00	00	06	00

Richard Noble	0280	03	00	10	03
Cobus Anderson	0170	02	00	06	09
Henry Wallrauen	0200	01	00	04	06
Derrick Williams	0250	02	00	05	06
Casparus Herman	1600	04	01	06	00
Daniell Smith	0200	00	00	02	00
William Padeson		01	00	02	06
Jane Taylor	0150	01	00	04	00
Hybert Laurance	0300	02	00	08	00
Oalla Toreson	0200	00	00	02	00
Magnus White	0170	01	00	04	03
Peter Allricks	0400	01	00	06	06
Jacob Artsen	0150	02	00	06	06
Roalof Anderson	0150	01	00	04	00
Jacob young	1070	00	00	10	09
Judah Crawford	0400	01	00	06	06
Augustine Dicks	0150	00	00	01	06
Thomas Spry	0300	00	00	03	00
Michall Offly	0300	00	00	03	00
Ellis Humpheris	0200	01	00	04	06
Cornelius Comoco	0150	00	00	01	00
			09	01	03

Land & tithebles of ye north of Brandy Wine

Isack Sauay & David Henrix	0500	00	00	05	00
William Cloud	0500	05	00	17	06
Oliuer Coope	0100	01	00	03	06
John Buckley	0100	03	00	08	06
John Grub	0200	01	00	04	06
Thomas Gulping	0100	01	00	03	06
Morgan Druet	0600	01	00	08	06
Thomas Clifton	0133	01	00	03	10
Stoffell Myers	0100	01	00	03	06
Olla ffranson	0233	01	00	04	10
Henrick	0150	01	00	04	00
Carl Peterson	0140	01	00	03	11
Olla Torson	0250	02	00	07	06
Elisabeth Paulson	0150	01	00	04	00
Peter Hallman	0150	01	00	04	00

Jacob Clements	0150	01	00	04	00
Justa Paulson	0100	01	00	03	06
Cornelius Empson	0600	05	00	18	06
Jacob Vanderueer	0535	03	00	12	10
Hans Peterson	0100	02	00	06	00
Vallan^t Hollingsworth	1000	03	00	17	06
Adam Sharply	0300	01	00	05	06
Robart Vaugans	0200	02	00	07	00
William Lester	0100	10	00	03	06
Conrade Constantine	0070	00	00	00	09

Land & Tithebles
S^{nt} Georges.

		£	s	d
Hans Miller	0200	02	00	07	00
John Elderkin	0820	02	00	13	02
John Darby	0800	02	00	13	02
John Willkingson	0300	00	00	03	00
			10	01	10

C 319. At a Court held at Newcastle for our Souaraign Lord ye King & ye Honble Propriatary and Govern^r on ye 20th & 21st of Aprill 1686

        John Cann
        Peter Allricks
        James Walliam   } Justices Present
        William Guest
        Corn^{ll} Empson

C 323. The Court order the Land of John Mattland be this day being ye 21st of Aprill sould at Publick outcry in order to Pay ye former Judgments of court wch was accordingly done & Cornelius Empson & Henrick Vanddenburg as highest bidders bought ye s^d Land for thirty one pounds & ten Shillings besides ye Vandue charges to be Paid in money corn or tobacco at Price currant by ye Last of october next at ye town of newcastle

C 326. The Court Adjurned until ye 20th of July next

At a Court held at Newcastle for our Souaraign Lord ye King & ye Honble William Penn Propriatary & Gouern^r of ye Prouince of Pensiluania & Territorys there unto belonging on ye 20th: 21st: 22nd & 23^d of ye 5th mo^t: called July 1686

John Cann
Peter Allricks
Edward Greene
James Walliam
William Guest
Henry Lemmens
Corn^{ll} Empson
Henricus Williams
} Justices Present

Samuell Land High Sherrief

Thes two acknowledgments for order sake are likewise Inserted among ye rest at ye latter end of this Courts Records

Thomas Clifton acknowledged a Deed of one hundred thirty thirty & three Acres of Land Scituat in ye Bowght near Verdreytyes Hooke to Peter Baynton as p^r ye Deed bearing date ye 24th of May 1686 C 328.

Neils Neilson Acknowledged a Deed of 133 acres of Land Scituat in ye Bowght near Verdretyes Hooke to Peter Baynton as p^r ye Deed beareing date this Instant July 1686

Samuell Land High Sherrief made return of an Execution on ye Estate of Thomas Woolaston which was served on ye one half of his Plantacon & Appraysed by Reneer Vander Coolen and Georg more at thirty Pounds for Payment of a Judg^t of Twenty six Pounds & fifteen Shillings obtain^d by John Gramton agst s^d Thomas Woolaston wch the Court allowed of C 329.

The Court order the Sherif to putt ye s^d John Gramton into Possession of ye Land according to ye Execution

John Gramton in open Court forwarneth Thomas Woollaston y^t he Presume not to cutt timber or to Plough or Sow y^t Part of ye Plantacon taken upon Execution

Edward Greene sen^r acknowledges a Deed of Mortgage to C 330.

William fframton for 3 tracts of Land called Rowls Sepulchre Lackford Hall & Phillips Poynt as p^r ye Deed beareing date ye 6th of May 1686

    Joseph Barnes   P^{lt}
    Thomas Woolaston   Deft

C 333.   The Plt declares y^t ye Deft hath invaded his Land & destroyed ye timber as by ye Declaracon more at larg may appear

The Deft denyeth y^t he hath Invaded ye P^{lts} Land or destroyed ye timber and alleadgeth ye Land which ye Plt claims was bought of John Nomers by ye Def^{t}s Predecessor which to Proue he Produced a certain Deed in Court: The Plt likewise Produced a good firm Deed of Enfeofment from John Nomers

Charles Bayly Attested sayth y^t at ye direction of Thomas Woolaston he cutt down trees on ye Plts Land within ye Plts Line & ye Deft Promised to Keep ye Attestant harmless

William White Attested saith ye Deft imploying Charles Bayly to make Pipe Staues ye s^d Bayly told ye Deft he had cutt down trees with ye Plts Line the Deft sayd I did not order you so to doe but for what you haue done I will bear you harmless in it

John Nomers Attested sayth hee Sould ye Land the one half to ye Defts Predecessor & the other half ye Plt bought & that he heard ye Plt & Deft discourse as if they would ffrindly Survay ye Land betwixt them when Dauy Powell came down

The Plt Produced ye suruayers Return to Court

Thomas Peirson Attested saith y^t ye Return of ye Suruay is true to ye best of his understanding

The Jury going out at their Return bring in their Verdict vizt

We find for ye Plt with three Pence demage & Cost of Sute

The Court give Judgment accordingly

Hybert Lawranson Plt
Tuncha Williams Deft

The Plt declares for a tract off Land & Plantacon formerly   C 333.
belonging to his brother Deceased & ye Plt as heir clayms y^e
Land now in ye tenure & occupacon of ye Deft as by ye Declaracon more at larg may appear

The Def^t by James Nevill hir ffriend in answare to y^e
Declaracon saith ye Defts late husband was Possessed of ye s^d
Land by Virtue of Suruiueorship in Joynt tenentcy as by y^e
answare of ye Deft more largly may appeare

The Plt alleadgeth ye s^d Land was deuided during the liues
of Dirk Lauranson ye Plts brother & Dirk Williams Def^{ts}:
husband lately deceased by consent

John Peirson Attested sayth being on ye Plantacon now in
dispute & some differences arrising betwixt Dirk Williamson
& Dirk Lauranson ye Attestant askt how ye Land was between
them. Dirk Williams said Dirk Lauranson was to haue y^t
Part that He Attestant did make his Crop on ye other Part
was for Dirk Williams & Dirk Williams was to doe as much
on ye Part of Dirk Lauranson & ye Lauranson had done on y^e
Part of Dirk Williams

Reneer Vand^r Coolen Attested sayth eleuen years since he
was upon ye Land in controversy & Dirk Williams & Dirk
Lauranson ware settling ye uper Part of ye Land & both told
ye Attestant there was to be another Plantacon of ye like bignes
for Dirk Lauranson & then one Party was to haue one Plantacon & ye other Party was to haue ye other   Dirk Lauranson
was to haue ye Lower Plantacon & there was a begining to
make ye s^d Plantacon & some houses built thereon

Henry Wallraven Attested saith he asked Dirk Lauranson
why he made his Will in his brothers absence he 's^d y^t he
gaue his Land to his mate because his brother was unkind to
him & his mate best deserved it & sayd if ye marsh had not
been cutt off it would be big enough for two Plantacons but
now it was not

The Pattent of ye Land granted to Dirk Lauranson & Dirk

Williams was read in Court & a true coppy of Dirk Lauransons Will was allso Produced & read in Court

After ye hearing ye cause ye Jury for awhile withdrew & at their Return bring in their Verdict Viz^t

Wee find for ye Deft with cost of Sute

The Court giue Judgment according to Verdict

The Deft Appealeth The Court grant ye appeal he Paying down ye Present Charges & guieing good Security according to Law

Hybert Lauranson & Abraham Man bind them selues Joyntly and seuerally in ye Penalty of one hundred Pounds cur^t money to Tuncha Williams Willow of Dirk Williams That he ye s^d Hybert Lauranson shall Prosecute to Effect his Appeal agst a Judgment obtained agst ye s^d Lauren Plt by ye s^d Tuncha Williams Deft this Court: & if ye s^d Hybert Lauranson shall again happen to be cast at ye next Provinciall Court at Philadelphia Sept^r: next to Pay all cost & damage according to Law

C 343. Upon ye Peticon of John Greene who haueing marryed one of ye daughters of Barent Egberts deceased claiming a Part in their fathers Estate

The Court order ye Execut^r to render an account to ye next orphans Court in Newcastle upon what account they hould ye Estate of Barent Egbert & to Produce Barent Egberts Will if Possible it may be done

C 343. Upon ye Peticon of John Quartermus y^t Justice Greene be ordered to Deliver a certain Pattent for Land John Wallker informing ye Court y^t ye Peticoner had no Right to ye Land The Court refused to meddle in it

July 22nd. 1686

C 345. Upon ye Peticon of diuers of ye Inhabitants of ye town of Newcastle complaining y^t seuerall Persons contrary to a former town meeting had cutt down ye Grass in ye common town marsh on ye Southwest side of ye town to ye great disapointed of other ye Inhabitants equally concernd and it appearing to ye Court diuers Wittnesses Attested y^t there was such an agreement in ye year 1684 that no Inhabitant should mow ye s^d marsh or hay thereon until ye 20th day of July yearly

The Court order ye grass cutt before ye 20th of this Instant July shall be equally deuided amongst ye Inhabitants they Paying ye Share of cutting & that henceforward no Person shall Presume to mow in ye town marsh until ye 20th day of July & that there be equall diuisions of ye marsh y^t all ye Inhabtants be accomodated as near as may be

Upon ye complaint of John White on ye behalf of ye Proprit^r agst Benjamin Blowfeild for not Administring on ye Estate of Herman Johnson whos widdow & Relict he marryed The Court order ye s^d Blowfeild to administer forthwith or another to be appointed so y^t ye children of ye deceased may not be depriued of their Right   C 345.

John White Acknowledged a Deed of Enfeofment for two hundred Acres of Land called ye barren Poynt Scituat on ye North side of Christina Creek to John Alloway as p^r ye Deed beareing date ye 21st July 1686   C 347.

John Alloway acknowledges a Deed of mortgage for two hundred acres of Land called ye Barren Poynt scituat on ye north side of Christina Creeke to Charles Jones Junr & company merch^ts at Bristoll as per ye Deed beareing date ye 21st of July 1686

Johanes De Haes acknowledges a Deed of Enfeofment from him ye s^d DeHaes & Mary Cantwell for ye Plantacon of Henry Jones betwixt ye town Dike & Mrs Mary Blocks Dike as by ye Deed may appear   C 347.

Henry Jones acknowledges a Mortgage of his Plantacon scituat betwixt ye town Dike & Mrs Mary Blocks Dike to James Sanderling as by ye Deed of Mortgage may appear   C 347.

Lucas Stiddem Acknowledges a convayance of a tract of Land Survayed for him in white Clay Creek containing 135 Acres of Land: to Wallter Powell   C 347.

C 347. The Letter of Attorny Proued by 3 Wittnesses & remains on yᵉ ffile

Erasmus Stedam being in open Court Proued yᵉ Lawfull Attorney of Jacob Vandeveer to convey overtain tract of Land to Thomas Peirson called Stony hill Scituat on yᵉ north Side of white Clay Creek containing ffower hundred Acres of Land Acknowledged in yᵉ name of yᵉ sᵈ Jacob Vanderveer yᵉ sᵈ Tract of Land to be conveyed from Vandeveer & his heirs to Thomas Peirson his heirs & Assigns forever as by yᵉ convayance beareing date yᵉ 20ᵗʰ Judy 1686

C 347. The Last Will & Testament of Capᵗ Edmund Cantwell Deceased was proued by Jnº Moll & Jnº Harmanson

July 22 1686

C 348. Benedict Stedham impowers his brother Adam as his Attorny Proued by 3 Wittnesses to acknowledge yᵉ Deed of Resignacon

Adam Stedman & Benedict Stedam doe acknowledge a Deed of Resignacon from & their heirs forever of all yᵉ Land houses & Plantacon Scituat on yᵉ South side of brandy Wine Creek being formerly yᵉ Plantacon marsh & Land of Timothy Stedham their ffather & is now assigned ouer unto Erasmus Stedham as by yᵉ Deed beareing date yᵉ 20ᵗʰ of July may appear

C 348. John Wallker & Wyburg his wife acknowledg a Deed of Enfeofment for a tract of Land called yᵉ high Hook Scituat on yᵉ North side of Apoquenimy Creek with a certain Parcell of marsh on yᵉ South east side of Drawers Creeke to Richard Noble as by yᵉ Deed beareing date yᵉ 7ᵗʰ of march 1681

C 348. Thomas Clifton Acknowledged a Deed of Enfeofment for 133 Acres of Land in yᵉ Bowght neer Verdreytys Hook to Peter Baynton as by yᵉ Deed beareing date yᵉ 24ᵗʰ of may 1686

C 348. Neils Neilson Acknowledged a Deed of Enfeofment for 133 Acres of Land in yᵉ Bowght neer Verdreytys Hooke as by yᵉ Deed beareing date yᵉ 20ᵗʰ of Judy 1686

C 348. Edward Greene Acknowledged a Deed of Enfeofment for yᵉ one moyety of a Pattent from Governʳ Andross to Bryan Omella containing in yᵉ whole Pattnᵗ 400 Acres of Land Scituat on yᵉ first Hooke of yᵉ Drawers Creek: to Henry Vandenburgh as by ye Deed bearing date ye 2nd of July 1686 may appear

Edward Greene acknowledges a Deed of Enfeofment for two hundred Acres of Land Scituat on ye north side of Drawers Creeke called Dyasons to Benjamen Blackleach as by ye Deed beareing date ye 21st of July may appear C 349.

James Claypoole Proued ye Lawfull Attorny: Benjamen Blackleach by his Attorny James Claypoole Junr acknowledgeth a Deed of Enfeofment for 200 acres of Land Scituat on ye north side of Drawers Creek called Dyasons to John Peterson as by ye Deed bearing date ye 22nd of July may appear: C 349.

Amos Nicolls Acknowledged a Deed of Enfeofment for 200 Acres of Land & building thereon Scituat near s^{nt} Georges Creeke to Edmund Perkus as by ye Deed beareing date ye 22nd of July may appear C 349.

Adjurnd until ye third tuesday in October

Vera Copia   To all Christian People to whom thes Presents shall come L^t: Collonell Paul Lite of ye Parish of S^{nt} Georg in ye Island of Barbados heretofore called Paul Lite of ye Island afors^d merchant sendeth Greeting in o^r Lord God Euerlasting Know y^{ee} y^t I ye s^d Paul Lite for very good & Valleuable consideracons me hereunto Effectually mouing but more especially for & in consideracon of ye trust and confidence which I haue & Repose in ye care & circumpeccon of my worthy & trusty ffriend William Dyer Esqr survay^r Gen^{ll} of his may^{ties} Customs in all his maj^{ties} Plantacons in America Haue by thes presents made nominated & Appointed & in my stead & place putt As well in my own Right Property and behoofe as allso as I am Execut^r to John Pitt Junior late of ye Island afores^d Deceased My s^d worthy & trusty ffriend William Dyer to be my true Lawfull & undoubted Attorny & Procurat^r in both & either of my s^d Acknowledgments Conclusions and Capacitys for me & in my name & to my use as I am respectiuely concerned & capaciated as afores^d. To aske demand require recover & receive C 351.

all & every such Sum or Sums of money tobacco hogs flesh & all other specie or merchandize as now are or hereafter shall be due or owing payable or accountable to me constituant in either of my capacity afores^d from any p^{r}son or p^{r}sons whatsoever in either of the Provinces of Maryland or Virginia or either of them but more especially from Capt. Henry Ward of ye s^d Province of Maryland his heirs Execut^{rs} & Adm^{rs} be ye same dew from him them or any of them by bill bond obligacon booke account Mortgage Deed couenant assumpsit Promise Judgment Execucon condemnacon or by anny ways or means whatsoeuer or howsoeuer Giuing & granting by thes Presents to my s^d Attorny & Procurator my full Power and Authority in both & either of my capacitys aforesaid and ye s^d seuerall p^{r}sons & euery of them but more espicially the s^d Capt. Henry Ward his heirs Execut^{rs} & Adm^{rs} and euery of them in upon touching and concerning ye p^{r}mises and Euery of them to Sue Arrest implead imprison & out of prison again to release all & euery such Person or p^{r}sons as is or shall be found indebted to me as afores^d in either of my s^d capacitys but more especially ye s^d Henry Ward as afores^d & upon recoverys made against him or them ye Effects so recovered to be sould & disposed of by my s^d Attorny & Procurato^r by sale or Markett Overt as ye custome of thos Provinces shall appoint & as my s^d Attorney & Procurato^r shall thinke meet & Requisite and ye same to sell & dispose of for my best advantage according to his discretion he being therefore accountable to me my Execut^{rs} Adm^{rs} or Assigns from time to time & to compound with ye s^d Persons or anny of them & especially wth ye s^d Henry Ward if he thinke it convenient & upon Payment composicon or other finall determinacon wth them or anny of them by my s^d Attorny to made Acquittances or other Lawfull discharges for me & in my name to make Sale & Deliuer & one Attorny or more under him for mannagment and recovery of ye Premises to make nominate substitute & Appoynt & at his Will & Pleasure again to Annihilate & make Voyd And generally to doe act & Execute all such further & other act & acts things deuises and other contriuances or con vayances whatso^r in ye Law or to my s^d Attorny shall seem necessary & convenient for management of ye Premises. Hereby Ratefying allowing and Confirming all & whatsoeuer my s^d Attorny Shall Lawfully doe or cause to be done in about ye execuōn of ye p^rmises in as full large ample & beneficiall manner & form to all intents constructions & purposes as I my self might or could doe if I ware p^rsonally Present In Witnes whear of I haue hereunto sett my hand & seale the second of July 1683 in ye 35th year of the Raign of o^r souaraigne Lord King Charles ye second ouer England &c^t:

And I doe before ye signing sealeing & Perfecting hereof hereby revoke annihilate disallow & make Voyd all former & other Letters of Attorny or procuracōn by me at anny time made to anny p^rson or p^rsons whatsoever touching ye p^rmises at anny time or times before ye date hereof

 Sealed & Deliuered
 in p^rsence of us   Paul Lyte   (seale)
  Robart Darkings
  Sam^{ll} Massey

The 7th of Aprill 1685

Then ye abouenamed Samuel Massey came & upon his corporall oath testefyed y^t in his presence & pressence of ye aboue named Robart Darkings ye aboues^d Paul Lyte Sealed & as his act & Deed deliuered ye aboues^d Letter of Attorney to & for ye uses thereon expressed expressed before me

C 353.

           G. Minveil Mayor

I doe hereby testefye y^t ye 7th day of Aprill 1685 I was Present when Sam^{ll}. Massey to ye afores^d Letter of Attorny Subscribed as a Wittnes upon his oath did proue ye same at ye City of Newyork before Gabriell Mineveil Esqr May^r of ye s^d citty to Such Effect as is afores^d: mencōned

(seale of the Province of Pensiluania)

 Wittnes my hand this 13^{nth} day of July 1685

          Tho Rudyard

Gouernor Tho Rudyard did signe yᵉ aboue before me this 13ⁿᵗʰ 5ᵗʰ moᵗʰ 1685

Wᵐ Markham

C 353. July 27ᵗʰ. 1686 Then the aforenamed Mʳ Samˡˡ Massey came & upon his corporall oath testefyed yᵗ in his pʳsence & pʳsence of yᵉ aboue named Robart Darkings aforesᵈ Paul Lyte Sealed as his Act & deliuered the aforesᵈ Letter of Attorny to & for yᵉ uses therein Expressed before us

John Cann
James Walliam

Lereˢ Admᶜᵒⁿ

C 354. At a County Court for Suffolke held at Boston 25ᵗʰ July Anᵒ: 1682

Vera Copia

Full Power and Authority to Administer all & singular yᵉ goods Estate & Credits of Mʳ William Taylor late of Boston Merᶜᵗ. deceased intestate is granted unto Mʳˢ Rebecca Taylor his Relict Widdow and his son in law Mʳ John Nelson of Boston Merᶜᵗ they giueing security to Administer yᵉ sᵈ Estate according to law & Exhibiting an Inventory thereof upon their Oaths

Attested pʳ Isᵃ: Addington Clre

Security is given as above
  Isᵃ Addington Clre

Copia Vera from yᵉ Records of Admᶜᵒⁿˢ Attested
               Isᵃ Addington Clre

Deliuered by yᵉ officer subscribed as a true coppy from yᵉ Record yᵉ 7ᵗʰ of January 1684 in pʳsence of
  William Dyer Junʳ
  Samuell Massey

Newyork Aprill yᵉ 11ᵗʰ 1685 Then appeared before me Wᵐ Dyer Junn: & Saml Massey & upon their corporall oaths declared y^t they saw ye within mencōned Letters of Administracōns signed sealed & Deliuered by Isack Addington of Boston & for ye uses within mencōned which I Certefie

J Spragg Secry

Recorded in ye Sec^{ryes} office for ye Province of New Yorke in liber No 27 fol (109) p^r

J Spragg Secr^t:

(Seale of ye province of pensil uania)

Vera Copia

Philadelphia ye 24th of ye 3 mo^t 1686

Wm Dyer Ju^r was then Attested before me according to ye Laws of this Province & did thereon declare y^t he saw ye Within Lett^r of Adm^{con} deliuered signed by ye officer subscribed. Witnes my hand & Seale of ye Province

Wm Markham Sect^r

Newcastle Territorys of Pensiluania 31st July 1686

Then the before named Sam^{ll}. Massey Gen^t came & upon his Ingagement according to ye Laws of this Prouince & Gouerm^t Attested y^t in his Presence & ye Presence of W^m: Dyer Junr the before named Isack Addington Signed sealed & as a Lawfull act & Deed deliuered ye before written & on ye other side of this Sheet mencōned Lett^r of Administracōn to & for ye ends & uses therein Expressed before us

C 355.

Edw Greene
James Walliam

Know all men by thes p^{r}sents that wee Rebecca Taylor Relict of Wm Taylor late of Boston Merchant & John Nelson of Boston mer^{ct} Administrat^r to ye Estate of Wm Taylor afores^d haue Assigned ordained & made & in our stead & place by thes p^{r}sents putt & constituted our trusty & well beloued ffriend Major William Dyer to be our true Sufficient & Lawfull Attorny for us & in o^r name & to our use to aske demand sue for Levy require recover & receive of all & every p^{r}son or p^{r}sons whatsoeuer all & euery such debt & defts sum

C 355.

& sums of money goods effects of things or other Estate whatsoever which is are or hereafter shall be dew owing belonging or Appertaining unto ye Estate of ye s^d Wm Taylor by anny manner of ways or means whatsoever & for Default of Payment & Deliuery ye s^d Debitors or either or anny of them to sue Arrest Attach implead imprison & condemn his & their bodys Lands Tenements goods & Chattles in Execution to take & out of Execucon to deliuer & upon receipt of anny Such debts sums of money &c^t due as afores^d Acquittance & other Sufficient discharges In due from of Law in our name to make Seale & Deliuer and if need be to Appear before anny Gouern^r Judges Justices or magistrates in

Vera copia.   anny Court of Judicature & therein our be-
anny Court of Judicature & there in our be-
matters & things relating to ye p^rmises Attornys one or more under him our s^d Attorny to make and substitute & at pleasure to revoke giuing & by thes p^rsents granting unto our s^d Attorny or his substitute our full & whole power strenght & authority to doe Execute p^rform and finish all & euery such other Acts things & Deuices whatsoeuer in ye Law needfull to be done about & relating to ye p^rmises and ye dependencys there of as fully amply and effectually to all intents & purposes as we might or could doe if personally p^rsent Ratefying allowing and houlding firm & stable all & whatsoeuer our s^d Attorny or his Substitute shall lawfully doe or cause to be done in & about ye p^rmises by Virtue of thes Presents In Witnes whereof we haue hereunto Sett our hands & seales the day of January Anno dom one thousand six hundred eighty & four R R Caroli secundi nunc Angliae &ct xxxvi

Signed Sealed & dd in
ye p^rsence of   Rebecca Taylor   (Seal)
   William Dyer Junr   Jno: Nellson   (Seal)
   Sam^ll Massey

   Newcastle territorys of Pensilvania 31st July 1686

C 357.   Then ye beforenamed Sam^ll Massey came & upon his ingagement Attested according to ye Laws of this Goverm^t that in his p^rsence & in ye p^rsence of Wm Dyer Junr the before named Rebecca Taylor & Jno Nelson signed sealed and as their act & Deed Deliuered ye before written & on ye other side of this sheet menc̄oned Letter of Attorny to & for ye ends & uses therein Expressed before us

Ed^w Greene
James Walliam

Vera Copia.   Know all by thes P^rsents that I Symon C 358. Dauis of Bristoll in ye Colony of New Plymouth in New England Eldest son of Nicholas Dauis late of Barnstable in s^d Collony mer^ct for good causes & considerac̄ons me thereunto mouing Haue nominated made ordained & by thes P^rsents do nominate make ordain & in my place & stead Depute & constitute my trusty & much Respected ffriend may^r William Dyer to be my true Sufficient & Lawfull Attorny for me in my name & to my use to Ask Demand take recover & receive all & singular such Lands & meddows y^t doth of Right belong unto me that was my deceased ffathers will at larg appear by Seueral Instruments Relating to ye Purchase ye s^d Lands Lying & being in East jarsay in ye Bay to ye Killca[ts] Rarritons Kills with all ye Privileges thereunto belonging from all euery p^rson or p^rsons that shall withould ye same and if need befo[re] P^rmises to appear & ye person of me ye Constituant to Represent in all Courts before all Judges there to Defend Reply & make answere allso to say Prosecute sue Attach Arrest implead imprison & condem all & every p^rson or p^rsons who shall delay or refuse to deliver anny such Lands as aboues^d after Legall Demand and for Prison again when need shall be to Deliuer their goods Estates prsons in Execution to take & from under Execution again to release Likewise one Attorny or more under him to make & Substitute & at Pleasure again to Revoke & release & generall in & concerning ye Premises and Dependencys thereof doe say Execute and accomplish all & whatsoever I ye constituant might or could doe if I were there in my own p^rson present all though ye matter Require more speciall charg thene herein is expressed all which I doe promis & engage to Retefye allow & hould of Vallew for ever In Witnes whereof I ye s^d: Symon Dauis haue hereunto sett my hand & seale this Twenty ninth day of January ano domini one thousand six hundred eighty fiue or six & in ye first year of his May^ties Raign Jeams ye second King of England

          Simon Dauis (seale)

Signed Sealed and Deliuered
in ye p^rsence of
  William Dyre Junr
  Edward Ewster

 June ye 28 1686.

This day p^rsonally appeared before me William Dyre Ju^r and Edward Ewster & made oath y^t they did see the above Specifyed Lett^r of Attorny signed Sealed & Deliuered to ye uses & purposes therein menconed

          Peiter Alricks

 At a Court held at Newcastle for our Souaraign Lord ye King & ye Honble Propriatary & Gouern^r the 20th of Aprill 1686

C 359. John Gramton P^lt
    Thomas Woolaston Def^t

 The Plt declares for ye Sum of twenty six Pounds & fiueteen Shillings Pensiluania money dew by a bill under ye hand & seale of ye Deft with cost of sute

 The Deft confesses Judgement for ye s^d Sum of 26^lb 15^s with Cost of Sute

 The Court order Judgment to be entered accordingly

C 359. Thes are therefore by ye Kings Authority & in ye name of ye Propriatary & Govern^r to Require thee to Levy by execution ye Sum of twenty six Pounds & fiueteen Shillings with ye costs of sute upon ye goods Chattels Lands or Effects (which according to Law are to be executed for ye Payment of Debts) belonging to Thomas Woolaston Deft and therewith to Satisfye ye s^d John Gramton his s^d Judgment of 26 ^{lb} : 15 and ye Costs of Sute and make return hereof & thy doings Herein at ye County Court to be held at .... in July next whereof fail not at thy Perill & for thy so doing this .... be thy sufficient War^{rt}: guien under my hand & seale this 24th of May in ye 2nd year of ye Kings Raign & 6th of ye Propriatarys Gouen[ment,] 1682

            Henry Lemmens

To Sam^{ll}: Land High Sherrief
of Newcastle County or his Dep^t:

 By Virtue of ye within menconed Execucon I seized upon ye C 360.
uppermost half of ye Plantacon of Thomas Woolaston which was appraised by Gorg more & Reneer Vander Coolen at thirty Pounds & was Exposed to Publick Sale upon condicon read at ye Publick outcry July ye 10th by me

          Sam^{ll} Land Sheririef

 Containing about two hundred Acres ye half of ye Plantacon   C 360.
& sould to John Gramton for thirty pounds and ten Shillings and was putt in Possession of ye s^d Land ye 26th of July by me

          Sam^{ll} Land Sheirrief

 July ye 10th 1686 I underwritten Samuell Land doe ack-   C 360.
nowledg to haue Received full satisfaction from John Gramton for ye half of ye Plantacon which he bought at ye Publick outcry y^t formerly belonged to thomas Woolaston taken upon Execution Witnes my hand at Newcastle upon Delaware River sam^{ll} Land Sherrief N C
John White Wittnes

 At a Court held at Newcastle by ye Kings authority & in ye name of William Penn Propriatary & Governor of ye Province of Pensilvania & Territorys begining on ye nineteenth day of october & continued to ye twenty third of ye same month one thousand six hundr^d & eighty six

	John Cann	
	Peter Allricks	
	Edward Greene	
Present	James Walliam	Justices
	William Guest	
	Henry Lemmens	
	Vall^t Hollingsworth	
	Corne^{ll}: Empson	

Sam^{ll} Land High Sherrife

C 367. Upon ye Peticon of Henry Vandeburg y^t ye Court would ord^r Major William Dyre to produce some papers belonging to ye Peticoner in ye hands of s^d Dyre ye Peticoner supposing ye s^d Dyre hath made allteracons contrary to his agreement therein The s^d Major Dyre alleadgeth he is not to be Surprised being ye Kings officer and craueth ye benefitt of a Statute of ye 14th caroli secundi Regis wch being read The Court Desired major Dyre to show his commission whereby he might proue himself wthin ye benefitt of that Statute & they would according to Law Proceed therein The s^d Dyre did Alleadg his commission was read in y[^{e}] Provinciall Counsell & declared y^t he did not think himself oblidged to shew it now The Court Therefore Decline to meddle in y^t affair & order ye Peticoner to Proceed as ye Law directs for ye gaining his papers

Henry Vandeburg desires Capt. Markham & Casparus Herman may be Attested The court allow it

C 368. Casparus Herman Attested y^t being at Vandeburgs dore Major Dyre askt ye Attestant if he Knew ye Land y^t. Vandeburg was Selling him ye Attestant replyed he Knew not much of it & after that Major Dyre went Into ye house & told Vandeburgh it was a bargain and shook hands & called ye Attest to be a Wittnesse The bargain was as followeth Henry Vandeburgh Sould Major Dyre 200 acres of Land & a horse & sixty pounds in money to be paid in two payments in consideracon whereof major Dyre Sould to Vandeburg & Deliuered a Brigantine Riding before ye Dore and s^d Dyre gaue Vandenburg the costome flree of thirty hogs^{sd} of tobacco wch was computed to be ye Loading of ye Brigantine at the confirming yᵉ bargain Vandeburg gaue major Dyre two guinnys wᶜʰ sᵈ Dyre Received

Capᵗ William Markham Attested saith yᵗ upon yᵉ best of his Knowledge upon yᵉ bargain of yᵉ brigantine there was Sixty Pounds to be paid at 2 Payments 200 acres of Land & yᵉ costom of thirty hosheads of tobacco ffree 2 guinnys & a horse

    William Dyre Esqʳ   Plt
    Justus Anderson   Deft

The Plt declares for a house & Plantacon as administʳ of John Law as pʳ yᵉ Declaracon may appear

C 378.

The Letter of Administracon was read and Mʳ bradshaw ownd he gaue it Capᵗ Markham Attested that James Bradshaw was Lawfully commissionated to Register & Survayor Genˡˡ of yᵉ County of Newcastle

The Deft alleadge John Law is yet Living & would haue yᵉ Plt proue him Dead

Robart Hutchinson Attested saith he heard at one Edmunds house in Mary Land yᵗ John Law was Dead at bush river as sᵈ Edmunds wife had heard

The Plt produced to coppys out of yᵉ Records where in Law acknowledges a mortgage of yᵉ house sᵈ Deft now liues in to yᵉ sᵈ Deft for one thousand guilders then yᵉ Deft produced a Deed of a latter Date to yᵉ Mortgage wherein John Law reconvays ouer his sᵈ house to yᵉ Defᵗ Epharim Herman saith being Attested that John Lawe hauing given bills of Exchange upon that yᵉ sᵈ Law reconvayed all his house & Lott back again to Justus Anderson & all former Deed were cancelled

And the Attestant saith the sᵈ Law was to haue in consideracon thereof as he doth suppose a Plantacon & 1500ˡᵇ of tobacco

Thomas Harris Attested he met wᵗʰ John Law & in discours Law said he had Excepted of a bill of 1500 ˡᵇ of tobacco from Justus Anderson in Tarkertons hand & that he would sell his Land to Cantwell this discourse was after ye reconvaying the house to ye Deft

Thomas Woolaston Attested saith he saw ye Def^t giue Law a bill of 1500 ^{lb} of tobacco on tarkinton which bill ye s^d Law did accept it being in consideraćon of ye bargain of ye house

There being diuers papers & Deeds read in Court The Plt withdrew his accon:

C 384. Whereas Joseph Bisse alias Spry being by a Court held at Newcastle June ye 3rd 1685 ordered to Liue with M^r: John Cann upon such condićons as are upon ye Records of ye s^d Court more at Larg Expressed The s^d Joseph Bisse haueing run away from his Mast^r John Cann & being now in ye costody of William Grant who is Willing to haue ye s^d Joseph Bisse if the Court pleas the s^d William Grant haueing ingaged in ye open Court to giue ye s^d Joseph one good cow & calf & one hundred acres of Land within this County Upon the s^d: condićons the Court order Joseph Bisse to serue William Grant seven years from ye date hereof being ye 22nd of october 1686 And Mr Cann is released from his former Ingagement

C 384. Upon ye Petićon of John Greene concerning Barent Egberts Estate in ye Right of his wife The Court Referr ye Peticoner to take his dew course at Law

C 385. Upon ye Petićon of Mathyas Vanderheyden concerning the Administraćon on ye Estate of Capt Henry Hard deceased scituat in this County The Court order Major Dyre to render the reasons of his Caueat which is not Sufficient The Court judg ye Peticoner ought to Administer

C 389. Justus Anderson acknowledged a Deed of Enfeofment being an Indenture bearing date ye 17^{nth} day of october 1686 to John Richardson for 200 Acres of Land scituate in ffern Hooke as by ye s^d Deed more at Larg may appear

C 424. Roalof Anderson & Jacob Artsen acknowledged a Deed of Enfeofment for a tract of Land containing three hundred Acres called Chelsy Scituat on ye South side of s^{nt} Georges Creek to Isack Decow Jacob Decow Robart Ashton and Richard Darkin as p^r ye s^d Deed bearing date the 20th of October 1686

John Moll & Christian his wife acknowledge a deed of Enfeofment for a house & Lott of ground wth all ye out houseing thereunto belonging Scituat in the town of newcastle betwixt ye house of Johanes De Haes and the Land Street to Arnoldus Delegrange as p^r ye Deed beareing date ye 15th of July 1686   C 389.

Woola Toolson Acknowledged a Deed of Enfeofment for a tract of Land at Pertee hooke to Adam Hay alias Skee as p^r ye Deed beareing date ye 19^{nth} of october 1686 may appear   C 389.

John Valck Acknowledged a Lott of ground betwixt Marys Street & Brewers Street in ye C town of Newcastle to John Hendrickson as p^r ye Assignment of ye War^{rt}: bearein date ye 15^{nth} of october 1686 may appear   C 389.

Erasmus Steedham Acknowledged an Assignment of his Warr^t & Certificate for a tract of Land called timber hill Scituat on ye South side of brandywine Creeke containing 200 Acres of Land to John Richardson as p^r ye Assignment beareing date ye 20th of october 1686:   C 389.

Gabriell Rappe acknowledged a Deed of Enfeofment for a tract of Land called Industry Scituat on the north side of ye Dragon Swamp containing 600 Acres of Land, to John Hayly as p^r ye Deed beareing date ye 20th of october 1686 may appear   C 390.

William Phillips Acknowledged a Deed of Enfeofment for two tracts of Land called Phillips Poynt & Rowls Sepulchre scituate scituat on ye Drawers Creek both the s^d tracts of Land containing 460 Acres of Land, to Edward Greene as by ye Deed beareing date ye 22nd of Aprill 1686:   C 390.

John Wallker ye Attorney of Benjamin Gumly acknowledged an Alianacon of ye tract of Land called Rowlls Sepulchre to William Phillips it being ye same tract of Land that Phillips hath Acknowledged to Edward Greene as by his Letter of Attorney bearing date ye 15th of october 1686   C 390.

Justus Anderson Acknowledged a Deed of Enfeofment for a house & 1 Lott of ground by ye River side toward ye olde flort to John Williams Neering as p^r ye Deed beareing date the 17^{nth} day of Aprill 1678   C 390.

C 390. Hendrick Vandenburgh and Anna his Wife acknowledged a Deed of Enfeofment for a tract of Land called Popler Neck Scituat near ye red Lyon containing 200 Acres of Land as by ye Deed ye s^d Deed (on ye backeside of ye Pattent) beareing date ye 22nd of June 1686

C 391. Symon Janson and Anna his wife Acknowledged by their Attorny Edward Land a Deed of Enfeofment for a tract of Land to Henry Lemmens as per ye Deed beareing date ye 29th of September 1685 may appear

C 391. Henry Garetson & John Erixson Acknowledged to haue received ffiueteen pounds at two Severall payments from John Jaquet of Swanwick being in part for his Land at Swanwick Sould by a former order of ye Court of Newcastle wch s^d Sums of ffiue pounds & ten pounds ware received June ye 8th: & 9th: 1686: 5 ^{lb} thereof being paid to Henrick Garetson

C 391. Y^e Court Adjurnd until ye 3rd tuesday in December next

C 392. At a Court held at Newcastle for our Souaraign Lord ye King & ye Honble William Penn Propriatary & Gouernor on ye 21: 22 & 23rd of X^{ber} 1686

Present
  John Cann
  Peter Allricks
  James Walliam   } Justices
  Cornelius Empson
  Vall^t. Hollingsworth

December 23rd

C 399. Lucas & Erasmus Stedham Administrat^r of ye Estate of Timan Stedham Plts

Jacob Vanderveer & William Vanderveer Defts

The Plts declare for a tract of Land Scituat at brandywine falls. The P^{lts} appear by their Attorny Corn^{ll} Empson & ye Def^{ts} by Abraham Mann

The Plt produced as Evidence two Depositions formerly taken & a copy of a former Declaracon & Judgm^t of court as allso a receipt for Quit Rent

Mathyas DeVoos Attested saith he Knew Mons Andrisen & Wallrauen Jansen Planted on ye Land now in controuersy

The Defts produce a Pattent from Govern^r Penn & a Pattent from york & a certificate from ye Deputy Survay^r & a Letter from Gouernor Andros as allso a Dutch paper

Thomas Peirson Attested Saith he resurvayed ye Land in controuersy for ye Defts according to ye tenor of ye Petent to ye best of his understanding by ye naturall bounds & one of ye Plts carryed ye chain

Epharim Herman was Attested who read Some of ye former records & declared ye Plts father had a former Judgement for ye Land & ye Def^t going to new york ye matter was to be reheard there but ye father of ye Plts said he would not be so troubled about it & it was not Determined at york as he Knoweth of:

The Jury haueing heard ye Plea on both sides goe out and at their return bring in their Verdict Viz^t

Wee of ye Jury find for ye Defts wth cost of sute—Judgm^t accordingly

Lylif Stedham acknowledged a Deed for a tract of Land called greene meddow Scituat on ye South side of brandywine Creeke containing 200 Acres of Land, to John Richardson ye Deed is dated 22 december 1686   C 405.

Humphry Best & Edward Greene Acknowledg a Deed of Enfeofment for a tract of Land Scituat in White clay creek being ye same Land that ye s^d Humphry Best & Edw: Greene bought of Broer Senexen being ye Just half part of 220 Acres of Land to John Grampton as p^r ye Deed beareing date 22nd December 1686:   C 406.

The Court adjurnd until ye 15^{nth} of ye 12 mo^t next ensuing   C 406.

ffabruary ye 15^{nth} 1686-7

At a Court held at Newcastle for o^r Souaraigne Lord ye King And ye Honble William Penn Propriatary & Gouern^r of y^e   C 408.

Province of Pensiluania & Territory on the ffiuetenth of Fabruary 1686/7:

Present
John Cann
Peter Allricks
James Walliam
Henry Lemmens
} Justices

C 408.   Upon ye Request of Broer Senexen concerning a certain Mortgage made & acknowledged by Humphry Best & Edward Greene Junr to ye s^d Broer Senexen for a Plantacon in white Clay Creek:

Epharim Herman & Arnoldus DeLagrange ware Attested who thereupon declare th^t to ye best of their Knowledge the money to be paid by Humphry Best & Edward Greene for ye Payment of a tract of Land Sould by Broer Senexen to ye s^d Best & Green & by them Mortgaged to s^d: Broer Senexen for payment was to be Siluer money. ye mortgage beareth date the 21st of 2nd mo^t 1685

C 408.   Joseph Leauesly being solemnly Attested did declare that he is a Wittness that Gerardus Wessells did sign & Deliuer a Deed of Mortgage of a house & ground to John Darby

C 409.   John Harmenson Acknowledged a Deed of Enfeofment for ffour hundred & forty Acres of Land called Knotsenburgh Scituat near ye Red Lyon Run: to Hendrick Vandenburgh as p^r ye s^d Deed & Assignment of ye Pattent beareing date the 15^{nth} of ffabruary 1686-7.

C 409.   Antony Bryant Acknowledged a Deed of Enfeofment for a tract of Land containing in Length 300: foot & in breadth 80 ffoot Scituat in ye town of Newcastle & bounded as p^r the Deed beareing date ye 15^{nth} of ffabruary 1686/7 to Hendrick Vandenburgh of ye town of Newcastle—

C 409.   Henrick Euertson Acknowledged a Deed of Enfeofment to Hendrick Vandenburgh for a certain Island and other tract of Land Scituat & being in ye Crane Hook butted & bounded as p^r ye s^d Deed beareing date ye 11th of ffabruary 1686/7

C 409.   John Mattson alias Screek Acknowledged a Deed of Enfeofment to Hendrick Vandenburgh for a certain Plantacon Scituat & being in Crane Hooke Butted & bounded as p^r ye s^d Deed beareing date ye 11th of ffabruary 1686/7

Edward Gibbs & Judith his wife as Administratrix of ye Estate of Agustin Dixen did acknowledge a Deed of Enfeofment to Cornelius Empson & Hendrick Vandenburgh for ye one moyety of a tract of Land Scituat in S^{nt} Georges Creek called Hampton containing 300: Acres of Land butted & bounded as p^r ye Deed beareing date ye 11th of January 1686/7:   C 409.

Hendrick Vandenburgh Acknowledged a Deed of Enfeofment to Henry Evertson for two hundred Acres of Land Scituat on ye north side of s^{nt} Georges Creek butted & bounded as p^r ye Deed beareing date ye 14^{nth} of ffabruary: 1686/7   C 409.

Hendrick Vandenburgh enters a caueat agst Jo: Burnams Lott to giue his reason by next Court   C 410

Joseph Hallman & Margaret Hallman Acknowledged a Deed of Indenture to Georg Taylor for a tract of Land Scituat on ye north west branch containing two hundred Acres of Land butted and bounded as p^r ye Indentures beareing date ye 10th of March 1685/6   C 410.

Adam Hay alias Ikeer acknowledged a Deed of Enfeofment to John Priestner for a certain tract of Land Scituat at Pert Hook containing: butting & bounding as p^r ye Deed beareing date ye 15^{nth} of fabruary 1686/7   C 410

Adjourned untill ye 15^{nth} of march next   C 410.

At a Court held at Newcastle for our Souaraign Lord ye King & ye Honble William Penn Propriatary & Govern^r of ye Province of Pensiluania & Territorys on ye 15^{nth} of march annoq dom̃ 1686/7   C 411

P^{r}sent
{ John Cann
Peter Allricks
James Walliam
William Guest
Henry Lemmens } Justices

C 412. Upon y* Peticon of Reneer Vandercoolen for y* Stopping all proceedings relating to a mortgage from Gerardus Wessels to John Darby the Peticoner alleadging the house intended to be mortgaged is not payed for to y* Peticoner The Court order y* Peticoner if he be agrieued to apply himself to y* Law

C 412. Upon y* Peticon of Hendrick Vandenburgh desireing all proceedings may be stopt relating to y* Sale of a Lott of ground belonging to one Joseph Burnham lately gone out of this govement in y* Peticoners Debt

The Court allow y* Peticoner to take out an Attachment agst y* Effects of y* s^d: Burnham

C 412. Georg more Acknowledged a Deed of Enfeofment for y* one moyety or half part of a tract of Land Scituat on y* South side of Christina Creek containing 185 Acres called Puttny as pr y* y* Deed to Job Nettleship beareing date y* 14^{nth} march 1687

C 413. Job Nettleship acknowledged a Deed of Enfeofment for the one moyety or half part of a tract of Land Scituat on y* South side of Christina Creeke containing 185 acres of Land called Puttny as p^r y* s^d Deed to Reneer Vandercoolen bearin date y* 15^{nth} of March 1687:

C 413. Sampson Atkings Acknowledged the copy of an originall Deed of Enfeofment for a tract of Land called Rich timber Scituat on y* Northwest branch of Duck creek containing four hundred & thirty Acres as p^r y* Deed beareing date y* 28th of January 1686 made & acknowledged to Epharim Herman

C 413. Reneer Vander Coolen acknowledged a Deed of Enfeofment to Job Nettleship for a tract of Land Scituat in y* town bounded to y* east with a Lott laid out for Hans Corderus to y* South wth y* Susquehanah Street to y* West wth y Land lately belonging Antony Bryant to y* North wth y* beaver Street as p^r y* Deed beareing date y* 14^{nth} of March 1687

C 413. Oalla Toarson Acknowledged a Deed of Enfeofment to Hendrick Vandenburgh for a tract of Land containing two hundred Acres Scituat betwixt s^{nt} Georges Creek & Arantys Creeke as p^r y* Deed beareing date 14^{nth} of march 1686/7:

Jacob young by his Attorny Edward Gibbs Acknowledged a C 413.
Deed of Enfeofment to Hendrick Vandenburgh for a tract of
Land called Doctors Commons Scituat on ye Southward side
of Georges Creeke containing one hundred & sixty Acres of
Land as p^r ye Deed beareing date ye 16^{nth} day of ffabruary 1686

Elisabeth Ogle Acknowledged a Deed of Enfeofment to Hen- C 413.
drick Vandenburgh for a house & Lott of ground Scituat in y^e
town of Newcastle bounding to ye northwest wth ye Brewers
Street to ye North east to ye Street w^{ch}: runs from ye River
to ye s^d brewers Street to ye South east wth ye market place
to ye south west wth Georgs mores house as p^r ye Deed beareing date ye 15^{nth} of march 1686/7

The Court Adjurns till the third Tuesday in Aprill next

At a Court held at Newcastle for our Sovaraign Lord ye King
& the Honble William Penn Propriatary & Governor of the
Province of Pensiluania & Territorys on ye 19^{nth}. 20th 21 & 22nd
of Aprill 1687

	John Cann	
Present	Peter Allricks	Justices
	Henry Lemmens	
	William Guest	

John Gramton   Plt   C 421.
Thomas Woollaston Deft

The Plt complains agst ye Deft in an acc̄on of trespass on
ye case for Plowing & sowing ye Plts Land & Remoueing the
bounds as p^r the Declarac̄on more at Larg may appear

The accon being called both partys appearing the Deft did
Alleadg he was Summoned only Eleuen days before the Court
& Desired ye benefit of ye Law in y^t case wch Law being Read
it did appear that the summons was to be at least ten days before the tryall & the Exhibition of ye complaint fourteen days
before

John White Attested did Declare that ye Plt did compain
of a trespass more then fourteen days before ye Court

The Plt was Attested that he did beleiue in his conscience y^t his caus was Just

both Partys Joyn Issue the Declaracon was Read and the Deft Exhibited his answere as p^r ye answere on ye ffile Referance being thereunto had may more at larg appear

William Woodhouse Evidence for ye Plt Attested saith y^t he heard his master ye P^lt to forewarn ye Deft from medling wth ye Land w^ch : was survayed by ye Survayor Genll out of ye Land lately belonging to ye Def^t : for ye Plt^s use: The Deft sayd he would not take his forewarning & after some time after ye Deft came when he and ye Plt ware at worke on ye s^d Land & ye Def^t did forbid the Def^t to break up anny ground or plant anny ffence there

The Plt Produced Diuers Records of former Courts to proue his Declaracon as Aprill Court 1686 July Court 1686 as allso ye copy of ye Execution & Return & order of Court wherein the Court allow ye Execucon of ye Land & order Possession

John Couche Attested saith y^t when M^r. Land came first with his execution to Thomas Woolastons about John Gramptons Judgment the s^d Woolaston haueing nothing to Lay ye Execution on the s^d Thomas Woolaston bid the Sherrief to Lay it on his Land & some time after John Gramton ye Plt offered to take his Negro again or to take him whilst ye Debt could pay him but ye Def^t Refused saying ye Negro shall neuer goe off his Plantacon again. the Attestant saith y^t about fourteen days since he saw Thomas Woolaston at Plow on ye Land y^t was Survayed by ye Survayor for Jno Gramton & Saith he saw him at Plow two or three times

The Plt produced a paper Subscribed by ye Deft as followeth

I Thomas Woolaston of white Clay Creek doe hereby certifye y^t I have Sould all my cows & a Mare wth ye Rest of my cattle affortnight agoe as Wittnes my hand this 28th of may 1686 Thomas Woolaston

John Mandy the Subsherrief being Attested saith he was

wth Samuell Land ye Sherrief at ye Defts and ye Sherrif told ye Deft he hd an execution against him upon ye account of John Gramton & ye s^d Deft Replyed to ye Sherrief Lay it upon my Land ye attestant saith the Sherrief took a horse from ye Deft at that time

John Couch as Euidence for ye Deft saith that about ye tenth of July last past he saw seuerall cattle driuen in order to pay John Gramton & that there was three cattle at ffern hooke & two more on ye other side of ye Creeke Mr Woolaston had a mare allso wch he presented in pay the Attestant thinks ye cattle & mare might be worth twenty pounds wch ware at flern Hooke and if they had been alltogather he supposeth they would haue ouer payd ye Deft the Attestant saith this was of a Saturday

William Alloway Attested saith y^t ye Defts wife came to desire the Attestant to help driue some cattle & saith on a Saterday they went & did driue two cows & calues & they would haue driuen a Steer but it run away & the Deft had a hors wch ye Attestant Supposeth was for pay at ffern hook and on the other side ye Creek there was a cow in a yard and a steer tyed by ye horns wth a roap

John White Attested said y^t some time in June last past he haueing heard y^t ye Deft made complaint to diuers persons y^t he had been unkindly dealt withall about ye Execution of Land & ye manner of selling it the Attestant saith y^t the Sherrief & he went on a munday as ye Attestant remembers to ye Defts house and they told him they de[s]ired he might redeem his Land and in order thereunto promised they would perswade ye Plt to Relinquish his Interest to ye Land if ye Def^t would betwixt that time & the next ffryday would be a Seuen night procure ye Judgment in cattle all at ffern hooke and that the whole Sum should at ye same time & place be tendered & putt into ye Possession of ye Sherrief (wth this caution that there should be no pretence of haueing some in one place & ye rest in another) & if these should be anny difference about ye price that either party should submit to ye Vallew y^t moderat persons should Vallew them at and if he y^e

Deft Should faile either as to place & time that then ye next day being Saturday & ye begining of July as ye Attestant Supposeth the Land Should be again Exposed by ye Sherrif to Publick sale to ye highest bidder without anny Reuersing ye Execution Sale & Possession of ye Land hereafter to all wch ye Deft did then fully agree & rested well contented therewith

Robart Darby Attested saith yt being at Wolla Thomas house in nouember last was atwelue month & talking wth ye Plt about ye Deft wch ye Deft owd him wch ye Attestant thinks was about 24 or 25 pounds the Attestant saith he offered to pay ye Plt then in in some ffatt & some Lean cattle if he ye Plt would take it ye Attestant saying he would take Woolastons bill for it ye Plt refused saying it is winter I Know not what to doe wth cattle

John Gramton ye Plt deyned yt euer such an offer was made to him by ye Attestant

The Jury haueing heard ye allegracons & Euidences on both sides goe out & at their return bring in their Verdict Vizt Wee find for ye Plt twelue pence damage wth costs of sute

Isack Weeldon fforeman.

The Deft desired an appeal the Court order him to giue in his reasons in writing wch he Did as ffolloweth

Aprill ye 21st obtaind against me Judgment against me under written this Present Court finding my Self agreued I craue an Appeal for thes Reasons following that is not haueing as I thought timely notice for providing Wittnes & haueing more Euidence then at this Court I could bring in wch would haue made my case more plain & clear to ye Jury & that the accon Depending haueing relacon to title of Land as well as trespasse & as I expect yt Equity may reliue me where the law may be short & therefore I appeale from this Court to ye next Provinciall Court in Equity to which I craue this Courts condicention

Thomas Woolaston

Judgment & Execu-
con gone out

The Court haueing heard the reasons & ordering the Law to be read concerning appeals they after serious consideracon unanimously declare they doe not Judg ye reasons sufficient & therefore giue Judgment according to Verdict:

Upon the Peticon of Peter Andree concerning a tract of Land sould by Edward Greene to ye Peticoner the sd Edward Greene haueing no title to it C 429.

The Court haueing spoak wth Edward Greene & Receiueing no Satisfactory answer Referr to ye Peticoner to take his cours at Law

Henry Jones by John White his Attorny Acknowledged a Deed of Enfeofment to Epharim Herman for a Lott of ground Scituat in ye town of Newcastle bounded to ye East wth Clas Daniell to South wth ye beauer Street to ye West w{th} Thomas Sprys Land as p{r} y{e} Deed beareing date y{e} 26th ffabruary 168$\frac{6}{7}$ C 431.

Charles Rumsey acknowledged a Deed of Enfeofment to John Richardson for three hundred Acres of Land being called non such Scituat in Christina as pr ye Deed beareing date ye 19{nth} of Aprill 1687 C 432.

Joseph Holding Administrat{r} of ye Estate of Francis Hutcheson Acknowledged a Deed of Enfeofment to John Mackony for a tract of Land called Persons Lodg Scituat on Duck Creek containing one hundred & Seuenty Six Acres as pr ye Deed beareing Date ye 19{nth} of Nouember 1686 C 432.

Henry Euerston Acknowledged a Deed of Enffeofment to John Gramton ffor a Lott of Land Scituat in Crane Hooke as p{r} y{e} Deed beareing Date y{e} 15{nth} of ffabruary 168$\frac{6}{7}$ C 432.

Thomas Gillet & Elisabeth Ogle acknowledged a Deed of Enfeofment to James Claypoole Senior of Philadelphia for a tract of Land Scituat in White Clay Creek containing one hundred & ffiuety Acres as pr Deed bearing date ye 15 march 1686/7 C 432.

Joseph Burnham Acknowledged a Deed of Enfeofment to John ffolk for a Lott of ground Scituat in Newcastle as pr ye Draft & Deed bearing Date ye 9th of march 1686 C 432.

John ffolk Acknowledged a Deed of Enfeofment for ye aboue C 432.

named Lott to Peter Godwin as p^r ye Deed beareing Date ye 20th of Aprill 1687

C 432. Arnoldus DeLegrange Acknowledged a Deed of Enfeofment to Georg Robinson Richard Mankin & John Pirkeld for one hundred ffiuety eight Acres of Land Scituat on ye North side of Christina Creek as p^r ye Deed bearing date the 17^rth of Aprill 1687

C 433. James Walliam ye Attorney of Gerardus Wessells Acknowledged a Deed of Mortgage to John Darby for a house & Lott in ye town of newcastle as p^r ye s^d Mortgage beareing date ye 8th day of July 1686

C 433. Edmund Perkus by his Attorny ffrancis Huckin Acknowledged a Deed of Enfeofment to John Simes for two hundred Acres of Land & houesing as p^r ye Deed beareing date ye 20th of Aprill may appear 1687

C 433. Justus Anderson Acknowledged a Deed of Enfeofment to Derrick Vandenburgh for ye one haff of his ground Scituat in ye ffront Street in ye town of Newcastle as p^r ye Deed beareing Date ye 20th of Aprill 1687

C 434. The Court order Casparus Herman to be Sommoned to Render an account of John Scots Estate by ye next Court

C 434. Adjurned untill ye 3rd tuesday in July next—

C 445. } On the 19th. 20. 21st Days of y^e
        } 5th mo^t called July 1687

    Peter Andree   Plt
    Edward Greene Senior   Deft

The Plt declares for one hundred pounds dew upon bond as p^r ye Declaracon may more at larg appear: the s^d bond was read to ye Court & Jury wherein the Plt bound the Deft in ye penalty of the s^d 100 ^lb to make good a title of Land wth other condicons wch condicons the Deft hath not performed

The Deft saith he Will in a uery Short time make a good title & desires the tryall maybe Suspended: the Plt beggs the benefitt of ye Law & that the cause may come to a tryall & produced a receipt for 2 negroos

The Jury haueing heard ye allegaco͞ns on both sides goe out and at their return bring in their verdict—Vidz^t

Wee of ye Jury doe ffind for the Plt wth Costs of Sute
        Peter Bainton fforeman

The Court giue Judgment according to Verdict

an Appeal
    The Def^t appeales The Court grant an appeale he guieing Security according to Law:

Edward Greene Richard Noble & Casparus Herman bind themselues their heires execut^{rs} & administrat^{rs} unto Peter Andree his heires & assigns in the Sum of two hundred pounds curr^t money of Pensiluania that ye s^d Edward Greene shall prosecute to effect his appeal at ye next provinciall Court in equity to be held at Philadelphia agst a Judgment now obtaind by Peter Andree for ye Sum of 100 ^{lb} & to pay all cost & damage according to Law as allso to pay ye present charges if s^d appellant Shall again happen to be cast

 Henry Jones Plt
 George Robinson Def^t   C 446.

The Plt declares for the accomplishment of a bargain of one hundred & ffiuety pounds to be paid by the Deft to the Plt for a house & Plantaco͞n or for ye Damage for Violating the bargain as p^r ye Declaraco͞n may appear

The Plt proues his Declaraco͞n by Wittnesses

John Priestner attested Saith the Def^t came to him & desired him to goe wth him s^d Def^t to ye Plts Plantaco͞n who accordingly did and ye attes^t Shewed ye Def^t the Land both ye good & bad & ye bounds of it then ye Deft desired ye attes^t to send for him when ye Plt came & he would pay the messenger wch ye attes^t did & then ye Deft came to the attes^t where he was & both went to ye Plts Plantaco͞n and there they made a bargain the Deft was to giue ye P^{lt} 150 ^{lb} wth some napkins & shirts for ye Plts house and Plantaco͞n & brewing tub the bargain was made & earnest giuen being a nine penny bitt the ye Deft Said it will be ten pound out of his way if he had not immediat Possession whereupon ye Plt agreed wth y^e

then tenant who was on ye Land to goe off & ye Plt deliuered ye Deft possession by turf & twigg the Deft was to pay 50 ^lb in goods & 100 ^lb in money ye attes^t thinks the Deft consented to pay ye 100 ^lb in money Saying he would pay James Sanderling quickly not being Willing to hyer money & ye Deft askt the Plt Seuerall times to goe home and receive his pay

Elisabeth Bellis Attested saith ye Deft came to ye Plts house & would buy ye land & did buy it for 150 ^lb : 100 ^lb in money & 50 ^lb in goods the Plt reserued ¼ an acre of Land behind ye garden for his own & his wifes life Sixty pounds in money was to be payd uery soon & 50 ^lb in goods and ye Plt was to Stay for ye other forty pounds wch was to be money the attes^t saith shee Saw ye Plt giue ye Deft possession of the house & Land by giueing him turf & twigg ye attest saith ye Deft was allso to guie some napkins to ye Plts wife

Roaloff Anderson Attested Saith he was not present at ye bargain but ye day after ye Deft came to Jno Priestners house and there said ye P^lt had been at his ye Deft^s house and had Layd out 40 ^lb in Linnen wch was to be received when the Deeds ware Deliuered wch Linnen was Layd out for pay for ye Land

William Robinson attested saith y^t ye Deft has father and ye P^lt made a bargain about ye Plts Land and came at length to this agreement y^t his father promised ye Plt to pay him 150 ^lb for his Land ye Plt sayd he owd money & would haue 100 ^lb in money to manage his trade but ye Deft promised only 60 ^lb in money 50 ^lb to pay Sanderling & the other ten pounds ye Deft said he would strain hard to raise but ye Deft did not promiss the other 40 ^lb in money because he had it not

The Deft ownd the bargain but saith he was wrought upon by reason of his ignorance & easyness at that time the Plt & John Priestner giueing the Deft Drams : & saith ye Plt was to receiue 50 ^lb for ye 1st payment wch s^d Deft was ready to pay but ye Plt refused to take any more than 40 ^lb

The Jury haueing heard the whole cause goe out & at their return bring in their Verdict Vidz^t

Wee of the Jury ffind for ye Plts with costs of Sute

        Peter Brainton fforeman

The Court giue Judgment according to Verdict

an appeall
The Deft appeales he giueing Security according to Law: Georg Robinson John Thirkild & Henry Hollingsworth bind themselues their heires Execut^{rs} & administrat^{rs} in ye Sum of three hundred pounds cur^{rt} money of Pensiluania; to Henry Jones of Philadelphia ffeltmaker his heirs & assigns that he ye s^d Georg Robinson Shall prosecute to effect his appeal now granted at ye next provinciall Court in equity to be held at Philadelphia agst a Judgm^t now obtained by ye s^d Henry Jones agst ye Appellant & to pay all costs & damage (if he again happens to be cast) according to Law as allso to pay the present Charges

Upon the request of John Wallker of newcastle to haue his Witnesses attested concerning a tract of Land called Spring garden containing 200 acres: C 457.

Casparus Herman attested Saith he asked James Smothers to buy his tract of Land called Spring garden but the s^d Smothers replyed I haue Sould it allready saith he to John Wallker and he hath payd me meaning Smothers for it

Casparus Herman Saith he would haue bought the Land of Smothers called Spring garden: then Smothers replyed as afores^d

Richard Noble & Epharim Herman Attested Say that John Wallker bought a tract of Land of James Smothers called Spring garden & s^d Wallker paid for ye Survay and other contingent Charges

John Wallker acknowledged a tract of Land called Spring garden containing two hundred acres of Land from him & his heirs for euer to William Phillips his heires & assigns for ever the s^d Land Scituat on ye Second Drawers Creek by ye Deed of Enfeofment beareing date ye 20th of July 1687: C 457.

William Phillips acknowledged a Deed of Enfeofment to ffrancis Richardson for ye aboues^d tract of Land called Spring garden Scituat & containing as by the s^d Deed beareing date the 21st of July 1687 C 457.

Robart Turner and Susannah Turner acknowledged a Deed of enfeoffment to Edward Blake for a house & Lott of ground C 458.

Scituat in ye town of newcastle bounded & containing as p^r ye s^d Deed beareing date the 24th of June 1687

C 458. Edward Blake acknowledged a mortgage of his house Scituat in the town of Newcastle Butted bounded & containing as by the s^d mortgage to Sarah Welch for ye payment of two hundred pounds as by ye mortgage beareing date 28th day of June 1687

C 458. Wolla ffranson acknowledged a Deed of enfeoffment to Peter Bainton for a tract of Land Scituat in ye Bougwt neer Verdreytys Hook containing one hundred thirty four acres as by ye Deed beareing date ye nineteenth of July 1687

C 458. Woolla ffranson acknowledged a bond of two hundred pounds to Peter Bainton for ye quiet Possession of the aboues^d 134 acres of Land as by ye bond beareing date ye 26th of the 2nd mo^t. 1687

C 458. Cornelius Vanderveer acknowledged a bond of two hundred pounds to Woolla ffranson to be Kept harmless from ye s^d Corn^ll. Vand^r his heires etct for a tract of Land containing about 50 acres as p^r ye bond beareing Date ye 20th of July 1687

C 458. Woola ffranson acknowledged a Deed of enfeoffment to Michall ffranson Son & heir of Michall ffranson deceased for fiuety acres of Land between dog Creek & Sony Creek as by ye Deed beareing date ye 20th of July 1687

C 459. Adam Stedham Benjamin Stedham Christian Stedham Lylif Stedham Lucas Stedham Erasmus Stedham acknowledged a bargain & Sale of one hundred acres of Land Lying on Brandy Wine Creeke neer Rattle Snake Creek to Henry Jacobson of ye County of Chester as by y^e s^d agreement beareing date y^e 20th day of y^e 1st month 1686

C 459. Casparus Herman acknowledged a Deed of enfeoffment to William Patteson for four hundred acres of Land Scituat neer a branch of s^nt augustins Creeke as by y^e Deed of enfeoffment beareing date y^e 17^nth of march 168$\frac{6}{7}$

Exam^d.

C 460. Whereas there was a Letter from Mr Secret^r Markham containing an order of counsell to the magistrates of this County as allso a coppy of a Peticon from Thomas Woolaston to y̅e̅ Pres^dt & Counsell & the minuits of counsell proceeding from that peticon Wherein the Magistrates are required to Stop all further proceedings in relacon to a Judgment lately obtained by Jno Grampton Plt agst Thomas Woolaston Deft as allso to grant s^d Woolaston an appeal The Court haueing with Due reverence to ye Pres^dt & Counsell: considered of ye premises doe ffind a great part of the Peticon (upon Which the s^d minuits & orders Semeed to be founded to be falss 2ndly the magistrates haue carefully considered the former tryall and the reasons then alleadged for an appeal and doe conceiue they haue not only acted according to the express Letter of ye Law but allso according to their own Judgment & conscience and doe not think they are oblidged to Depart from their first Judgments of Court there being no Law to compell them so to doe or that will Secure them in their compliance wth anny orders not founded on Law

Arnoldus DeLegrange acknowledged a Deed of Enfoeffment C 469. for his Plantacon in Cristina Creeke as allso for a tract of Land called Content containing in both places four hundred forty four acres of Land & Marsh as p^r ye s^d Deed to John Richardson bearing date ye 21st day of September 1687

John Richardson Acknowledged a bond & mortgage of all C 470. the Land and Plantacon bought of Arnoldus De Legrange for the true Payment of one hundred thirty & two pounds cur^rt Lawfull money of old England as by ye bond & mortgage to the s^d Arnoldus Delegrange beareing date ye 21st of 7^ber: 1687

John Wallker acknowledged a Deed of entaile to William C 470. Phillips and the heires begotten on ye body of Ann the Present wife of the s^d William off & for a tract of Land Scituat on ye head of Drawers Creeke, called by ye name of the Mill neck & Bounded as by ye Deed beareing date ye 22nd. 7^ber: 1687

Jurian Andriesen acknowledged the receipt of fiue hundred C 470. Guilders from his father in Law Broer Senexen being in full for his Portion & further alloweth & confirmeth what was done by ye Court of Newcastle concerning his Late ffathers

Estate on ye 7th & 8th of may 1678 as per ye Deed beareing date ye 19th of 7^ber 1687

C 471. Arnoldus DeLegrang Broer Senexen & Gisbert Johnson Devos mutually acknowledged & consented to certain Articles of agreement for the Division of their Severall Plantacons on Cristina Creek where they now liue as by the s^d Articles beareing date the 20th of Aprill: 1683

C 470. Broer Senexen acknowledked a Deed of enfeoffement to Jurian Andries for one hundred acres of fast land and fiue acres of Marsh as by ye Deed beareing date the 19^nth of 7^ber 1687

At an orphans Court held by ye Kings authorty & in the name of a Propriatary & Govern^r at the town of Newcastle october the 4th & 5th annoq dom 1687

John Cann   Johanes Dehaes
Peter Allricks Edwd Blake   } Justices Present

Upon a motion concerning the Estate of Dr Spry Deceased

C 471. It is ordered that Ann Greene & Abiah Egberts haue notice to appear at ye next Court in order to advise wth the Administrator about the most effectual means for ye preseruacon of the house & orchard in town

C 473. At a Court held for the County of Newcastle by the Kings authority and in the name of the Propriatary & Governor october ye 18: 19th: & 20th 1687

John Cann: Peter Allricks William Stockdale
Cornelius Empson Johannes Dehaes Edward
Blake Richard Hallywell: } Justices Present

C 478. Mr Peter Bainton Reseireing to haue a Deed from Abraham man acknowledged to the attorny of s^d Peter Bainton the Court conceiues s^d Peter Bainton cannot acknowledg ye s^d Deed to his own attorny not being impowred So to doe by authority from ye s^d Abraham man

Thomas Ellis enters a Caveat agst ye Land of William C 478.
Morris

Edward Greene Senior tendring a Decree of Pronciall Court C 479.
relating to him as appellant and Peter Andree Appelle whereby the s^d Edward Greene was to doe Severall things therein contained the Court Demanded the s^d Edward to comply with the Decree relating to the personall Security of 50^{lb} and the Deed of 400 acres of Land the s^d Edward Greene Replyed, in consideracon that Andree ye Appelle was not present he did not think himself obliged to comply therwith this court

Jacob Clasen & Grety his wife acknowledg a Deed of enfeof- C 480.
ment for a tract of Land at Pert Hook twenty ffiue rod broad and Six hundred rod dutch measure long as by ye Deed bearing date ye 24th of December 1686: and Claus Andrews in open Court renounces all Claim & pretention to the s^d Land, to John Priestner according to ye Deed

Arnoldus De Legrang & Cornelia his wife acknowledged a C 481.
Deed for a house & Lott in ye town newcastle to Mathyas Vanderheyden as ⅌ ye Deed beareing date ye 18^{nth} of 8^{ber} 1687 may more at larg appear

Jutus Anderson acknowledged a Deed of enfeoffment to John C 481.
White for the house & Lott of ground which formerly belonged at ye s^d Justus Anderson Scituat by ye water side as by the Deed bearing date ye 19^{nth} of october 1687 may more at larg appear

John White acknowledged a Deed of enfeoffment for the C 481.
Land he formerly bought of Antony Bryant to Justus Anderson as ⅌ ye Deed bearing date ye 19^{nth} of 8^{ber} 1687

Joseph Bowles by his Lawfull attorny acknowledged a Deed C 481.
of enfeoffment to Arnoldus DeLegrange for a tract of Land called middle way Land containing three hundred acres of Land as ye Deed bearing date ye 16^{nth} of 7^{ber} 1687

To all Christian People to whom thes Presents may come C 481.
Greeting Know yee that for diuers good reasons hereunto me moueing I haue made ordained & constituted my loueing loueing ffriend Mr Peter Bainton of ye Bowght in Delawar River in the County of Mer^{ct}. to be my true & Lawfull attorny in my

name place & Steed for me to his use to aske receiue demand recover by law anny Debts dues and demand bills or anny pay anny ways by anny ways or contracts what ever y^t Shall appear to owing due or belonging to Abraham Mann of Cristina in ye County of Newcastle and what my s^d attorny Shall act and doe in and touching anny thing belonging to the s^d Mann Shall at all times allow thereof to stand good in law in as full and ample manner as if I was there in person my self Ratefying and confirming at all times what my s^d attorny Shall act and doe according to Law allowing this to be as firm and Stable in all my concerns as the Law can allow if in words anny thing may by me wanting giueing and granting to my s^d attorny full power and Lawfull authority in and touching the premises to make ordain and appoint one attorny or more at his pleasure allso giueing and granting my s^d attorny power to make ouer one parcell of Land or plantacon as appears by contract to Uster Anderson of the Same County and to receive made over to me again from the s^d Uster Anderson all that shall appear by contract or bargain to be made over to me and to receiue of the s^d Uster all moneys that shall appear to be due or when due to rece them giue and granting & owning all releases or discharges by him to be Sufficient as Wittness my hand and Seale this 7th day of July 1687

Signed Sealed & Deliuered
in ye pressence of us   Abraham Man

    the mank H I of Hans Uster
    Thomas pacdvns(?)

                    Proved by Hans Uster who was attested in open Court 8^{ber} 18^{nth} 1687 at newcastle

C 482.   The Court adjourned to ye Sixt day of December.

C 483.   At a Court held at Newcastle by ye Kings authority and in the name of the Propriatary & Governor on the Sixt: Seventh eight & ninth days of December one thousand six hundred & eighty Seven

| John Cann Peter Allrichs Vall^t Hollingsworth | Justices |
| Corn^{ll} Empson Edward Blake Richard Hallywell | Pres^{nt} |

Xber 9th 1687

Andrew Tilly acknowledged a Deed for half his Marsh to   C 492.
Elisabeth Ogle as by ye Deed bearing date ye 19 of June 1686

Justus Anderson appeared in open Court & made a tender   C 494.
of two Deeds of enfeofment one to John Burgraue & one
other to John Smith of Newcastle

Upon ye Peticon of John Gramton concerning a Decree of   C 495.
ye Provinciall Judges relating to ye s^d Gramton and Thomas
Wooleston

The Court refer the answere of the s^d Peticon to a further
consideracon

Arnoldus De Legrange acknowledged to haue receiued forty   C 496.
pounds from Jno Richardson being in part paid for his Plantacon bought by John Richardson

Arnoldus DeLegrange acknowledged the aliancon of his   C 496.
Pattent for a Lott of Land below ye ffort in ye town of newcastle containing in breadth 60 ffoot & in length three hundred
ffoot as by ye Pattent, and the assigment thereon bearing date
ye 8th of December 1687: unto Edward Greene Senior

Arnoldus DeLegrange acknowledged the alianacon of his   C 496.
Pattent for a Lott of ground Scituat & bounded as by ye Pattent being the Second Lott from ye Dike in length 300 ffoot &
in breadth 60 ffoot as by assignment on ye back of ye Pattent
beareing date ye 8th of December 1687

John Moll & Christian his wife acknowledg a Deed of en-   C 496.
feofment ffor a certain Pattent & the Land contained therein
being the ground where the magazen Stood & butted & bounded
as by ye Pattent from Sr Edmund Andross beareing date y^e
25th of march 1676: the Assignment to James Claypool beareing date ye 6th of December 1687

James Claypoole acknowledged a Deed of enfeofment ffor   C 497.
the before menconed Pattent & Lott of Ground wch. he bought

of John Moll: to Elisabeth Courtry as by the Deed beareing date ye 6th of December 1687:

C 497. Hendrick Vandenburgh acknowledged a Deed of enfeofment for a certain tract of Land Scituat on ye South side of Cristina Creeke butted & bound{d} according to ye sd Deed to Engelbert Lott as by ye Deed beareing date ye 29th of november 1687

C 497. Jonas Arskin acknowledged a Deed of enfeofment for two hundred acres of Land Scituat on White Clay Creek to Robert Courtny and Sam̄ll Hickman as by ye Deed beareing date ye 9th of December 1687

C 497. John Sybrance acknowledged a Deed of enfeofment for a tract of Land & Marsh at Perden hook in ye County of Newcastle to Robart ffrench as by ye Deed bearing date ye 6th day of December 1687

C 497. Robert ffrench Desireing to haue Some Witnesses attested concerning the title of ye aboues{d} Land

C 497. Sybram Johnson & John Hulk being attested doe declare yt the sd Land now Sould by John Sybrance to sd Rob: ffrench was formerly the Land of John Sybrance ffather to this John & by reason the eldest Son of the sd John ye ffather did offende him ye sd ffather said he would giue this Land to this his Son John & accordingly after the death of the sd John the ffather the aforesd Land was alloted to ye sd John ye Son who hath been in ye quiet Possession therof for many years

C 499. Engelly Hallyday attested Saith Hendrick Sybrance Sould the Marsh belonging to ye Woodland of a certain Pattent Severall years before anny writings ware made & that ye Land now Sould by John Sybrance was allways called his ye sd Johns Land

C 497. The County Court adjurned untill ye next third Tuesday in ffabruary next

C 499. At a meeting of the Justices January ye 17{nth} 1687

John Cann Peter Allricks Corn{ll} Empson
Johanes Dehaes Edwd Blake . . . . . . } Justices Presnt

The bussines of the Levys was again moved there being noe

meeting at ye time appointed before by reason of the unseasonableness of ye weather

Upon the peticon of Charles Rumsey that the Court would order the execucon to be extended to all the effects of Robart Darby for a Satisfying a Judgm^t obtained against s^d Darby the effects attached not being Sufficient The Court conceiue the execucon may extend to all his effects until ye Judgm^t be Satisfyed C 500.

Thomas Gillett acknowledged a Mortgage of his Plantation called the Devises to Nicholas Allum & Mathyas Mattson as ℔r ye Deed bearing date ye 17^nth January 1687 C 501.

A List of the Lands Lotts Tithebles of the Constablery of Newcastle 1687 C 502.

Edward Gibbs & Robert Hutchinson John Garetson	400	00	1	..	18	
Robart Hutchinson	500	00	1	1	1	
John White	635	01	3	2	0	1
James Walliam for Spry	200	03	00	00	15	00
Edward Land	100	00	01	00	09	00
John Penington	200	00	02	00	18	00
Dorcas Land	200	03	00	00	15	00
Charles Rumsey	640	00	02	01	11	02½
Powell Lawson	200	00	02	00	18	00½
John Richardson	200	00	02	00	18	00
Arnoldus De Legrange	0300	03	00	00	18	00
Urian Boreson	0354					
Jacob Clason	0250	00	02	00	19	06
Peter Jaquet	0300	00	02	01	01	00
Widdow Lemmens	0800	00	01	01	10	00
Mathyas Lawson	0120	00	01	00	09	07
Danel Smith	0012	00	02	00	12	04
Hendrick Anderson	0150	00	01	00	10	06
John Screek	0120	00	02	00	15	07
Hendrick Evertson	0100	00	01	00	09	00
Sybran Johnson	050	00	01	00	07	06
John Sybrance	0050	00	01	00	07	06
Widdow Priestner	0100	00	00	00	03	00
James Hallyday	0100	00	02	00	15	00
John Jaquet	0200	00	02	00	18	00
Abrman Haym	0100	00	01	00	09	00

Adam Hays	0100	00	01	00	09	00
Mary Block	0400	00	02	01	04	00
Isack Slover	0000	00	01	00	06	00
Hendrick Williams	0000	02	00	00	06	00
James Walliam	0000	02	01	00	12	00
John Biscus	0000	02	01	00	12	00
Josyne Hamilton	0400	01	01	01	01	00
Richard Hallywell	0050	01	00	00	04	06
John Williams	0550	02	03	01	17	06
Johanes Dehaes	0050	02	01	01	13	06
Mathyas Vanderheyden	0000	01	00	00	03	00

A conuacon of the Land Lotts and Tithebles of the Constablery of newcastle

Hendrick Vandenburgh	0039	03	03	1	08	2½
John Bower	0000	01	01	00	09	0
John Harmanson	0000	02	02	00	18	0
Epharim Harman	0400	02	02	00	18	0
Emelius De Ring	0000	03	01	00	15	0
Isack Tine	0000	04	01	00	18	0
Edward Boulton	0000	00	01	00	06	0
Robart Dyer	0248	00	01	00	13	5½
Edward Blake	0248	01	01	00	16	5½
Justa Anderson	0000	01	01	00	09	0
John Hendrickson	0000	01	01	00	09	0
Peter Allricks	1471	02	07	04	12	3
Antony Bryant	0000	01	00	00	03	0
Mathyas De Ring	0000	02	01	00	12	0
Domine Testmaker	0000	02	00	00	06	0
Englebert Lott	0150	03	00	00	13	6
Sarah Welch	1000	01	00	01	13	0
John Cann	0000	02	00	00	06	0
Garret Johnson	0000	03	01	00	15	0
Widdow Mandy	0000	01	00	00	03	0
John Smith	0000	02	00	00	12	0
Claes Daniell	0000	01	01	00	09	0
Moses DeGam	0000	01	01	00	09	0
John ffloreat	0000	01	01	00	09	0
John Moll	0350	04	00	01	02	6
Reneer Vandercoolen	0000	04	01	00	18	0
John Darby	0000	01	00	00	03	0
William Marham	1100	00	00	01	13	0
Jacob Cornelison	0000	00	01	00	06	0
Thomas Longshaw	0000	00	01	00	06	0

RECORDS OF THE COURT OF NEW CASTLE. 169

Leneord the Glazier	0000	00	01	00	06	0
John Burgraue	0000	00	01	00	06	0
Symon & John Cock & Jnº Hales....	0000	00	03	00	18	0
Tennis DeWitt Claes Anderson Rand: Hauke	0000	00	03	00	18	0
Ambross Baker	0050	03	02	01	02	6
John Dan Hybert } Laurence Sick Olle }	0000	00	03	00	18	0
Peter Goddin Matt Coulson } Matt Erixson }	0000	00	03	00	18	0
James Bradshaw Ja } Claypool: Wm Chambers }	0000	00	03	00	18	0
Zacariah Vandercoolen } Josep: Clayton }	0000	00	02	00	12	0
Widdow Murrey	0300	00	00	00	09	0
Richard Noble	0000	02:	01:	00:	12:	0

A List of the Land & Tithebles of the north Side of Brandy Wine Creek

Jacob Vanderveer	0500	02	01	07	0
Cornelius Vanderveer	0000	01	00	06	0
Cornelius Empson	0500	06	02	11	0
Mouns Justy	0100	01	00	09	0
Jonas Scogging	0150	00	00	04	6
Hans Peterson	0550	04	02	00	6
Jacob Clemens	0150	01	00	10	6
Peter Anderson	0100	01	00	09	0
John Mouns	0150	01	00	10	6
Peter Mouns	0100	01	00	09	0
Thomas Jonas	0250	03	01	05	6
Stoffell	0100	01	00	09	0
Neils Neilson	0100	00	00	03	0
Peter Bainton	0400	02	01	04	0
Morgan Druet	0300	01	00	15	0
Mathew Sanders	0000	01	00	06	0
Thomas Gelping	0100	01	00	09	0
Wm Stockdale	0000	02	00	12	0
John Grubb	0260	01	00	13	10
John Buckly	0100	01	00	09	0
Oliver Coope	0100	01	00	09	0
John Prew	0100	01	00	09	0
Wm Cloud	0500	03	01	13	0
Jeremiah Cloude	0000	01	00	06	0
Edward Eglington & Isack Warner.......	0400	00	00	12	0

Vall[t]. Hollingsworth	0400	02	01	04	0
Henry Hollingsworth	0200	04	01	10	0
Thomas Conway	0200	01	00	12	0
Thomas Hollingsworth	0200	01	00	12	0
Robart Vance	0200	02	00	18	0
W[m] Lester	0100	01	00	09	0
Adam Sharpley	0300	01	00	15	0
Thomas Clifton & W[m] Hanly	0000	02	00	12	0
Richard Beacham	0000	01	00	06	0

A List of the Lands & Tithebles of the North Side of Christina Creek

William Guest	1250	02	01	19	0
William Gessop	0200	01	00	12	0
Christopher White	0000	01	00	06	0
Wolla Thomas	0200	03	01	04	0
Aron Johnson	0200	02	00	18	0
Broer Senexen	0660	02	01	11	10
Christian Vrianson	0100	01	00	09	0
Gisbert Wallraven	0235	01	00	13	0
Arnoldus Legrange	0300	01	00	15	0
Israell Helm	0474	00	00	14	3
Charles Pickering	0776				
Benjamen Stedham	0150	01	00	10	6
Jacob Hendrickson	0250	01	00	13	6
Mathyas Devoos	0400	01	00	18	0
Sam[ll] Peterson	0750	02	01	14	9
Christian Stalcop	0225	04	01	10	9
Robart Robinson	0500	04	01	19	½
Richard Robinson	0200	00	00	06	0
Erasmus Stedham	0300	01	00	15	0
Lucas Stedham	0265	02	00	19	11
W[m] Griggs	0400	01	00	18	0
John Grigg	0200	01	00	12	0
Henry ffournis	0260	00	00	07	10
Joseph Cookson	0200	00	00	06	0
Jonas Arskin	0600	02	01	10	0
Andrew Tilly	0250	01	00	13	6
Eliasbeth Ogle	1000	01	01	16	0
Hugh Marsland	0300	01	00	15	0
James Claypoole	0500	00	00	15	0
John Brewstor	0300	01	00	15	0
John Omerson	0240	02	00	19	3
James Reed	0800	01	01	10	0

Henry Dull	0100	01	00	09	0
John Alloway	0200	02	00	18	0
Thomas Langshaw	0250	00	00	07	6
Bryan Macdonell	0200	01	00	12	0
Giles Barrett	0550	01	01	03	6
Thomas Peirson	0600	01	01	04	0
John Smith	0200	00	00	06	0
Thomas Wollaston	0400	01	00	18	0
Joseph Barnes	0250	01	00	13	6

A Continuacon of the Land and Tithebles of North Cristina Creek

Henry & Paul Jacobson	0400	03	01	10	0
Wm Rakestraw	0750	01	01	08	6
John Cann	0700	01	01	07	0
Abraham Mann	0850	01	01	11	6
Wm Mann	0000	01	00	06	0
Andrew Stalcop	0225	02	00	18	9
Thomas Gillet	0300	01	00	15	0
Neiles Lawson	0700	00	01	01	0
Thomas Graues	0200	00	00	06	0
Henry Jacobson	0250	01	00	13	6
Georg Hogg Senr & Junr	0600	00	00	18	0
Thomas Mathews	0350	02	01	02	6
John Collet	0400	00	00	12	0
W^m & John Rawlings	0600	00	00	18	0
Zacarah Patrick &c^t	0600	00	00	18	0
ffrancis Smith Senior etc^t	0900	00	01	07	0
ffrancis Smith Junr	0400	01	00	18	0
Anthony Burgis	0300	00	00	09	0
Anthony Weston	0300	00	00	09	0
David Sharply	0500	00	00	15	0
Oliver Taylor	0200	01	00	12	0
Nathaniell Cartwell	0200	00	00	06	0
James Standfeild	0500	00	00	15	0
John Bradshaw	0200	00	00	06	0
Wm Osborn	1000	00	01	10	0
John Couch	0200	01	00	12	0
John Huns	0100	03	01	01	0
Peter Stalcop	0100	01	00	09	0
Phillip Davis	0200	01	00	12	0
Nicholas Daw	0200	00	00	06	0
Thomas Greene & company	0500	00	00	15	0
John Mackomb	0300	00	00	09	0
Wm Stockdale	0350	00	00	10	6

Symon Cock	0200	00	00	06	0
George Harland	0200	02	00	18	0

A List of the Lands & Tithebles of North side of St Georges Creeke

Hendrick Vandenburgh	0900	00	01	07	0
Peter Woollaston	0000	01	00	06	0
John Moll	1000	01	01	16	0
Hans Hansen	0400	01	00	18	0
John Darby	0800	03	02	02	0
Mathyas Vanderheyden	0500	00	00	15	0
John Hayly	0400	00	00	12	0
Jacob Young	1200	00	01	16	0

Rowlif Anderson }
John Wilson } A List of the Lands & Tithebles of the North side of Apoquenimy

Rooloff Anderson	0400	04	01	13	0
Georg Baker	0200	01	00	12	0
Alexander Cammell	0350	00	00	10	6
Epharim Herman & John Dehaes........	0400	00	00	12	0
Robart Hutchinson	0400	00	00	12	0
Adam Peterson	0590	02	01	09	8
John Boulton	0300	00	00	09	0
John Webster & Ryly	0600	00	00	18	0
Nicholas Doller	0150	00	00	04	6
James Brookes	0250	00	00	07	6
John Walker	0400	01	00	18	0
Wm Phillips	0	01	00	06	0
Wm Burrows	0200	02	00	18	0
Richard Hemlott	0200	00	00	06	0
Hans Hanson	0500	00	00	15	0
Richard Hudden	0370	02	01	03	2
Otto Otto	0100	01	00	09	0
John Otto	0100	00	00	03	0
Hendrick Vandenburgh	0770	00	01	03	2
Thomas Salloway	0200	01	00	12	0
Peter Johnsoe	0250	02	00	19	6
Edmund Perkus	0730	00	01	01	11
Edward Greene Senr	3167	01	05	01	2
Gabriell Rappe	0200	02	00	15	0

Peter Andree	0400	04	01	16	0
ffrancis Richardson	0200	00	00	06	0

The continuacon of the Lands and Ththebles of North Apoquenimy

Richard Noble	0300	00	00	09	0
Widdow Anderson	0150	01	00	10	6
Hendrick Wallraven	0200	02	00	18	0
John Hayly	0150	01	00	10	6
Hybert Laurance	0480	00	00	14	5
Casparus Herman	3200	01	05	02	0
Sam^{ll} Pudding bagg maker	0000	01	00	06	0
John Cole	0300	02	01	01	0
John Jarvice	0400	01	00	18	0
Wm Grant	0400	00	00	12	0
Edmund Lindsey	0200	00	00	06	0
Thomas Laws	0500	02	01	07	0
John Simes	0200	02	00	18	0
Amos Nicolls	0500	00	00	15	0
John Willson	0500	02	01	07	0
Ellis Humpherys	0200	02	00	18	0
Peter Allricks	0400	02	01	04	0
Jacob Decow & Robert Ashton	0300	04	01	13	0
Doctor Staples Success^r	0400	00	00	12	0
Hendrick Vandburgh & Corn^{ll} Empson	0150	00	00	04	6
Edward Gibbs	0640	02	01	11	3
John Peirson & W^m: Scarfe	0000	02	00	12	0
Daniell Smith	0200	00	00	06	0

A List of the Lands & Tithebles of North side of Duck Creek: hundred

Richard Hallywell	4398	07	08	14	0
John Mackarty & Rob: Moreton	0470	01	01	00	1
Justa Anderson	0200	00	00	06	0
William Grant	0550	03	01	14	6
Henricus Williams	0450	01	00	19	6
Basilia osborn	0400	00	00	12	0
Robart money	0400	00	00	12	0

A continuacon of the Lands and Tithebles of North side Duck Creeke

James Sickes	0000	01	00	16	0
Walter Smith	0500	01	01	01	0

Lucas Michall	0000	01	00	06	0
John Hartops Children	0850	01	01	11	6
Thomas Snelling	0450	01	00	19	6
Isack Weeldon	0460	01	00	19	9¼
An Westingdale	0480	00	00	14	5¼
Thomas Gelping	0480	00	00	14	5¼
Benjamin Gumley	0280	01	00	14	5¼
Joseph Harris	0208	00	00	06	3
ffrancis Cook	0000	01	00	06	0
Owen ffawks	0200	00	00	06	0
Morris Liston	0650	04	02	03	6
Epharim Herman	1800	00	02	14	0
Joseph Hallman	0000	01	00	06	0
Joseph Houlding	0900	02	01	19	0
John Taylor	0200	01	00	12	0
Georg Taylor	0200	02	00	18	0
Andrew Loue	0200	01	00	12	0
Thomas Harrison	0200	01	00	12	0
Richard Mitchell Execut^r	0200	00	00	06	0
Edward Gibbs	0400	00	00	12	0
Richard Quince	0200	01	00	12	0
ffrancis Johnson	0200	01	00	12	0
Michall Offley	0600	01	01	04	0
Sybrant Valk	0200	00	00	06	0
Wm Hatton	0600	02	01	10	0
Antony Tomkings	0500	02	01	07	0
Edward Owen	0370	02	01	03	1½
Robart Courtney	0000	01	00	06	0
Thom: Harris & Wm Osborn	1000	04	02	14	0
Lewis Owen	0200	01	00	12	0
Peter Byard	0850	02	01	17	6
ffrancis Letts	0050	01	00	07	6
John Harris	0070	00	00	02	1½
Henry Barns & Richard White	0000	02	00	12	0

C 511. At a Court held at Newcastle by the Kings authority and in the name of the Propriatary and Governor on the 21st 22^d 23 & 24th days of the 12th mo^t called ffabruary Anno dom 168¾

  John Cann Peter Allricks William Stockdale ⎫
  Johanes Dehaes Vall^t Hollingsworth . . . . ⎬ Justices Present
  Corn^{ll} Empson Richard Hallywell . . . . . ⎭

C 517. Edward Greene Senior presenting a copy of the late Decree at the provinciall Court relating to him as appellant and Peter Andree appelle which being read and Some questions arrising concerning the fullfilling the s^d Decree at length both partys vids^t Edward Greene & Peter Andree Recognize & bind themselves their heires execut^{rs} and Administ^{rs} to each other their heirs execut^{rs} & Administ^{rs} in the Sum of two hundred pounds lawfull money of Pensiluania to Submitt all former Judgments appeals Decrees & accons to the Justices on the Bench and to obey fullfill & perform the Judgm^t of the s^d Justices under the penalty & upon payment of the s^d Sum of two hundred pounds by the party Delinquent & non observant to the party observant:

Whereupon the Court haueing duely considered the allegacons and Evidences on both sides doe give Judgement & followeth vidz^t.

the s^d Justices order Edward Greene to make a good and firm Deed in Law to the s^d. Peter Andree for all the Land which the s^d Andree formerly bought of the s^d Edward Greene being flour hundred acres but more especially of two hundred acres thereof being the Land lately belonging to Bryan Omella and to invest the s^d Andree in a good estate of Inheritance Such as Shall be good & ffirm in Law which the s^d Edward Greene ffor want of a Title to it himself cannot the s^d Edward Greene cannot or doth not make a good & ffirm & Lawfull assurance & Inheritance to the premises at or before the twenty fourth day of may next ensuing but in case the s^d: Edward Greene cannot or doth not make a good & ffirm Title as afores^d that then the s^d Edward Greene on the s^d ffour & twentyeth day of may as afores^d Shall pay down to the s^d Peter Andree or his Lawfull assigns or attorny the ffull Sum of Sixty pounds in currant Silver or gold money of this province, and shall allso the Same day pay down in currant money of Pensuilvania So much as John Hayly & Jacob Decow Shall Judg & Vallew the improuements & building done by the s^d Peter Andree or his order on the s^d Land to be worth & the s^d Edward Greene is allso to give imeadiatly to the s^d Andree such good and Sufficient Security ffor performance of the afores^d conditions or payment of the s^d moneys as the Justices shall approue & like off and upon payment of the s^d moneys in manner afores^d the Justices order Peter Andree to giue unto the s^d Edward Greene quiet possession of the s^d Land Which being the Judgment of the Justices was read to the s^d Edward Greene & Peter Andree both partys declared they ware content therewith

C 521. Upon the Peticon of Joseph Holding concerning Some Land pr tended to be Sould by his predecessor Christopher Ellit to Some persons who neither pay for the Land or improue or answer the Levys

The Court in answer to the Peticoner advice him to proceed in all Lawfull matters referring to ye improuement of the estate of Christopher Ellit of which he is administ^r

C 521. Luliffant Stedham & Erasmus Stedham acknowledged a Deed of enfeoffment to Corn^{ll} Empson ffor Six acres of Land on ye South side of Brandy Wine Creek as ⅌ ye Deed bearing date ye 17^{nth} of ffabruary 1687 may appear

C 522. Justa Anderson acknowledged a Deed of enfeoffment for Six Lotts of Land in the Towne of newcastle to John Burgraue as by the Deed beareing date the 21st of october 1687:

C 522. Justa Anderson acknowledged a Deed of enfeoffment ffor the northwest moyety or Lott of Land (wch s^d Justus fformerly bought of John Moll) to John Smith as by ye Deed bearing bearing date ye 23nd of ffabruary 1687

C 522. John & Mary Smith acknowledged a Deed of enfeoffment ffor their house & Lotts of ground in newcastle to Justus Anderson as by the Deed beareing date ye 23rd of ffabruary 1687

C 522. Edward Greene Senior acknowledged a Deed of enfeoffment ffor two Lotts of Land Scituat on the northeast Side of town of necastle to James Claypoole as by ye Deed beareing date ye 22nd of ffabruary 1687

C 522. Reneer VanderCoolen acknowledged a Deed of Enfoeffment for one hundred & ffiuety acres of Land in white Clay Creek to John Burgraue as by ye Deed beareing date ye Sixth day of January 1687

John Burgraue acknowledged a Deed of mortgage ffor the aboue s^d Land to Reneer Vandercoolen ffor payment of fforty pounds curr^t money of holland as by the Deed beareing date the 23rd of ffabruary 1687 C 522.

Andrew Tilly acknowledged a Deed of enfeoffment ffor two hundred and ffiuety Acres of Land to Reneer Vandercoolen as by the Deed bearing date the 22nd of october 1687 C 522.

Reneer VanderCoolen acknowledged a Deed of Enfeoffment ffor the moyety of one hundred eighty ffiue acres of Land to Andrew Tilly as by the Deed beareing date 22nd of oct^r 1687 C 523.

John Willkingson acknowledged a Deed of enfeoffment ffor thr hundred acres of Land on ye north side of Christina Creeke to Conrade Constantine as by the Deed beareing date the 22nd of ffabruary 1687 C 523.

John Moll & Christian: & John their Son acknowledged a Deed of enfeoffment for two Lotts of Land in the Town of newcastle as by the Deed bearing date ye 21st of ffabruary 1687 C 523.

Hugh mackgregory & Prudence Barns acknowledged certain agments & conditions to each other as by the instrument of agreement bearing date ye 21st of ffabruary 1687 C 523.

The Court demanding of Edward Greene would tender his Security according to their Judgm^t: betwixt him & Andree he not bringing his Security the Court Judg he hath violated the award C 523.

At a Court of Quarter Sessions held for the Town and County of Newcastle by y^e Kings authority and in the name of the Propriatary and Governor on y^e twentyeth twenty first and twenty second & twenty third of the first month called march 168$\frac{7}{8}$: C 524.

John Cann Peter Allricks Johanes Dehaes
Corn^{ll} Empson Edward Blake Richard } Justices Present
Hallywell

    Joseph Harris Plt C 526.
    Edward Owen Deft

The Plt declares against the Deft for nott giueing the Plt

a title to a certain tract of Land & for damages for non performance as by the declacon may more at large appear

The Deft by his attorny George Martin Saith the Deft is Willing to make & confirm a good title to ye s^d Land but first demandeth payment of the moneys dew and Saith ye Land is not anny other persons then the Defts who can & Will guie a good title

Which title being Demanded in Court upon examinacon of the powers of the Defts attorny it did appear by the Lett^r of attorny that he had no power to dispose of ye Lan.

Edward Greene Senior attested saith he heard ye Deft offer to pay the Societys Debt if Isack Weeldon would be quiet not disturb his title: Isaac Welldon attested an evidence

Thomas Harris attested Saith he was building a Sixty ffoot house on the Land Some years past and demanding his money of William Morris who was then upon it the s^d Morris the attestant goe to Edward owen for his pay Saying J   e nothing to doe with it: John White attested

ffour papers relating to ye Land ware produced, 2 bi(?)

The Jury heareing the the allegacons on both sides bring in their Verdict Vidz^t Wee of the Jury find for ye Plt by reason of not making good the title and giues the Plt one Shilling damage wth costs of Sute.

The Court guie Judgment accordingly

C 527.
    Peter Andree   Plt
    Edward Greene Deft

The cause being left to ye Justices, they order the Deft to perform the Judgment of the last court and Vallew the improuements at twenty fiue pounds curr^t money and the Plt to haue liberty to take away afframe Lying in ye Woods & the Deft to haue immediat possession the Plt to take off his crop now growing on ye Land and the Deft to pay all cost of Sute

Richard Hudden   Plt
John Willson   Deft   C 527.

The Plt declares against ye Deft for nott giueing the Plt a Title to a tract of Land bought of ye Defts predecessor & payd for as appeared by good euidence in Court, both partys leave ye cause to ye Justices on ye Bence who giue Judgment that ye Deft giue ye Plt a Title to ye Land and pay cost of Sute

Justa Paulsen acknowledged a Deed for twenty Acres of Land to William Lester as by ye Deed beareing date ye 21st of March 1688   C 535.

William Lester asknowledged a Deed for the aboue twenty acres of Land to Mathew Sanders as by ye Deed bearing date ye 15^{nth} of March 1688   C 535.

John Cann acknowledged a Deed of enfeoffment for his Plantation at Apoquenimy, to Peter Andree as by ye Deed may more at larg appear   C 535.

Charles Peterson acknowledged a Deed of enfeofment for three hundred & forty acres of Land to Hans Peterson as by the Deed beareing date ye 20th of march 1688 may appear   C 535.

Neils Neilson acknowledged a Deed of enfoeffment for one hundred acres of Land to Peter Bainton as by ye Deed beareing date of ye 21st of march 1688 may appear   C 535.

Neils Neilson acknowledged a Deed of enfeofment as afores^d and acknowledged a bond of ffiue hundred pounds to maintain certain titles of Land as by ye bond beareing date the 20th of march 1688 may appear to Peter Bainton   C 535.

Isack Slover acknowleged a Deed for two Lotts of ground in y^e town of newcastle to Hendrick Vandenburg as by the Deed bearing date y^e 7th of December 1687   C 535.

ffrancis Richardson acknowledged a Deed in trust to Josyn Hamilton for a tract of Land & Lott of ground as by ye Deed bearing date y^e 21st of ffabruary. 168$\frac{7}{8}$ C 535.

Justus Anderson Acknowledged a Deed for a Lott of ground Scituat in newcastle, to James Walliam & John Darby as by y^e Deed beareing date y^e 20th of march 168$\frac{7}{8}$:   C 536.

Hans Peterson Neils Neilson & Woolla ffranson acknowl-   C 536.

edged a Deed to Peter Bainton for the mill in Stony Creeke and for the s^d Creek allso as by y^e Deed bearing date the 10th of ffabruary 168⅞

C 537.   Adjurned until y^e 3rd tuesday in June next

End of Book C.

May y^e: 5th & 7th 1688.

D 1.   At a Speciall Court held at Newcastle by ye Kings authority and in the name of William Penn Propriatary and Governor of the Province of Pensilvania and Territorys on ye fifth day of may ann dom̅ 1688

John Cann Edward Blake	
Charles Rumsey Peter Bainton	Justices Present
Georg Robinson Rob: Ashton	

May 7th 1688.

D 2.   Upon the Peticon of Abraham Man concening the rehearing of a certain cause wherein William Guest obtained a Judgment against ye Peticoner, as by ye s^d Peticon may more at large appear

The Court grant ye Peticoner to haue a reahearing of the accon betwixt William Guest & ye Peticoner at ye next Quarter Sessions to be held at Newcastle Provide ye Peticoner consent the s^d. rehearing Shall be affinall end & determinacon without anny further delay or appeall & not otherwise and y^t William Guest haue due notice to appear

Abraham Mann consented to ye answere of ye Peticon

June ye 19^nth 1688.

D 3.   At a Court of Quarter Sessions held at ye Town of Newcastle by ye Kings authority And in the name of the Propriatary & Governor on the 19th 20th & 21st days of the 4th mo^t: 1688

John Cann   William   Stockdale   Vall^t ⎫
Hollingsworth   Edward   Blake   Peter   ⎬ Justices Present
Bainton   Charles   Rumsey   Robart Ashton ⎭

The Accōn between Abraham Mann and William Guest C 6. being called Mr Edward Jones appeared in the behalfe of Abraham Mann as his Attorny and the Letter of Attorny was duely proued and ye s^d Attorney allowed

The Court offered him a rehearing of the cause according to the order of the Governor & Counsell' and of the order of the Court of Newcastle upon ye Peticōn of the s^d Abraham Man and his consent to the conditions of the Rehearing but ye s^d: Attorney declared he could not proceed to ye rehearing on those conditions it being contrary to his Instructions & further Saith he is in Some measure Surprized and being askt by the Court if he had anny more to offer replyed he had no more to Say:

Whereupon William Guest craued a confirmacōn of the first Judgment from which the s^d Abraham Man did appeall and that the execucōn might proceed   The Court order the Sheriff to proceed with his execucōn & to make a return the next Court   The s^d. William Guest exhibiting a bill of Charges Since the Appeal   The Court tax ye Charges at three pounds

John Gramton Desired a caueat and Protest might be en- D 12. tered against Thom: Woollastons allianating anny part of the Land wch ye late Sheriff Sam^ll Land putt the s^d Gramton in possession off fformerly belong to ye s^d Woollaston

John Willson appoints in open Court John Wallker to be D 12. his attorny to acknowledge a tract of Land to Richard Hudden

Mathyas Devoos by his Attorney to Charles Pickering Ack- D 13. nowledged a Deed of Enfeoffment for his Plantacōn in Christina as by the Deed of Enfeoffment to Charles Pickering bearing date ye 17^nth day of the tenth mo^t 1685 Thomas Peirson being the Attorny

Robart Courtney Acknowledged a Deed of Enfeoffment to D 13. Jonas Arskin for Land Scituat in white Clay Creek as by y^e

Deed bearing date ye 19^nth day of June 1688 may more at larg appear

D 13. Justa Paulson ackuowledged a Deed of Enfeoffment & reconvance ffor a tract of Land Lying upon Crain hooke to Hans Peterson as by the Deed beareing date the June 20th : 1688 may more at larg appear

D 13. Dorcas Land Acknowledged a Deed of Enfeoffment ffor one hundred Acres of Land Scituat in Christina Creeke: to Edward Land as by the Deed bearing date the 19^nth of June 1688 may more at larg appear.

D 13. John Garetson by his Attorny Robart Hutchinson acknowledged a Deed of Enfeoffment for a house & Lott in Newcastle to Mary Mandy as by ye Deed beareing date the 18^nth of June 1688

D 13. William Guest Acknowledged a Deed of Enfeoffment ffor two hundred Acres of Land being part of a tract called Wedgburg, to Richard Mankin: as by the Deed bearing date ye 19^nth of June 1688

D 13. Jonas Arskin Acknowledged a Deed of Enfeoffment ffor a tract of Land on ye South side of White Clay Creeke contaiug 200 Acres to Zacariah Vandercoolen as by ye Deed beareing date ye 2nd of Aprill 1688:

D 13. Edward Eglington Acklowledged by his Lawfull Attorny Jeremiah Collet a tract of Land Lying on boath Sides of Namans Creek containing two hundred Acres, to Georg fforeman as by ye Deed bearing date ye 16^nth of march: 168⅞ may appear

D 14. Wee Underwrtten being Chosen & Appointed by ye Court held at newcastle the 21st of the 4th month 1688 to View examin and adjust ye acc^ts between John Darby & Robart Dyer in a matter of differance there depending betwixt the s^d partys which s^d. matter wee takeing upon us and after Sundry demands differances & objections on both sides it was by them Selues Agreed & consented to that the s^d Dyer Should pay to the s^d Darby within the Space of ten days next after the s^d Darby hath deliuered up a certain Deed of bargain and Sale concerning Swart nutten Island with ye Appurtenances

&ᵗ. to the sᵈ Dyer the Sum of Twenty pounds Siluer money and the Sum of twenty pounds like money in three months after yᵉ first time of payment to yᵉ sᵈ Darby or his order: Not at all makeing anny account or takeing anny notice: of ten pounds placed in Dyers accounts due from Dʳ Wessells but remaining So Still: and this Wee giue as our Judgment concurring with their consent and Request Wittness our hands & Seales yᵉ 22ⁿᵈ day of yᵉ 4ᵗʰ month June 1688

       Edward Blake
       Edward Greene
       Edward Gibbs
       Charles Pickering

D 14. Edward Blake & John White being Legally Attested Declareth that on yᵉ 25ᵗʰ day of yᵉ last month June they Deliuered to Robart Dyer By the Request of John Darby one Deed of mortgage Specifyed in the aboue award. Taken this 4ᵗʰ of yᵉ 5ᵗʰ moᵗ. July 1688

       John Cann

Edward Blake Edward Greene & Edward Gibbs being allso attested did Declare the aforesᵈ Judgment was their act & Deed

D 16. Know all Men by these presents that I Sarah Welch of Philadelphia Widdow doe Depute ordain & make & by these pʳᵉsents Depute ordain authorize and make my ffriend Charles Pickering of yᵉ Same place my true & Lawfull Attorny or Agent to Sell Lett Sell or otherwise to dispose of anny or all my Lands houses & Tenements with their & every of their improuements for ready moneys goods or Security to be paid at certain days to come for my use as my Attorny And Allso to aske receive & Demand of all that Stands indebted to me in the County of Newcastle in money wheat porke beeffe tobacco etc: if payd them to acquit & discharge & for want thereof to take Such lawfull ways & means as the law Shall direct in euery respect giueing & by these presents granting my full power & lawfull authority to my sᵈ. Attorny to act & doe as he Shall see meat in as full larg & ample manner as if my Self ware there personally present & will ratefy allow & make good all & whatsoeuer my s^d Attorney Shall lawfully doe or cause to be done in ye premises as wittness my hand and Seale this 18^nth day of ye 6th mo^t. 1688

Signed Sealed & Deliuered
In ye presence of   Sarah Welch
   his marke
William W kened^ay
Susanah Turner

D 17.   At a Court held at Newcastle by ye Kings authority and in the name of the Propriatary & Governor on ye 18: 19: 20th & 21st of September 1688

William Stockdale Edward Blake Robart Ashton Peter Bainton Charles Rumsey } Justices Present

D 20.   Ann Greene & Abiah Egberts Coheirs of the estate of Barent Egber   their late father deceased & daughter in law to Thomas Spry dec   doe desire the Court would direct them about their s^d ffathers   James Walliam the Administrator of the estate of Thomas Spry be   in court and Desireing to Deliuer up his charg:

The Court promiss to consider of it

D 22.   William Codington and Elisabeth his wife by their Attorny Charles Pickering and James Sanderling } Plts
Robart Ashton & Hannah Decow   Deft

The Plts declare for a tract of Land called Chelsy Scituat in Sn^t Georges Creek in ye County of Newcastle granted by Governor Edmond to Ann Whale & Sould by Georg More the Son & heir of Ann whale to John Ogle & from John Ogle to John Test and from John Test to Marmaduke Randall & by him given to Elisabeth Codington for proof whereof the Plts produce the Pattent to the s^d Ann Whale and Deed from the s^d Georg More John Ogle John Test and Deed of Guift from

Marmaduke Randall all which ware read in open Cor and allso a certificate of the s^d Elisabeth her marryage wth William Codington and a Letter from ye Gouernor Penn and a coppy of a Verdict obtaind

The Defts alleadg the Land in Controversy was fforfeited by the Laws of the Country then called ye Dukes Laws & for Proof bring a record of their Peticon to ye Court of newcastle and the Courts anwere thereunto and allso a Pattent from Gouernor Andross to Roaloff Anderson and Jacob Actsen from whom the Plts doe deriue their Title

The book called the Dukes Laws was allso produced and a Law read relating to purchasers of implanted Lands and allso a Paper of Articles Signed by the Gouernor Louelace and an Indian Deed

The Plts alleadg the s^d marmaduke Randall was taken into captiuity and there Dyed whereby it was impossible for him to improue the s^d Land and unreasonable to take it away from him:

James Sanderling was Attested that he paid ye Quit Rent & offered if anny was behind to make immediat payment & petitioned the Court not to grant away the s^d Land by reason the owner was in captiuity and he offered to improue it as Soon as anny person as by his Attestacon more at larg may appear

John Cann did declare he gaue James Sanderling notice and that the s^d James Sanderling made applicacon to ye Court of newcastle that they would not grant the Land from Marmaduke Randall:

Johanes Dehaes did declare the booke containing the Laws then produced ware the laws they formerly ware guided by

The Defts deny the Sufficiency of the Pretended Deed of gift which was referred to the Jury:

The Plts alleadg they ware not turnd out of the Land by a Legall tryall either of the laws of England or the Dukes Laws

After diuers Allegacons & Pleas on boath Sides the cause is commitd to a Jury who going out bring in their Verdict Vid^tz:

Wee of the Jury in an accōn between William Codington & Elisabeth his wife Plts And Robart Ashton & Hannah Decow Defts: ffind for the Defts

Robart ffrench fforeman

The Court giue Judgment according to Verdict

The Defts appeal to haue ye cause tryed ouer again in Equity The Court grant an appeal they giueing Security which was done. uid ffol :33—(& Folio 481: of this Book)

D 28. The Court order the estate of Nathaniel Sturkes Deceased to be committed to the care of Robert Ashton who is desired after the Debts are payd to giue in his account of ye s^d Estate ye next Court in order to send ye remaining effects to the wife of the deceased and John Hayly and John Willson appointed to apprays ye s^d estate

D 31. Reneer Vandercoolen acknowledged a Deed of enfeoffment of his house & ground Scituat on ye Greene or markett place to Anthony Greene as by the Deed bearing date ye 22nd of June 1688

D 31. Justus Anderson acknowledged a Deed of enfeoffment ffor his Kitchen and halfe of the Lott. to George ffisher as by the Deed bearing date the 30th of August 1688

D 31. Hugh mackgregory demanded of Justus Anderson an acknowledgment of the Deed of enfeoffment Signed & Deliuered by the s^d Justus to ye s^d Hugh Mackgregory being for his house & half the Lott Scituat in ye town of newcastle, which Justus Anderson refused to doe in ye open Court

D 32. Jonas Arskin Acknowledged a Deed of enfeoffment for a tract of Land called Aelsbury to Reneer Vandercoolen as by the Deed bearing date the Second day of Aprill 1688

D 32. Corneluis Empson acknowledged a Deed ffor ffree grinding of corn to Lolifand & Erasmus Stedham & their heires for euer as by the Deed bearing date the 28th day of ye 3rd mo^t 1688:

D 32. Peter Godin acknowledged a Deed of enfeoffment for a Lott of Land in town to Robart Dyer as by the Deed bearing date ye 20th of 7^{ber} 1688 may more at larg appear

John Wallker Acknowledged a Deed of enfeoffment for two D 32.
hundred Acres of Land on ye Drawers Creek: to Richard
Hambly as by the Deed bearing date ye 19^{nth} of July 1687:
may more at larg appear:

Corneluis Derrickson by his Attorny John White acknowl- D 32.
edged a Deed of enfeoffment for a Lott of Land in ye Town of
Newcastle to Edward Greene mer^{ct}: as by Deed bearing date
ye 18^{nth} of July may more at large appear 1688

Richard Noble by his attorny John White acknowledged a D 32.
Deed of enfeoffment ffor a parcell of Land Scituat in ye Town
of newcastle, to Robart Dyer as by ye Deed bearing date the
18^{nth} of July 1688 may more at larg appear

Reneer Vandercoolen acknowledged a Deed of enfeoffment D 32.
for a Lott of ground between the Land of Gerardus Wessells
and Anthony Greene, to William Markham as by ye Deed
bearing date the Sixth of 7^{ber} 1688: may more at larg appear:

The Sherriff makeing a return of the Land taken upon the D 32.
Seuerall execucons for Satisfying the Judgments obtaind
against Abraham man, the s^d Sherriff alleadging the Land
hath been appraysed and exposed to Sale for the use of the
Creditors but no person appeared to buy the s^d Land:

The Court order the Sherriff Edward Gibbs: to give the
Creditors possession as the Law directs:

Edward Gibbs made a return of an execucon laid on the D 33.
house of Justus Anderson for Satisfying a Judgm^t: obtain
by Peter Stalcop agst s^d Anderson

Charles Pickering & James Sanderling recognize them D 33.
Selues both & either of them their heirs execut^{rs} & Adminis^{rs}
in the Sum of one hundred pounds curr^t money of Pensiluania unto Robart Ashton & Hanah Decow. etc that they y^e
s^d Charles Pickering & James Sanderling Shall prosecute to
effect Their appeale now obtaind as Attorny of William &
Elisabeth Codington agst Robart Ashton & hannah Decow
Appelles: before the Provinciall Judges at their Sessions at
Philadelphia & to pay all cost & damage if they again happen
to be cast and allso to pay the Present charges:

188 RECORDS OF THE COURT OF NEW CASTLE.

D 34.   John Smith & Hugh macgregory Present a Peticon concerning an execucon layd on the house of s^d. Justa Anderson

The Court order the moneys dew to Justus Anderson for the house from Hugh macgregory be payd to the s^d John Smith and the Creditors who haue Judgments so far as the money will extend.

D 34.   The Court adjournd to ye 3rd Tuesday in october

D 35.   At a Court held for ye County of Newcastle by the Kings Authority & in the name of our Propriatary and Governor on ye 16: 17: 18 & 19^nth days of october anno dom: 1688:

> William Stockdale Edaward Blake Peter Bainton Charles Rumsey Robart Ashton John fforeat John Hayly } Justices Present

D 35.   James Bradshaw in behalf of ye Governor entered a Caveat against John Moll that he might not acknowledge a Deed four Tracts of Land

The Court Suspend the acknowledgment of the s^d Land untill the next Quarter Sessions in December next at which time at which time James Bradshaw promises to be provided: with the reasons of his Caueat:

D 35.   At the request of John Moll Peter Bayard & Herman Borkells being Legally attested did declare they Saw John Moll sign Seale and Deliuer a Deed of enfeoffment for four Tracts of Land to Henry Coursey bearing date ye 27th of September 1688:

D 36.   Georg fforeman   Plt
        Edward Owen   Deft

The Deft being attached by his lands to answer ye complaint of George fforeman ye Plt for fforty eight peices of eight the accon haueing continued three Courts & the Deft haueing had due notice and not appearing The Court according to their former order giue the Plt judgment for forty eight peices of eight wth cost of Sute and the Land Attached to be according to Law Sould for Satisfaction

Upon the Peticon of John Darby concerning an execucon D 39. lately Serued on ye body of Robart Dyer for Satisfaction of Judgm^t etct The Court order the estate of Robart Dyer to be executed and appraysed at Siluer money price for Satisfying the Judgm^ts obtained by the s^d John Darby agst the s^d Robart Dyer

John Moll in open Court acknowledged a Deed of enfeoff- D 41. ment to John fforeat ffor a house & Lott of ground in newcastle, as by the Deed bearing date the 16^nth of october 1688:

Conrade Constantine acknowledked a Deed of enfeoffment D 41. ffor ffiuety acres of Land to Paul mounson as by the Deed beareing date the 16^nth of october 1688:

Hans Peterson acknowledged a Deed of enfeoffment for one D 42. hundred acres of Land in Crane hooke to Hendrick Anderson as by the Deed bearing date the 16^nth october 1688:

Justus Anderson in open Court ordereth Hugh mackgregory D 42. to pay all Such moneys as is dew to s^d Justus Anderson for his house by an obligacon of 80 ^lb for the Conditionall payment of 40 ^lb for the Satisfying Such Judgments and execucons as are Layd on the s^d house and Hugh mackgregory Promiseth in open Court to pay and discharg all Such Judgm^ts & execucons as now lye on the s^d Justus Anderson So far forth as money will extend that is dew for the s^d house And on that condicon alone the Court allow the acknowledgment of the house now to be acknowledged and no otherwise

Justus Anderson acknowledged a Deed of enfeoffment for a D 42. house and peice of ground in ye Town of newcastle to Hugh mackgregory as by the Deed beareing date the 3rd day of August 1688:

Henrick Toulson acknowledged a Deed for one hundred D 42. acres of Land to Thomas Jones as by the Deed dated the 16^nth day of ye 2nd mo^t: 1688

At a Court of Quarter Sessions held by the Kings authority D 43. and in the name of o^r Propriatary & Governor, at the Town of newcastle on ye 18^nth 19^nth & 21st days of December Anno Dom 1688:

William Stockdale Vall^t. Hollingsworth
Edward Blake   Peter Bainton } Justices Present
John fforeat Charles Rumsey & John Hayly

D 43.   John Moll exhibited a Peticon relating to ye Caueat entered by James Bradshaw to Stop the alianating the Land lately offered to be acknowledged and alleadgeth ffluety pounds damage: both partys appearing and certain bills from a person in Holland drawn payable by John Moll unto the Governor and a letter from the Governor relating to a certain Debt ware produced & read in Court   James Bradshaw refered the matter in controversy to the Bench and the Peticoner Desired it might be refered to a Jury. The s^d James Bradshaw begging that John Moll might giue Security for payment of the Debt

The Court continue the caueat until further order

John Moll Peticoning for a Speciall Court to determine the matter of the Peticon   The court grant the Peticoner a court on ye 1st tuesday in ffabruary next

D 45.   Hans Peterson   Plt
Thomas Jones   Def^t

The Plt declares against the Deft in an accon of trespass for the Defts entring on ye Plts Land &ct as by the Declaracon   The Deft Denyeth the trespass and Saith the Land on which he entered is not the P^{lts} Land

The Plt produceth a Deed from Oalla Toarson to Paull mounson, & Chales Peterson & an other Deed from Charles Peterson to Hans Peterson with Seueral Pattents

The Deft produceth an old Pattent as allso Vall^t. Hollingsworth who being attested did declare he heard Paul mounson Say he neuer gaue anny thing for the Land. John Darby was allso attested who being shewed the Deed from Oalla Toreson to Paul mounson Saith that he beleiueth it is the mark of Christophers Barnes   after divers pleas & allegacons on boath sides the Jury going out bring in their Verdict (Vidz^t:) Wee find for ye Deft with cost of Sute   Wm Rakestraw fforeman:

The Court giue Judgm^t according to Verdict

The Plt appeales: The Court grant him his appeale

Hans Peterson & Cornelius Empson Recognize themSelues their heires execut^rs and administ^rs in the Sum of forty pounds to Thomas Jones his heires and assigns that the s^d Hans Peterson Shall prosecute to effect his appeal now obtaind: before ye Provinciall Judges at the next Provinciall Court to be held at Philadelphia and to pay all cost & damage if he again happen to be cast as allso to pay the p^rsent charges

    Robart Dyer   Plt
    John Garetson Deft   D 46.

The Plt Declareth against the Deft for cutting & carrying of hay off from the Plts Marsh as by ye Declaracon may more at larg appear—

The Deft alleadgeth that he doth not Know it to be the Plts marsh & Saith he hath cutt hay there Seuerall yeares:

John Darby attested Saith it was allways counted that the Creek that did run under the Dike made the Island

Robart Hutchinson was allso attested and a Pattent produced: The cause being fully heard the Jury goe out and bring in their Verdict Vidz^t: Wee find for the Plt with cost of Sute and twelve pence damage.

                       William Rakestraw fforeman

The Court giue Judgm^t according to Verdict

    Justus Anderson Plt.
    Georg ffissher   Deft   D 47.

The Plt declares for Satisfaction ffor a house & Lott of Land Vallewed at twenty pounds: as by the Declaracon:

The Deft alleadgeth he hath giuen Satisfaction for the s^d house & Lott of ground and for prooff brings the Deed: and allso John Smith & Hugh mackgregory who ware both attested: both the Plt & Deft Submitt the cause to the Justices on the Bench: Who haueing Seriously considered of the allegacons & evidences of both partys The Justices understanding the Plt was Somewhat disordered with drink at the time of the first pretended agreement & they being allso informed that the Deft had offered eighteen pounds for the house & land it appearing to them very likely to be So in that the Deft doth alleadge he hath payed the greatest part of eighteen pounds, They considering the Premises giue Judgment that the Deft make Payment of the Sum of nineteen pounds for the s^d house & Lott & goods to him Sould & deliuered the Plt to allow & discount So much out of the s^d nineteen pounds that the Deft can now in court make appear to be payd thereof

And if the Deft doe not think ffitt to pay the s^d nineteen pounds he hath liberty to deliuer back the house & goods the Plt repaying all he hath receued for them: and the Deft to pay cost of Sute

D 50. Woolla ffranson Stoffell Myeres & Neils Neilson acknowledged an Instrument of Diuission & Partition of their Land to Peter Bainton as by the Instrument bearing date ye 18^{nth} of December 1688:

D 50. William Guest acknowledged a Deed of Mortgage of his Plantacon called Wednesbury to Alexander Creeker & John Donaldson as by the Deed bearing date the 20th of December 1688

D 50. Hans Peterson had acknowledged a Deed of enfeoffment to him from Corneluis Empson for a tract of Land called the Mill Land as by the Deed bearing bearing date ye 20th day of December 1688:

D 50. Hugh Mackgregory acknowledged a Deed of enfeoffment ffor a house and Lott of ground in newcastle as by ye Deed bearing date ye third day of December 1688: unto John White of Newcastle

D 51. Thomas Gasper and Anneky Lemmens his wife acknowledged a Deed of enfeoffment for a house & Lott of ground at Crane Hooke as by ye Deed bearing date ye 20th day of December 1688: unto Henry Euertson

D 51. John Boulton acknowledged a Deed of enfeoffment for one hundred & fiuety acres of Land to John Cock as by the Deed bearing date ye 19^{nth} of December 1688

Edward Gibbs acknowledged a Deed of enfeoffment for a Lott of ground in the Town of newcastle as by ye Deed bearing date ye 30th day of november 1688: unto Robart Evans of newcastle   D 51.

Hugh Mackgregory acknowledged a Deed of Mortgage contained in a bond to Hendrick Vandenburgh for the payment of 80 ^{lb} being for the conditional payment of 40 ^{lb} as by the s^d obligacon bearing date ye 11th day of December 1688   D 51.

Hendrick Vandenburgh acknowledged a Deed of enfeoffment for a house & Two Lotts of ground in the town of newcastle unto Hugh Mackgregory as by the Deed bearing date ye 11th December 1688   D 51.

Upon the Peticon of Hugh Mackgregory & James Reed to be discharged of the penaltys of certain recognizances in behalf of Abraham Man his appeales: The Court discharg the Peticoners of their recognizances   D 52.

A Peticon being exhibited relating to orphans of Anthony Thomkings The Court takeing the matter of the Peticon into Serious consideracon and ffinding there hath not been due care taken of the estate of the s^d Orphans as the law directs The court orders a Sommons be issued out to Elisabeth Tomkings to appear at ye next court to be held on the 11th of march ensuing to render an account of ye estate of Anthony Tomkings & in ye mean time Richard Hallywell John Hayly & Isack Weeldon are or anny two of them appointed & Desired to Inspect the estate & take Care the orphans Suffer not by anny Imbezlement untill the s^d next Court   D 52.

Upon the Peticon of Jonas Wright the Son of Josyne Hamilton in behalf of himself and the rest of the orphans. The haueing considered the matter of the Peticon doe appoint James Walliam & Edward Blake who are desired to be Supervisers of the estate & usuage of the s^d orphans and John Biscus John Hendickson & Emelius De Ring are appointed Administrators in the behalf of ye orphans   D 53.

The s^d John Biscus Jno Hendrickson & Emelius De Ring Joyntly & Seuerally doe Recognize themselues & heires &ct in the Sum of one thousand pounds to the Court of Orphans for

the time being of ye County of newcastle to render a true
accopt make good pay of all the estate of the s^d orphans to
them committed: when thereunto lawfully required

D 55.   Received this Seventeenth day of January 1688 of Georg
ffisher the Sum of nineteen pounds being in full Satisfaction
for a Judgmnt obtained at a Court held at newcastle on y^e
18^{nth} day of December last past as allso in full of all other
accounts whatsoeuer from the begining of the world to the
day of ye date hereof as Wittness my hand and Seale the day
& year first aboue written

the word nineteen was interlined before the Sealing & Deliuery hereof:

Sealed & Deliuered in
the pressence of us   Justa Anderson (Seale)
  John White
  R^d aynolds

D 55.   At a Speciall Court held at Newcastle on the 5th day of y^e
12th mo^t 168$\frac{8}{9}$

  Edward Blake Robart Ashton Charles Rumsey ⎰ Justices
  John fforeat John Hayly . . . . ⎱ Present

D 57.   In Pursuance to an order from y^e Govenor & Counsell bearing date of the 7th day of y^e 12 mo^t 168$\frac{8}{9}$ directed to y^e
Justices of the County of Newcastle to putt the s^d order in
execuçon Wee the Justices of y^e s^d County haueing mett at
the house and Lands mençoned in y^e Petiçon annexed to the s^d.
order upon the 11th day of y^e 1st mo^t. 168$\frac{8}{9}$ did find John
Grampton and his wife on y^e s^d Premises who haueing readyly
& willingly on our Command Departed thence Wee put Thomas
Woolaston in full and peaceable possession thereof whereby
wee conclude the s^d order fully executed & haue hereunto
Sett our hands this 13^{nth} day of y^e 1st mo^t. 168$\frac{8}{9}$

 To the Clark of y^e County Court . .
of Newcastle who is hereby required   John Cann
to record the same & return   Edw Blake
a copy thereof to y^e Governor
& Counscill

October y^e 4th 1684

In the name of god Amen I Joana Gouldsmith of Baltamore D 58. County in the Province of Maryland being weak of body but of perfect Strength of mind & memory praysed be to god for it I doe by thes Presents renounce all former Wills & Testaments of what Nature or form Soeuer they ware and make this my last Will & Testament in maner and form as followeth first I bequeath my Soul to god my creator that gaue it me my body to ye earth to be buryed in decent manner hopeing that through ye merrits of Jeasus Christ my only Sauiour and redeemer for a Joyfull resurrection of the last day & for what estate god of his mercy hath bestowed upon me I giue & bequeath in manner & form as followeth

Itim I doe giue unto my beloued daughter Blanch Wells wife to Mr George Wells my dyamond Ring that She now hath in her costody

Itim I giue & bequeath to my well beloued Daughter Susanna Richardson now wife to Mr Mark Richardson all ye estate which is properly mine or anny ways belolonging or appertaining to me either in goods plate money Ster^l or tobacco which is due by bill bond or account or anny other ways to me belonging or appertaining of what nature Soeuer it Shall be found Willing this to pay all my Just Debts & Legacys aboues^d And as for the half of my deceased husband Sam^{ll} Gouldsmiths estate which was left in my hands by Will of my s^d Deceased husband for the use of my aboues^d daughter Susanah to receiue & possess after my Death with improuement therefore I doe hereby giue one thousand pounds of tobacco improuement of ye s^d estate and all ye rest of my estate I giue unto my beloued daughter Susannah Richardson to her & her heires for euer In order hereto I Will my fores^d daughter Richardson to be my whole Sole and absolute executrix of this my last Will & Testament & no other In Wittness whereof I haue hereunto Sett my hand & Seale the day & year aboues^d

Signed Sealed & Deliuered
In the Pressence of us   Joanna Gouldsmith   (Seale)
    Isack I Jackson
    Edward Eb burgh   Vera copia   Jam Heath { Reg }
    Thomas P ffloyd

D 59.   At a Court of Quarter Sessions held by the Kings authority and in the name of our Propriatary & Gouernor on the 11th 12^{nth} 14^{nth} 15 & 16^{uth} days of march 168$\frac{8}{9}$ ffor the Town & County of Newcastle:

John Cann Peter Allricks Johanes De Haes Sitting the latter end of the Sessions:

March y^e 12th

John Cann   William Stockdale ⎫
Edward Blake   Charles Rumsey ⎬ Justices Present
John fforeat   John Hayly— ⎭

15^{nth} March

D 66.   Upon the motion of Cornelius Empson for erecting a more Safe Speedy and constant passage over the Brandy Wine Creek and upon his Promise to constantly attend the Same and keep it in continuall repair The Court grant the s^d Cornelius Empson upon his So doing the liberty the liberty to take for the passage of Man or beast as the law directs which is to be made at y^e Mill Damm:

D 67.   Andrew Loue acknowledged a Deed of enfeofment to Lewis Owen for two hundred acres of Land as by y^e Deed bearing date y^e 16^{nth} day of march 168$\frac{8}{9}$

D 67.   Paull Mounson acknowledged a Deed of enfeofment to Hans Peterson for a tract of Land called Monson Hooke as by y^e Deed bearing date the 21st day of January 1688

D 67.   John Hayly acknowledged a tract of Land called Industry containing Six hundred acres. to Hendrick Wallraven: as by the Deed bearing date y^e 12th day of march 168$\frac{8}{9}$

D 67.   Derrick Vandenburgh acknowledged a Deed of enfeofment to Georg Hogg for a parcell of ground in y^e ffront Street in newcastle p^r Deed dated 26th ffabruary 168$\frac{8}{9}$

Joseph More acknowledged a Deed of enfeoffment to Bryan Buckworth as by the Deed bearing date y^e 29th December 1688   D 67.

John Anderson acknowledged a Deed of enfeoffment for three hundred and ninety acres of Land to Peter Stalcop as by the Deed bearing date the 13^{nth} of march 168$\frac{8}{9}$ D 67.

Hendrick Vandenburgh & Anna his wife acknowledged a Deed of enfeoffment ffor a Tract of Land called Doctors Commons & containing one hundred and Sixty acres of Land to Robart Ashton as by the Deed bearing date y^e 11th day of march 168$\frac{8}{9}$ D 67.

John White acknowledged a Deed of enfoeffment for a tract of Land called Westminster, to Joseph Clayton as by the Deed bearing date the 14^{nth} day of march 168$\frac{8}{9}$ D 68.

End of Book D.

By the King and   in the name of the Honble. Wm Absolute propriatary of the Province Pennsilvania and Counties annexed   America.

Att a Court of Quarter Sessions held at New Castle for town and County aforesaid June 17th 1690 before Peter Alrichs, John Cann, Edward Blake and Charles Rumsy

Edward Blake & Robert Dyer P^{lts}	
John Penington . . . . Def^t	plea of trespass

The Plts and Deft appear and Joyn issue The Plts declare for 40s damage for the Def^{ts} entring upon and with holding their land, and falling the wood &c and produceth a pattent and deed with map of Survey and Severall evidences, The Deft for plea saith, the land he is Seated on was Surveyed to him by a warrant, and produceth a certificate with other evidences &c whereupon a Jury is called and impannelled who upon their attestations find for the Def^t with cost of Suit, which the Court confirm, and Judgment is awarded against the P^{lts} for the cost

Came into Court James Bradshaw Register; and produceth a will therein called the last will and Testament of John Hendrickson, and desireth the approbation of this Court in relation to the Administration of the said estate to be given to John Harms and John White Executors therein named and appointed thereby. John Harms appears and declares that the intent of John Hendricksons words upon the making the said will was to appoint them only as Overs and the widdow to have the power of Administration, and declines the probate of the said will, whereupon the Court adjudge the widdow and Relict to be the fittest person in law for administration on the estate of her deceased husband

Came into Court Elizabeth Ogle widdow and Administratrix of John Ogle deceased and made appear by Inventory and other papers and accounts in Court produced, that she hath over and above paid the Value of the Inventory of goods belonging to the said Ogle deceased, and committed to her Administration whereupon the Court grant her a Quieta est and discharge her from paying any more debts of the said John Ogle

Conveyances, obligations, bills, Articles, & letters of Attorny proved and acknowledged in open Court

Letter of Attorny { Derrick Vanderburgh to Henry Vanderburgh & from him to Isaac Wheeldon . . . } proved & allowed vid: fil.

Letter of Attorny { Henry Vanderburgh to Isaac Wheeldon } proved & allowed vid. fil.

Release: Corneluis Derrickson & Abraham Inloes— to Peter Alrichs & Johannes DeHaes Edmond Cantwell & Ephraim Herman deceas^d Guardians — bearing date 17th day June 1690 from all things relating to the estate of Martin Rosamond & Derrick Albertson deceased from the begining of the world to this day

assignment of a Conveyance: William Alloway to Richard Reynolds — bearing date the 16th June 1690 for a lott in New Castle bought of Adam Ikey

Conveyance: James Walliams to Saml. Brewerton — bearing date the 17th day of June 1690 for one hundred and eight acres and a half land on the North Side of Augustine Creek bought of Thomas Rothwell 17 $\frac{7}{m}$ last

Came into Court John Mackarty and John Hartop and did Assign and make over from them & their heirs unto Richard Hallywell and his heirs & assigns for ever, all their right title and interest in and to certain Articles of agreem^t bond of performance, and obligations of payment of 120 ℔ by Robert & Wm Goforth, and acknowledged to have received full Satisfaction in hand therefor, which witness were proved in open Court.

Articles of — agreem^t between { Robert & Wm Goforth— and Jno Mackarty & Jno Hartop }

bearing date the 13^d day of the 11th month 1689 for a plantation & housing q^t ab^t. 270^a. situate on hangmans Creek, Sold to Robert & Wm Goforth; proved in Court

Obligation { Robert & Wm Goforth to John Mackarty and John Hartop } bearing date 13th January 1689 for two hundred forty pound for performance of the above Articles, proved in Court

Adjourned to the next Quarter Sessions September the 16th 1690.

By the king and Queens authority and in the name of Wm Penn Absolute Proprietary of the Province of Pennsilvania and Counties annexed in America.

Att a Court of Quarter Sessions held at New Castle this 16th of September 1690 before Peter Alrichs, John Cann, Edward Blake and John Heally Justices & Henricus Williams—

Hans Peterson Pl^t
Wm Lester . . Deft
} Plea of trespass on the case
The Pl^t & Def^t appear and joyn issue

The Plt declares for four pound ten shillings damage for the Deft by force and violence entring his meadow and cutting and destroying his grass thereon growing—The Deft for Plea saith he hath not entred and destroyed the grass on the P^{lts} meadow but it is his own, which he hath mowed—Severall evidences were attested and papers produced whereupon a Jury is called impannelled and attested who upon their attestations say they find for the Def^t with cost of Suit, the Court give Judgm^t thereon—

Letter of Attorney	Joseph Holdin to Isaac Wheeldon	bearing date 14 March 1689 proved and allowed	vid fil
Letter of Attorney	Robert Logan to Robert ffrench	bearing date 12th September 1690 proved and allowed	vid fil
Letter of Attorney	Benj^a ffordham to Isaac Wheeldon	bearing date 16th May 1690 proved and allowed	vid fil
Conveyance	Benj^a ffordham to Benj^a Gumley	bearing date the 16th of May 1690 for a tract of land on the South side of Blackbirds Creek, formerly belonging to the said B Gumly acknowledged by Isaac Wheeldon attorny of Benj^a ffordham and proved	
Conveyance	Jno & Christina Moll to John Richardson . . .	bearing date the 17th day of September 1690 for a piece of land in New Castle was proved & acknowledged	

Conveyance { John & Christina Moll to James Read ...... } bearing date the 17th day of September 1690 for a piece of land in New Castle with housing & improvem'ts was proved and acknowledged

Release { Humphry Best & Ed: Green to Broer Senexon .... } bearing date the 16th day of September 1690 from all claim & demand of a p's of land &c on both sides w't clay creek formerly bought by them of him.

Att a Court of Orphans held at Newcastle October 7th 1690 before Peter Alrichs, John Cann, Edward Blake, and Ch: Rumsy

Conveyances { John Smith .. to Sampson Atkins to W'm Osborn } bearing date the Seventh day of October 1690 for a lott in New Castle was acknowled by James Read Executor et another lott adjoyning

adjournd to the time appointed by law

Att a County Court held at New Castle the 18th day of November 1690 before Peter Alrichs, John Cann, Edward Blake, Charles Rumsey, & John Heally

Assignment of a Conveyance	Robert Mercer— to John Champion Christopher White	bearing date the 17th day of November 1690 for 200 acres of land bought of Joseph Moor was acknowledged

By the king and Queens authority and in the name of the Right hon[bl] W[m] Penn absolute Proprietor & Governor of Pennsylvania and lower Counties

Att a Court of Quarter Sessions held at New Castle the 16th day of December before Peter Alrichs, John Cann, Edward Blake & Charles Rumsy—

Edward Gibbs produceth a Comission from Sam[l]. Jenings to be receiver of the Quit Rents of this County dated December 4th 1690.

By the King and Queens authority and in the name of the right hon[ble] W[m] Penn absolute Proprietor & Governor of the Province of Pennsilvania & Counties annexed

Att a Court of Orphans held at New Castle the 3d day of March 1690 before Peter Alrichs, John Cann, Edward Blake, Cornelius Empson and Charles Rumsy—

Edward Gibbs high Sherif returns a warrant from Justice Cann & Blake as p file.—that according to the said warrant he went to the Plantation and took the Same into his Possession and left two to look after it, whom Percifull Westingdale forced out and kept out, who being brought hither by a warrant Saith he knoweth not his age, but Elizabeth Barker being Solemnly attested declares that he was born the 5th December 1670 whereupon it is concluded that the Administration of the said estate of Ann Westingdale most properly be committed to the hands of Benj[a] Gumbley as the next of kin and the power of Administration granted by James Bradshaw Register to Percifull Westingdale be consequently void, and the Administration to be comitted to Benjᵃ Gumbley—

By the king and Queens authority, and in the name of the right honorable Wᵐ Penn absolute Proprietor and Governor of the Province of Pennsylvania & Counties anexed in America

Att a Court of Quarter Sessions held at New Castle the Seventeenth day of march 1690 before John Cann, Edward Blake, Cornelius Empson, Peter Baynton, Charles Rumsey, Robert Ashton, Henricus Williams & John Heally—

John Darby and Rowlif Anderson are appointed & attested Publick Appraisers of the town & County, to appraise all lands, goods and chattells to be exposed to their view both by Coroner and Sherrif—

The Grand Jury having from time to time presented Peter Alrichs for not draining the Swamp near his ground at the South end of the town, and the same being Still neglected to the anoyance of the inhabitants of the said town—the Court adjudge the claim & property of the said Peter Alrichs therein to be void & forfeited—

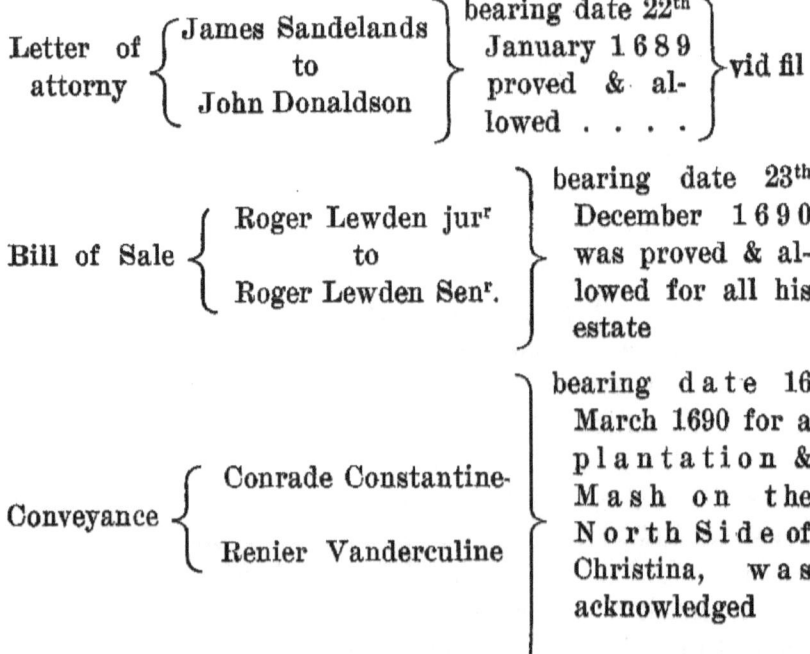

Letter of attorny { James Sandelands to John Donaldson } bearing date 22ᵗʰ January 1689 proved & allowed . . . . } vid fil

Bill of Sale { Roger Lewden jurʳ to Roger Lewden Senʳ. } bearing date 23ᵗʰ December 1690 was proved & allowed for all his estate

Conveyance { Conrade Constantine Renier Vanderculine } bearing date 16 March 1690 for a plantation & Mash on the North Side of Christina, was acknowledged

Conveyance { Henry Vanderburgh to Cornelius Kettle .. } bearing date 13th January 1689 for a lott in New Castle next to Anthony Bryant 45 foot Broad—

Conveyance { John & Ellin Mackarty to Richard Hallywell } bearing date

31th December 1690 for a plantation & improvements On the north side of Hangmans Creek q^t 279 acres land acknowledged by John Mackarty & Edwd Gibbs attorny of Ellin Mackarty to R. Hallywell

Mortgage { Edward Blake . . . . . to Robert Ashton in behalf of Abraham & Hannah Decow— } bearing date

22th March 1688 for the lower half of black Walnut Island and the lower half of the Out lett, for the payment of 149-7-6 when Abraham & Hannah Decow come to age—

Articles between { John fforatt . . . . . & Elizabeth Cousturier } bearing date the 6th ffebruary 1689 about an intended marriage between them, to keep their estates distinct & to their particular heirs, acknowledged to each other—

By the king and Queens authority and in the name of the right honb^{le} William Penn Proprietor and Governor of the

Province of Pennsilvania and Counties annexed in America

Att a Court of Quarter Sessions held at New Castle the 16th day of June 1691 before Peter Alricks John Cain, Edward Blake, Henry Williams & Charles Rumsey

The Coroner returns an Execution levyed on the lands of Jacob Young to Satisfye a Judgment obtained by Edward Gibbs for 205 ℔ with cost—and assigns over to the said Edward Gibbs the Said plantation and land appraised at 220 ℔, he promising to return the Overpluss back to the Coroner—

Edward Gibbs Sherrif assigns over the said land to John Cole for to Satisfye a Judgment obtained Against him for two hundred pound, the said John Cole promising to return the Overpluss, and likewise dischargeth the said Edward Gibbs and his heirs from the Said Judgment, as having herby received full Satisfaction

The Sherrif returns an Execution levyed on the lands of Edwd Green to Satisfye Saml. Atkins of a Judgment obtained and assigns over the Same

Assignment of a Conveyance { Robert Dyer to Nicholas Wansford } bearing date 15th June 1691, for a lott sold by Rich^d: Noble in Mary Street New Castle

Letter of attorny { Edmond Linsy to Edward Gibbs } bearing date 6th June 1691 proved & allowed

Assignment of a Pattent.. { Edmond Linsy to John Burk.. } bearing date 6th June 1691 for 200^a land called Dublin situate on Georges Creek proved & acknowledged by Edwd Gibbs attorny of Edmond Linsy

Letter of Attorny	Artman & Mathew Hayn to Edward Gibbs	bearing date 18th May 1691 proved & allowed
Conveyance	Artman & Mathew Hayn to Nicholas Lockier	bearing date 18th May 1691. for a piece of Mash in Swanwick 41¾ rodd broad proved & acknowledged by Edwd Gibbs Attorny of Artman & Mathew Hayn—

By the king and Queens authority &c^t: (as before)

Att a Court of Quarter Sessions held at New Castle the 15th day of September 1691 before Peter Alrich; John Cann, Edward Blake & Charles Rumsy

Thomas Gasper Pl^t
Hans Hanson Def^t } trespass

The Pl^t and Def^t appear and joyn issue

The Plt declares for four pound tenn Shillings damage for the Def^{ts}. entring the Pl^{ts} meadow & cutting & destroying the grass, the Def^t. for Plea Saith he is not guilty, whereupon the Jury is called impannelled and attested, who upon their attestations find for the Pl^t. one penny damage with cost of suit, which the Court confirm.

The Def^t desires an Appeal to the Provincial Court in equity, which is granted—

Hans Hanson and Rowlif Anderson doe bind themselves joyntly and Severally in the Summe of One hundred Pound corant mony to Thomas Gasper, conditioned that Hans Hanson doe pay down the present cost of this Court, and to effect prosecute his appeal (this day granted against Thomas Gasper) at the next Provincial Court in equity to be held for the County of New Castle, and to pay all costs & damages that Shall be there awarded against him

Hans Peterson Plt } trespass
Thomas Jones. Deft

The Plt and Deft appear and joyn issue

The Plt declares for three pound damage for the Def^{ts} etring the Pts meadow & cutting and destroying the grass— the Def^t for plea Saith he did not cut the Pl^{ts} grass. Whereupon a Jury is called impannelled and attested, who upon their attestations find for the Pl^t one Shilling damage and cost of Suit, which the Court confirm—

By the King & Queens authority

Att a Court of Quarter Sessions held at New Castle for the Town & County afores^d the 19th of March 1694—

Peter Alrichs, Edward Blake, Richard Hallywell and Adam Peterson & John Grubb—

March 20th. 1694—

Peter Peterson Pl^t } in a plea of trespass on the
Val. Hollinsworth Dft case

Hans Peterson &c Pl^t } in a plea of traspass on the
Val. Hollinsworth &c Dft case & joyn issue

The Pl^{ts}. declare for damage for the Df^{ts} cutting grass & carrying away hay from the Pl^{ts} marsh, the Def^{ts} plead not guilty whereupon a Jury is called, impannelled and attested, who say they find for the Def^{ts} and Judgment awarded accordingly

James Read Pl^t } upon a lease of Ejectment
Edward Cole Dft

Edward Blake & Richard Hallywell as Trustees of Henry Cousturier & Elizabeth Dunkarton appear by Griffith Jones their Attorny Pl[ts]

John fforatt by David Lloyd his attorny as Df[t]

The Pl[ts] declares for five hundred pound damage for a house & ground at the North end of the Town of New Castle as ⅌ the declaration—the Def[t] pleads not guilty and Joyn issue, whereupon a Jury is called impanelled & attested who find for the Dft

The Plts desire an appeal to the Supream Court in law which the Court grants, whereupon—Edward Blake and Richard Hallywell do recognize themselves joyntly and Severally in the Summe of forty pound corant mony to be levyed of their lands goods and chattells for the use of John fforatt conditioned that they will prosecute this Appeal at the next Supream Court to be held at New Castle in law, and to pay all Costs & damages that shall be there awarded against them

Conveyance { John Moll to Hans Hanson } dated the 19th March 1694 for a plantation of 1000[a] by Dragon Swamp was acknowledged

Mortgage { Hans Hanson to John Moll } dated as above for Said Land was acknowledged

Conveyance { Walraven Otto to James Read } dated 30th October 1694 for a tract of land at Apoquinamink landing wth a peice of Marsh.

Conveyance { James Read— to Jeffry Martin } dated 7th November 1694 for the Said land & Marsh—

Conveyance { Jeffry Martin to James Read } dated 7th November 1694 for 40[a] of the Said tract on Drawers Creek

Conveyance	James Read to Walraven Otto	dated the 30th October 1694 for the above 40ª
Conveyance	Thomas Ogle to Edward Gibbs	dated 20th March 1694 for 100ª at Georges Creek
Conveyance	Wyborough Walker to John Howe	dated the 21th March 1694 for 346ª at Drawers Creek was acknowledged
Conveyance	William Markham to Jasper Yeates ..	dated the 1st January 1694 for a tract of land near the Town of 1078ª & 3 lotts at the South end of the Town acknowledged by John Donaldson

this deed was acknowledged

By the Kings authority and in the name of William Penn absolute Proprietor and Governour of the Province of Pennsilvania & Counties anexed—

Att a Court of Quarter Sessions held at New Castle for the Town & County aforesaid the 18th day of June 1695—

Before

John Donaldson, Cornelius Empson, John Richardson and Nicholas Lockier—

A Comission for John Donaldson & James Claypoole to grant probates of wills & letters of Administration was read

Upon Severall complaints that the fferry at Christina Creek is very much neglected, and noe due attendance given, Ordered that if Peter Jaquett doe not forthwith procure a Substantiall boat fit for a ferry and look well and attend the same, so that farther complaints be made, his recognizance entred on record be put in Suit against him—

Conveyances acknowledged

Conveyance { Joseph Holden to Joseph Allman } bearing date the 18th June 1695 for a plantation q^t 286^a land at Blackbird Creek acknowledged by Isaac Wheeldon as Attorny

Conveyance { John Moll to John Dunn } bearing date the 18th June 1695 for a piece of land between the town Marsh & the land of Edward Lison & Gerhard Smith—

Assignment { George Hogg .. to Hypolit Lefevor } bearing date the 18th June 1695 on the back of a pattent for a lott at the North end of the Town in the front Street—

By the Kings authority &c^a: as before—att a Court held at New Castle the 6th Augst 1695 Before

John Donaldson Cornelius Empson, Nicholas Lockier and John Hanson

Nathaniell Janes & uxor Plts } Plea of land
Val: Hollinsworth &c   Defts }

The Pl^{ts} and Def^{ts} appear and joyn issue

The Pl^{ts} declare for a piece of Marsh, which the Df^{ts} have disseired them of, the Df^{ts} plead not guilty, whereupon a Jury is called and impannelled who upon their Attestations find for the Dft with cast of Suit which the Court confirm and grant Judgment—

Wm Sharply P^{lt} } plea of land
Hans Peterson D^{ft}

The Pl^t and Df^t appear & joyn issue by consent

The Pl^t. declares for a peice of Marsh which the Df^t hath disseired him of, the Df^t pleads not guilty whereupon a Jury is called and impannelled who upon their attestations find for the Pl^t with cost of Suit, which the Court Confirm & grant Judgm^t

Indenture of ... division or partition { Wm Crosee & Thomas Janvier to John Bisk & Elizabeth his wife } bearing date the 28th of May 1695 for a lott and housing in the front Adjoyning to Amelius De Rings lott.

Indenture of ... division or Partition { John Bisk & ... Elizabeth his Wife to W^h Crosee and Thomas Janvier .. } bearing date the 28th May 1695 for the Same lott--

Conveyance { Charles Rumsey to John Hussey .. } bearing date the 1st of July 1695 for his land & Plantation at Christina

Assignment { John Richardson to John Hussey .. } bearing date the 6th of August 1695 for the other P^t: of the above Plantation q^t. 300^a:

Mortgage { Richard Reynolds to Hans Peterson — } bearing date the 4th June 1695 of a house & lott in Town for 75^{lb} at 2 Years payment

Conveyance	Edward Gibbs— to John Donaldson	bearing date the 1st August 1695 of 400^a land with Stock at Georges Creek
Assignment	Edward Land to John Rayne	bearing date the 7th Augst 1695 on the back of a deed of 100^a land at Christina
Conveyance	James White to John Lewden	bearing date the 6th Augst 1695 for a plantation & land at Christina Creek q^t 435^a
Letter of Attorny	John Heally to James Read	bearing date the 17th March 1694 proved and allowed
Letter of Attorny	William and Marget Price to Adam Peterson	bearing date the 1st day of June 1695 proved and allowed
Conveyance	William and Marget Price to John Heally	bearing date the 5th of November 1694 for 200^a land in hang Mans Creek in Apoquinamink

By the Kings authority and in the name of the Honble William Penn absoluate Proprietor of the Province of Pennsilvania and Counties annexed—

Att a Court held at New Castle for the Town & County aforesaid the 15th day of October 1695 Before

John Donaldson, John Williams, Cornelius Empson John Richardson & Nicholas Lockier. Justices

Letter of Attorny	Corneluis Derrickson to Richard Reynolds	bearing date the 17th Sep^t 1695 to acknowledge a p^s of land to John Watts proved and allowed
Letter of Attorny	Jacob Hendrickson to Hendrick Hendrickson	bearing date the 15th day of May 1695 to acknowledge a p^s of land to Erick Anderson proved & allowed.
Assignment on the back of a Conveyance	Abraham Inloes .. Cornelius Derickson to John Watts	bearing date the 17th Sep^t 1695 for a p^s of ground in the

Town between Otter & Bevor Street was acknowledged

Conveyance	Jacob Hendrickson to Errick Anderson .	bearing date the 26th Aprill 1692 for a p^s of land at Brandywine Creek q^t 300^a acknowledged
Conveyance	James White to George Hogg	bearing date the 17th day of Sep^t 1695 for half a lott in Town adjoyning to the house of G. Hogg acknowledged
Mortgage	George Hogg to James White	bearing date the 18th Sep^t 1695 for the Said half lott was acknowledged

Conveyance { Wyborough Walker to John Wilson .... } bearing date the 17th day of October 1695 for a p^s land at Drawers Creek called Mill forke with a p^s Marsh q^t 111^a was acknowledged

Conveyance { John Wilson .. to Kenhelm Clark } bearing the 17th day of October 1695 for the above Land was acknowledged

By the kings authority &c.^a—Att a Court held at New Castle the 19th day of November 1695—Before John Donaldson, John Williams & Nicholas Lockier

Letter of Attorny { Ann King ... to Marinus Dewit } bearing date the 9th day of November 1695 to receive a Conveyance of land proved & allowed

Conveyance { Edward Gibbs Adam Hay John Heally to Ann King & Marinus Dewit } bearing date the 31th day of October 1695 for a tract of land on the North Side of Apoquinamink Creek—

Assignment on the back of a Conveyance { Margarett Sherry to Hypolitus Lefevor } bearing date the 19th day of November for a house and lott in the front Street of New Castle

Conveyance { John Heally ... to Richard Cantwell } bearing date the 19th day of November for a tract of land in Apoquinamink called Poplar hill q^t. 200^a.

By the Kings authority & in the name of the Honble William Penn Proprietor & Governor of the Province of Pennsilvania & Counties anexed

Att a Court of Quarter Sessions held at New Castle the 17th day of December 1695 Before — John Donaldson, John Williams, Cornelius Empson, Nicholas Lockier and John Richardson

Wm Woodland   Pl^t
Jacob Young   Df^t

The Pl^t declares for two hundred pound damage for Slandering his title of land, the Def^t pleads Justification to the words, whereupon a Jury is called and impannelled who upon their attestations find noe cause of action which the Court confirm.

Letter of Attorny from Mary Mayle to James Read for making over a Conveyance to John Heally bearing date the 31st day of October 1695 proved and allowed—

Conveyance { Mary Mayl to John Healy } bearing date the 31th of October 1695 for a plantation called the change in Sassafrass Creek q^t 500^a.

Assignment on the back of a Conveyance { Renier Vanderculin to Luke Emly .... } bearing date the 17th day of December 1695 for a plantation q^t 100^a on the North Side of Christina

Mortgage { John Ellis to Mathias Vanderhyden } bearing date the 23th of March 1693 for 2 lotts in New Castle for payment of 10 lb the 10th of October 1695

Conveyance { Timothy Atkinson to Thomas Babb ... } bearing date the 17th day of December 1695 for 100ª land & 20ª mash in Rocklands

Assignment on the back of a Conveyance { Sam¹ Brewerton . to Lymon Massillant } bearing date the 17th day of December 1695 for 108½ª land at Augustine Creek

Conveyance { from Leonard Ostarhaven Administrator of Æmelius De Ringh by consent of the Orphans Court acknowledged the South ⅔ of a lott at the North end of the Town qᵗ in breadth 132 foot & in length 289 foot dated the 17th of December 1695

By the Kings authority and in the name of the Honble William Penn absolute Proprietor of the Province of Pennsilvania & Counties anexed—

Att a Court of Quarter Session held at New Castle the 17th day of March 1695 — Before

John Donaldson, Cornelius Empson, John Richardson and Nicholas Lockier—

Mortgage { Peter Yokum ...... to Charles Sanders & compª } dated the 1st of January 1694 for a tract of land at white Clay Creek, amongst other lands else where acknowledged by John Donaldson Attorny of Peter Yokum to Joseph Pidgeon Attorny of Charles Sanders & Comp[a]

Conveyance { Isaac Warner to W[m] Tally .. } dated 16th March 1695 for 200[a] land by Namans Creek was Acknowledged

Conveyance { John & Abiah Garretson to Edward Gibbs ..... } dated the 16th March 1695 for 300[a] land at George's Creek was acknowledged by George Moor Attorny of John & Abiah Garretson

Release { Paul Barns ... to Hilitie Anderson } dated the 3[d] of March 1695 of his right on the back of a Pattent dated the 14th of August 1671 for 300[a] of land & Marsh at Apoquinamink granted to Barent Hendrickson was acknowledged

Assignment { Neil Cook .. to John Latham } dated the 17th of March 1695 on the back of a deed for 200[a] land at Christina was acknowledged—

Assignment { John Ogle ... to Edward Harrison } dated the 17th of March 1695 on the back of a deed for a lott in Town was acknowledged

Conveyance { Hans Peterson . to Patrick McKarty } dated the 17th of March 1695 on a deed for a tract of land and Marsh at Verdredyhook was acknowledged

By the Kings authority & in the name of the Hon[ble] William Penn Absolute Proprietor of the Province of Pennsilvania & Counties annexed in America.

Att a Court held at New Castle the 16th day of June 1696
Before—Peter Alrichs, Richard Hallywell, John Donaldson, Adam Peterson & John Hanson

Peter Jaquett presented for deficiency in keeping the fferry at Christina, appears and promiseth to keep the ferry better for the future, therefore the Court consider that he be continued till the next Court upon his better attendance

Letter of Attorny { Bisk & Spark to Richard Reynolds } dated 31th March 1696 proved and allowed

Letter of Attorny { Peter Lester to Richard Askew } dated 17th June 1696 proved & allowed

Conveyance { John & Eliza: Bisk & Wm & Margarett Sparks to Benjamin Swett . . . } dated the 31th March 1696 for half a lott in the front Street was acknowledged by Richard Reynolds Attorny

Conveyance { Cornelius Post to John Ellis . . } dated the 22th of July 1695 for a house and lott in the front Street at the South end of the Town.

Conveyance { Renier Vanderculine & his wife . . . . . to John Thompson . . } dated the 16th of June 1696 for a house & lott in the Market place—

Conveyance { James Claypoole to Robert ffrench . } dated the 16th of June 1696 for two lotts in the front Street at the North end of the Town

Conveyance { ffrancis Smith & his wife .. to George fforman to
Conveyance { Ann Smith ... } for 500 Acres of land at Brandywine with all the Stock

Conveyance { Jacobus Alrichs to John Parris .. } dated the 17th of June 1696 for a lott in Otter Street in Town—

Conveyance { Peter Lester to John ffox .. } dated the 10th May 1696 for 100 acres of Land and ten Acres of Marsh on the North Side of Brandywine

By the Kings authority and in the name of the Honouble William Penn absolute Proprietor of the Province of Pennsilvana and Conties anexed

Att a Court held at New Castle the Seaventeenth day of November 1696 —— Before—

Richard Hallywell, John Donaldson, Cornelius Empson and John Richardson

Conveyances, deeds assignments &c acknowledged in Court—

Conveyance { Henry Wright & Jocabus Alrichs to James Read ... } dated the 17th day of November 1696 for a house and lott next to John Williams house and ground

Conveyance { Edward Lison .. to William Howston } dated the 13th of October 1696 for a tract of land in Town with housing, a negroe woman, a Cow, & Cafe, a horse &c acknowledged by George Hogg the Attorny of Edward Lison

Assignment { Henry Vanderburgh to John Watts .... } on the dack of a Pattent dated the 12th of the 2d month 1686 for a brick yard at the West end of the Town for thirty nine acres the assignment dated the 3d July 1696

Release { Peter Anderson to Broer Senex .. } dated the first of September 1696 for his portion of 3500 guilders

Conveyance { Paul & Elizabeth Paulson ... to Errick Errixon . } dated the 17th October 1696 for two lotts at Crane hook

Obligation { John Tosson . to Hans Peterson } dated the 27th of the 4th month 1696 for sixty pound for the payment of thirty pound in three payments

Lettery of Attorny { Edward Lison .. to Margarett Sherry } dated the 28th of September 1696 proved and allowed

Conveyance { Renier Vanderculine to Cornelius Empson . } dated the 17th of November 1696 for a house and parcell of ground between the ground of Edward Blake and Peter Alrichs, & the ground of James Claypoole

Conveyance { Paul & Elizabeth Paulson to Peter Anderson ...... } dated 16th November 1696 for 220a land and 25 acres of mash near Red Lyon Creek

Release { Errick Anderson to Paul Paulson .. } dated 21ᵗʰ of September 1696 of all his right to the estate of Olla Paulson

Conveyance { Henry Vanderburgh to John Richardson } dated the 4ᵗʰ of July 1696 for 440 acres land at Red Lyon Creek

Asignmᵗ { James Read ... to John Richardson } dated 17ᵗʰ November 1696 on the back of a Conveyance for a pˢ of ground in Otter Street

Conveyance { Richard Carr ... to John Donaldson Richard Hallywell Robert ffrench } dated the 3ᵈ of August 1696 for all the Mash at the North end of the Town

By the Kings authority in the name of the Honᵇˡᵉ William Penn Proprietary of the Province of Pennsilvania and Counties anexed

Att a Court held at New Castle the 16ᵗʰ day of March 1696 —Before

Peter Alrichs, Richard Hallywell, John Donaldson, Cornelius Empson & John Richardson Justices

Nicholas Lockier obligeth himself to James Read that Hillitie Anderson shall fully perform all the Articles & agreement She hath made with him about a house and lott in Town

Amos Nicholls Plᵗ
Bennony Clark Dft } upon a lease of Ejectment

Jacob Young the proper Plᵗ being dead the Court discontinue the action

John Richardson .... Plᵗ
Wᵐ Burroughs Admrs of Richard Hambly . } Dft   in an action of debt

The Pl^t by his Attorny appears & proves three bills for nine thousand pound of tobacco under the hand and Seal of Richard Hambly & the Def^t having nothing to object the Court give Judgment for the Same with cost

Henry Vanderburgh Pl^t.
Olla Olson ..... Df^t } breach of Articles

The Pl^t and Df^t appear, and the action depending on a tract of land about St Georges Sold to the Def^t and not paid for, the Def^t in open Court Surrenders up to the Pl^t the said land, with all the houses and improvements, the Plt consents thereto and releaseth him from the Articles, And admits him to remain on the premises till his crap now in the ground be taken off, which the Court confirm with cost.

Letter of Attorny { Edward Green to John Watts } dated the 12th day December 1696 proved & allowed

James Read acknowledged an Instrument dated the 5th of May 1693 to John Heally in trust, of his dwelling house and lotts in the Town of New Castle as a Joynture to his wife Anna, and to her heirs by him

Conveyances, deeds of Sale, Assignment & Releases for houses and lands acknowledged in open Court

Conveyances { John Bisk and Elizabeth his wife to Benjamin Swett } dated 17th December 1696 for a house and lott in the front Street of the Town

Conveyance { Henry Vanderburgh to Richard Askew.. } dated 17th November 1696 for four hundred acres of land at Georges Creek

Assignment on the back of a Conveyance... { Jacob Rotier.... to Renier Vanderculine } dated the 16th March 1696 for a lott of land & houses at Cranehook

Conveyance	Samuel Barker .... to Christopher Woolcock	dated the 16th March 1696 for two hundred acres of land at Redclay Creek
Mortgage	to Richard Mankin,	of the Same date for the Said land
Conveyance	James Read .... to Hillitie Anderson .	dated the 18th March 1696 for a house & lott in the front Street of New Castle
Release	Thomas Wollaston to Hillitie Anderson .	dated the 19th March 1696 of his right to the aforesd house & lott
Conveyance	Mathias Errixon to Errick Errixon .	dated the 3d ffebruary 1696 for a lott of land at Cranehook
Conveyance	Errick Errixon . . to Renier Vanderculine	dated the 16th March 1696 for a lott of land at Crane hook
Conveyance	Edward Lison to James Miller.	dated 24th September 1696 for a house and lott in the front of New Castle acknowledged by Edward Gibbs Attorny
Assignment of a deed .	John Ogle . . to John Latham	dated the 16th March 1696 for seaventy five acres of land at Christina bridge
Assignment on the back of a deed...	Edward Green to Robert Rotier	dated 17th day November 1696 for two hundred acres land at Christina Creek

Conveyance { John Hales to John Roe } dated 18th March 1696 for three hundred Acres of land near Georges Creek

Conveyance { John Ogle to John Crawford } dated 16th March 1696 for the upper half of a tract of land at White Clay Creek q^t three hundred acres

Conveyance { Renier Vanderculine & Margarett his wife to Mathias Vanderhyden } dated the 17th March 1696 for a house and lott in the front Street of New Castle

Conveyance { Renier Vanderculine to John Reynolds } dated the 16th March 1696 for a hundred and twenty five acres land at White Clay Creek

Conveyance { John Crawford to Edward Gibbs } dated the 16th March 1696 for a Plantation at Georges Creek, now in the possession of the Said Edward Gibbs

By the Kings Authority And in the Name of the Honble William Penn absolute Proprietary & Governo^r of Pensylvania and Counties annexed

Att a Court Held at New Castle the 21st November 1699
Before
Richard Halliwell Cornelious Empson Jno Richards & Jno Heally Justices

Jacob Young Pl^t } Upon a Title of Land by lease
William Woodland Def } of Ejectment

The P^{lt} and Def^t appeare and joyn Issue

The Plt declares for ffive hundred pounds Damage for the Def^{ts} unlawfully Holding possession of a Plantation and Tract of land at Georges Creeke

The Def^t Pleds not Guilty Whereupon a Jury is Called Impanneled and attested who upon their attestations doe find for the Plt twelve pence Damage with Cost of Suite which the Court Confirmed and gave Judgm^t

Att a Court held at Newcastle the fifteenth August 1699

Indenture { Nicholas Locker and his wife to John Heally .... } bearing date the 19th of August 1699 for a certain plantation Marsh and houses upon Delaware river, acknowledged in trust to John Healy

Conveyance { Joseph Cleyton to John Ogle ... } bearing date 15th of Augt 1699 for 444 acres of Land at White Clay Creek

Conveyance { Hans Peterson .. to The Sweedes Church } bearing date the 15th of August 1699 of a tract of land & Marsh at Verdredee hook Acknowledged to the Church Wardens in trust.

Conveyance { Edward Gibbs .. to Mathias Erickson } bearing date the 15th of August 1699 for two hundred Acres of Land at Scotts run Acknowledged in open Court

Conveyance { Jacobus Alrichs ffrom Mathias Erickson } bearing date August 1699 for two hundred Acres of Land neer the head of Toms run Acknowledged in Court

Conveyance { Hyppolitus lefevre To Joseph Pidgeon . } bearing date the 29th of August 1698 for a lott in the front Street of New Castle Acknowledged in open Court

Conveyance { James Read To John Richardson To John Donaldson } bearing date August 1699 for a parcell of ground the Otter Street and high Street Alias Wood Street contayning about Six Acres acknowledged in open Court

Conveyance { James Read To John Richardson } bearing date the Elevennth day of March 1699 for a house and two lotts of ground between Otter Street and bever Street Acknowledged in open Court—

John Gardner Pl^{tf}
Neill Cook Def^t Upon a Lease of ejectment

The proper Pl^{tf} William Guest in person and Cornelius Empson in Person Def^t Come into Court and Joyn Issue

The Pl^{tf} declares for a certain Messuge and Tenement with three hundred & Seventy Acres of Land lying and being between Whiteclay and Redclay Creek att the Upper end of bread and Cheese Iseland which the Def^t hath taken possession of The Def^t for plea Sayeth that ye s^d tract of Land is his proper right whereupon a Jury is called Impannelled and attested who find for ye Pl^{t}f the land in Contraversy and [torn] pounds damage with Cost of Suit. The Def^t: Craves an apeall to the provinciall Court in Equity which the Court grant from the Verdict of the Jury

Cornelius Empson recognizeth himself in the Summ of one hundred pound Currant money to be levyed of his land goods and Chattells for the use of Wm Guest Conditioned that he Shall prosecute this apeall before the Judges of the next provinciall Court in Equity to be held at New Castle and to pay all Costs and damages that Shall be there decreed ag^t him.

Lower Counties on Delaware Ss.

In pursuance of a Resolve of the Honorable House of Assembly of the Lower Counties on Delaware appointing us a Committee for causing the several Records of Transactions in the several Courts within the County of Newcastle, relating to the Titles of Lands, before the Year One thousand seven hundred, and of Warrants, Surveys, Patents, Deeds and Wills, signed, executed and Recorded before the same Year, in the several public Offices within the County aforesaid, to be Transcribed by the Officers respectively in whose custody they remain, and to compare them with the Originals, and make Report to the House of our Proceedings in the Premises. We Do now humbly report to the Honorable House that we have carefully caused such parts of the same Records to be transcribed as related in any wise to the Titles of the Lands within the said County, and have diligently compared the same with the Originals, and do certify that the foregoing Book marked (A) beginning with Folio one, on the tenth day of October in the year one thousand six hundred and seventy six, and ending with Folio five hundred and thirty, and on the twenty first day of November in the Year one thousand six hundred and ninety nine, contains nothing but true and genuine Proceedings faithfully and literally copied from Original Records.

                Evan Rice
                Tho M:Kean

INDEX OF PERSONS

Owing to the various nationalities of the Swedish, Dutch, English and Welsh settlers in Pennsylvania, together with the general illiteracy of the time, much diversity in the spelling of names will be found in the early court records. Some attempt has been made to represent the later accepted forms in this index.

Aside from the fact that with some the father's first name became the surname of the children we find that some names were changed so that they give no trace of identity, and others greatly changed from the original spelling.

Only one reference is given to a name on the same page.

Abrinck, Peter, 8, 9, 37, 85, 101, 110.
Abrink, see Abrinck.
Absinck, see Abrinck.
Addington, Isaac, 136, 137.
Aertsen, Jacob, 37, 38, 125, 144, 185.
Aertsen, Paul, 99.
Albertsen, Derrick, or Dirk, 70, 199.
Albertsen, John, 54, 55, 56.
Albertson, see Albertsen.
Aldrets, Evert, 21.
Allman, Joseph, 84, 211.
Alloway, John, 122, 131, 171.
Alloway, William, 114, 153, 199.
Allricks, see Alrichs.
Allum, Nicholas, 167.
Alman, see Allman.
Alrich, see Alrichs.
Alrichs, Jacob or Jacobus, 220, 227.
Alrichs, Peter or Pieter, 3, 12, 32, 35, 37, 45, 48, 50, 61, 67, 69, 71, 72, 80, 85, 93, 96, 101, 105, 109, 110, 113, 120, 125, 126, 127, 140, 142, 146, 148, 149, 151, 162, 165, 166, 168, 173, 174, 177, 196, 197, 199, 200, 202, 203, 204, 206, 207, 208, 219, 221, 222.
Alricks, see Allrichs.
Ambrooses, 71.
Anderson, see Andries, Andrieson and Andriessen.
Anderson, Alchy, 92.
Anderson, Andrew, 73.

Anderson, Erick or Errick, 214, 222.
Anderson, Gustavus, 123.
Anderson, Hendrick or Henrick, 27, 51, 68, 77, 79, 98, 115, 119, 189.
Anderson, Hillite or Hilitie, 218, 222, 224.
Anderson, John, 197.
Anderson, Justus, 92, 100, 112, 143, 144, 145, 156, 163, 165, 176, 179, 186, 187, 188, 189, 191.
Anderson, Lace or Lasse, 98.
Anderson, Widow, 173.
Andrews, George, 19.
Andries, see Anderson.
Andries, Claes, 37, 94, 98, 163, 169.
Andries, Eskell, 51, 53, 79.
Andries, Hendrick or Hendrik, 51, 53, 167.
Andries, Jacobus, 37, 85, 100, 125.
Andries, Jurian, 161, 162.
Andries, Justa, 7, 10, 15, 39, 79, 81, 84, 96, 120, 164, 168, 173, 176, 188, 194.
Andries, Lace or Lasse, 98.
Andries, Peter, 155, 156, 157, 163, 169, 173, 175, 176, 177, 178, 179, 221.
Andries, Roelof, Roalof, Roaloff or Rowlif, 9, 11, 12, 37, 38, 85, 92, 100, 101, 124, 125, 144, 158, 172, 185, 204, 207.
Andries, Widdow, 123.
Andrieson, Lauranc, 81.

INDEX OF PERSONS.

Andriessen, see Anderson and Andries.
Andriessen, Cristiaen, 37.
Andriessen, Mons or Moens, 147.
Andros, see Andross.
Andross, Edmond or Edmund, 5, 11, 12, 14, 15, 17, 18, 56, 57, 58, 62, 64, 65, 165.
Andross, Governor, 132, 147, 184, 185.
Appelthight, Joseph, 46, 47.
Appelthigt, see Appelthight.
Archer, Jacob, 86, 101.
Arskin, Jeane, 15, 16.
Arskin, Jonas or John, 7, 13, 15, 16, 27, 83, 95, 99, 103, 114, 116, 122, 166, 170, 181, 182, 186.
Artsen, see Aertsen.
Ashman, John, 65.
Ashman, John, Junior, 62.
Ashman, John, Senior, 63.
Ashton, Robert or Robart, 144, 173, 180, 181, 184, 186, 187, 188, 194, 197, 204, 205.
Askew, Richard, 219, 223.
Atkings, see Atkins.
Atkingson, see Atkins.
Atkins, Richard, 10.
Atkins, Sampson, 10, 123, 150, 202.
Atkins, Samuel, 206.
Atkins, Timothy, 217.

Babb, Thomas, 217.
Bainton, see Baynton.
Baker, Aeltie, 70.
Baker, Ambroos, Ambrose, Ambross or Ambros, 8, 37, 69, 70, 80, 89, 98, 169.
Baker, George, 100, 124, 172.
Bakers, see Baker.
Bandfall, William, 97.
Barecroft, Thomas, 68, 78.
Barentsan, see Barentsen.
Barentsen, John, 37, 46, 70, 81.
Baretsan, see Barentsen.
Barnes, Branchee, 91.
Barnes, Christopher, 190.
Barnes, Engelty, 91.
Barnes, Henry, 174.
Barnes, Joseph, 13, 16, 18, 37, 44, 75, 83, 103, 122, 128, 171.
Barnes, Paul, 218.
Barnes, Prudence, 177.
Barns, see Barnes.
Barker, see Berker.

Barret, Giles or Gyles, 13, 38, 40, 77, 80, 83, 103, 122, 171.
Barrett, see Barret.
Barrot, see Barret.
Barrott, see Barret.
Bayard, Peter, 37, 84, 99, 122, 174, 188.
Bayly, Charles, 103, 128.
Baynton, Peter, 127, 132, 157, 158, 160, 162, 163, 169, 179, 180, 181, 184, 188, 190, 192, 204.
Beacham, Richard, 170.
Beaston, George, 34.
Beekman, Matheus, 7.
Bell, Thomas, 13, 79, 84.
Bellis, Elizabeth, 158.
Bercker, see Berker.
Berker, Agnis, 17.
Berker, Elizabeth, 203.
Berker, John, 84, 100, 106.
Berker, Samuel, 6, 14, 15, 17, 75, 83, 103, 122, 124.
Best, Humphry, 106, 122, 147, 148, 202.
Beswick, see Beswike.
Beswike, Francis, 4.
Beswike, James, 4, 73, 95.
Bilderbeek, David, 37.
Bisck, see Bisk.
Biscus, see Bisk.
Bisk, Elizabeth, 212, 219, 223.
Bisk, Jan or John, 12, 27, 29, 37, 69, 80, 92, 97, 120, 168, 193, 212, 219, 223.
Bisk & Spark, 219.
Biske, see Bisk.
Biskus, see Bisk.
Bisse, Joseph, 144.
Blackleach, Benjamin, 133.
Blake, Edward, 116, 159, 160, 162, 165, 166, 168, 177, 180, 181, 183, 184, 188, 190, 193, 194, 196, 197, 200, 202, 203, 204, 205, 206, 207, 208, 209, 221.
Blake, Justice, 203.
Block, Mary, 27, 81, 98, 107, 120, 131, 168.
Blocq, see Block.
Blowfield, Benjamin, 131.
Boatsman, Jurian, 37, 79.
Boeyar, see Boyer.
Bond, Joseph, 122.
Booyar, see Boyer.
Boreson, Jurian, Urian or Urion, 82, 99, 119, 167.
Borkells, Herman, 188.

INDEX OF PERSONS.   231

Borsman, see Boreson.
Borsman, Urian, 119.
Boulton, Edward, 89, 98, 120, 168, 172.
Boulton, John, 192.
Bower, John, 81, 168.
Bowles, Joseph, 83, 163.
Boyer, John or Jan, 37, 71, 97, 120.
Bradshaw, James, 143, 169, 188, 190, 198, 204.
Bradshaw, John, 171.
Bradshaw, Mr., 143.
Brainton, see Baynton.
Brasie, Thomas, 23.
Brewerton, Samuel, 199, 217.
Brewstor, John, 170.
Bro, Christian, 121.
Brockholls, Anthony, 23.
Brooks, James, 172.
Bridgman, Richard, 116.
Brisco, John, 82.
Bristoll, John, 122.
Brown, James, 103, 111.
Bryant, Anthony, Antony or Antonous, 37, 69, 70, 80, 96, 116, 120, 148, 150, 163, 168, 205.
Buckley, John, 103, 125, 169.
Buckly, see Buckley.
Buckworth, Bryan, 197.
Burch, H. V. D., 62.
Burgin, Philip, 59.
Burgis, Anthony, 171.
Burgraue, see Burgrave.
Burgrave, John, 165, 169, 176, 177.
Burk, John, 206.
Burnam, see Burnham.
Burnham, Joseph, 97, 149, 150, 155.
Burroughs, William, 172, 222.
Burrows, see Burroughs.
Byard, see Bayard.

Cain, John, 206.
Cambell, Alexander, Elixander or Alixander, 100, 124, 172.
Cammel, see Cambell.
Can, see Cann.
Cann, John, 13, 14, 16, 17, 18, 23, 25, 26, 35, 43, 45, 48, 50, 51, 53, 67, 69, 80, 83, 87, 88, 89, 90, 91, 92, 93, 94, 95, 96, 97, 103, 104, 105, 107, 109, 110, 113, 116, 117, 118, 120, 122, 126, 127, 136, 142, 144, 146, 148, 149, 151, 162, 165, 166, 168, 171, 174, 177, 179, 180, 181, 185, 194, 196, 197, 200, 202, 203, 204, 207.
Cann, Justice, 203.
Cann, Mary, 16, 17.
Cantwell, 144.
Cantwell, Captain, 33, 34, 72, 114.
Cantwell, Captain Edmund, 132.
Cantwell, Edmund or Edmond, 3, 8, 12, 19, 26, 31, 33, 40, 42, 61, 62, 78, 81, 84, 88, 91, 95, 96, 97, 100, 105, 111, 112, 120, 121, 199.
Cantwell, Mary, 131.
Cantwell, Richard, 216.
Carelton, Arthur, 58.
Carr, Patrick, 87.
Carr, Richard, 222.
Carr, Sir Robberd, 16.
Carter, John, 81, 90.
Cartwell, Nathaniel, 171.
Cauging, Jonas, 83.
Chambers, Benjamin, 111.
Chambers, William, 169.
Champion, John, 203.
Chandler, Philip, 101.
Charles II, King of England, 23.
Cheeke, William, 86.
Choes, John, 85.
Christian, 85.
Claassen, Grety, 163.
Claassen, Jacob, 37, 79, 82, 94, 98, 119, 163, 167.
Claassen, Pieter, or Peter, 13, 37.
Claeson, see Claassen.
Clark, Bennony, 222.
Clark, James, 83, 103.
Clark, Kenhelm, 215.
Clasan, see Claassen.
Clasen, see Claassen.
Clason, see Claassen.
Clausan, see Claassen.
Claypole, see Claypoole.
Claypool, see Claypoole.
Claypoole, James, 103, 122, 133, 155, 165, 169, 170, 176, 210, 219, 221.
Clayton, Joseph, 169, 197, 226.
Clemens, see Clementsen.
Clemensen, see Clementsen.
Clemensen, Oele or Oela, 37, 48, 49, 50.
Clements, see Clementsen.
Clementsen, Jacob, 37, 48, 49, 50, 83, 103, 126, 169.
Clementson, see Clementsen.
Clementss, see Clementsen.
Clifton, Thomas, 113, 125, 127, 132, 170.
Cloud, William, 125, 169.

INDEX OF PERSONS.

Cloude, Jeremiah, 169.
Coch, Otto Ernest, 64.
Cock, Jan Eskelsen, 37.
Cock, John, 169, 192.
Cock, Lasse, Lausa, Laussa, Laurane or Laurens, 63, 64, 65, 66, 77.
Cock, Peter Eskelsen, 37.
Cock, Symon, 169, 172.
Cock, Symon Eskelsen, 37.
Coderus, Hans, 6, 19, 37, 80, 92, 150.
Codington, Elizabeth, 184, 185, 186, 187.
Codington, William, 184, 185, 186, 187.
Coeckoe, Oele, 20.
Cole, Edward, 208.
Cole, John, 173, 206.
Collet, Jeremiah, 182.
Collet, John, 171.
Comoco, Cornelius, 125.
Cook, Francis, 174.
Cook, Neil or Neill, 218, 227.
Cookson, Joseph, 13, 44, 83, 122, 270.
Constantin, see Constantine.
Constantine, Coenraet, Conrad or Conrade, 13, 37, 82, 103, 126, 177, 189, 204.
Constantinus, see Constantine.
Conway, Thomas, 170.
Coop, see Coope.
Coope, Oliver, 103, 125, 269.
Corderus, see Coderus.
Cornelison, Jacob, 99, 120, 168.
Corseer, William, 81.
Couch, John, 152, 153, 171.
Couche, see Couch.
Coulson, Matt, 169.
Coursey, Henry, 188.
Courtney, Robert or Robart, 100, 166, 174, 181.
Courtny, see Courtney.
Courtry, Elizabeth, 166.
Coustourier, Elizabeth, 205.
Coustourier, Henry, 209.
Crawford, James, 38.
Crawford, John, 225.
Crawford, Judith, Judah or Judy, 38, 39, 81, 85, 101, 110, 123, 125.
Creeker, Alexander, 192.
Croesie, William, 9, 37, 97, 121, 212.
Crosee, see Croesie.

Daniell, Claes, 80, 81, 97, 121, 155, 168.
Darby, John, 13, 73, 80, 85, 101, 116, 126, 148, 150, 156, 168, 172, 179, 182, 183, 189, 190, 191, 204.
Darby, Robert or Robart, 88, 124, 154, 167.
Darkin, Richard, 144.
Darkings, Robert or Robart, 135, 136.
Darvall, William, 72.
Daston, John, 53, 54, 55.
Dauis, see Davis.
Davis, Lewis, 4, 34, 95, 98.
Davis, Nicholas, 139.
Davis, Phillip, 171.
Davis, Simon or Symon, 139, 140.
Daw, Nicholas, 171.
DeBrina or Debrina, Catalinta, 117.
De Coomink, Peter, 37.
De Cou, Abraham, 205.
De Cou, Hannah, 184, 185,187, 205.
De Cou, Isaac or Isack, 144.
De Cou, Jacob, 144, 173, 175.
De Cow, see De Cou.
De Does, John, 120.
Defoss, Mathyas or Mathias, 92.
De Gam, Moses, 37, 81, 83, 97, 121, 168.
De Haen, Justa Andries, 37.
De Haes, Johannes or John, 3, 12, 16, 17, 18, 19, 21, 23, 29, 32, 43, 45, 50, 61, 67, 71, 81, 86, 97, 100, 107, 111, 116, 120, 124, 131, 145, 162, 166, 168, 172, 174, 177, 185, 196, 199.
Dejam, see De Gam.
De Lagrang, see De Lagrange.
De Lagrange, Arnold or Arnoldus, 23, 25, 26, 31, 35, 37, 45, 48, 67, 77, 79, 83, 90, 91, 97, 102, 119, 121, 145, 148, 156, 161, 162, 163, 165, 167, 170.
De Lagrange, Cornelia, 163.
Denny, John, 56, 57, 58.
De Ring, Emilius or Aemilius, 29, 30, 31, 37, 60, 70, 72, 81, 96, 114, 120, 168, 193, 212, 217.
De Ring, Mathias or Matheus, 37, 39, 71, 80, 96, 120, 168.
De Ringh, see De Ring.
Derrickson, see Dircksen.
Devoos, Giesbert, 82.
Devoos, Gisbert Johnson, 162.
Devoos, Mathias or Mathyas, 5,

INDEX OF PERSONS. 233

12, 37, 38, 98, 103, 116, 121, 147, 170, 181.
Devoos, Walraeven Jansen, 18.
De Vos, see Devoos.
Dewit, Marinus, 215.
Dewit, Peter, 37, 39, 46, 81, 113.
Dewit, Tennis or Tunis, 81, 101, 125, 149.
Dewson, John, 81.
D' Haes, see De Haes.
D' Hinjossa, Alexander (Governor), 70, 71.
D' Honeur, Giljam, 71.
Dircksen, Cornelius, 187, 199.
Dircksen, Gisbert or Gysbert, 31, 32, 41, 42.
Dirksen, see Dircksen.
Dirksen, Aeltie, 30.
Dirksen, Anna, 30.
Dirksen, Cattalyntie, 29, 30.
Dirksen, Cornelius, 214.
Dirksen, Gysbert or Gybert, 29, 30, 72.
Dirksen, Susanna, 29, 30.
Dirkss, see Dircksen.
D' Lagrange, see De Lagrange.
Doedus, John, 98.
Doll, see Dull.
Doller, Nicholas, 172.
Donaldson, John, 192, 204, 210, 211, 213, 215, 216, 217, 218, 219, 220, 222, 227.
Drewet, see Druit.
D' Ring, see De Ring.
Druet, see Druit.
Druit, Morgan, 20, 21, 38, 82, 125, 169.
Dulgar, Hendrik, 37.
Dull, Henry or Hendrik, 10, 37, 83, 102, 122, 171.
Dunkarton, Elizabeth, 209.
Dunn, John, 211.
Duthay, Daniel, 90.
Dyer, Robert or Robart, 116, 168, 182, 183, 186, 187, 189, 191, 197, 206.
Dyer, William, 133, 139, 143, 144.
Dyer, William, Junior, 136, 137, 138, 139, 140.
Dyer, William (Major), 137, 142, 143.
Dyre, see Dyer.

Eb burgh, Edward, 196.
Edmunds, 143.
Edmunds, John, 14.
Egber, see Egberts.

Egberts, Abiah, 162, 184.
Egberts, Barent, 108, 130, 144, 184.
Egberts, Eldert, 80.
Eglington, Edward, 19, 103, 169, 182.
Eglinton, see Eglington.
Elderkin, John, 86, 126.
Ellet, see Ellit.
Ellis, Humphry, 114.
Ellis, John, 217, 219.
Ellis, Thomas, 163.
Ellit, Christopher, 61, 66, 67, 84, 92, 176.
Ellit, Widdow, 99.
Ellitt, see Ellit.
Emly, Luke, 216.
Empson, Cornelius, 108, 110, 113, 117, 126, 127, 142, 146, 149, 162, 165, 166, 169, 173, 174, 176, 177, 186, 191, 192, 196, 203, 204, 210, 211, 213, 216, 217, 220, 221, 222, 225, 227, 228.
Emsen, see Empson.
Enloos, Abraham or Abram, 37, 85.
Erickson, see Erikson.
Erikson, Errick, 221, 224.
Erikson, Jan or John, 48, 49, 146.
Erikson, Mathias, 169, 224, 226, 227.
Erixon, see Erikson.
Erixson, see Erikson.
Errixon, see Erikson.
Erskin, Jonas, 10.
Eskelson, Jan or John, 29, 39.
Eskelson, Margaret, 29, 39.
Eskelson, Mathias, 29, 39, 40.
Eskelson, Peter, 29.
Eskelson, Symon, 29, 39.
Euertson, see Evertson.
Evans, Robert, 193.
Everts, see Evertson.
Evertsen, see Evertson.
Evertson, Hendrick or Henry, 37, 51, 52, 79, 98, 119, 148, 149, 155, 167, 192.
Ewster, Edward, 140.

Fabee, 84.
Faulkenburg, John, 119.
Fawks, Owen, 174.
Field, John, 100.
Field, Samuel, 44.
Fisher, George, 186, 191, 194.
Floyd, Thomas P., 196.
Folk, John, 80, 155.
Folk, Sybrant, 80, 85.

INDEX OF PERSONS.

Folcher, Peter, 107.
Folchr, see Folcher.
Foratt, see Foreat.
Fordham, Benjamin, 201.
Foreat, John, 97, 121, 168, 188, 189, 190, 194, 196, 205, 209.
Foreman, see Forman.
Forman, George, 87, 182, 188, 220.
Forsbeen, see Forsben.
Forsben, Eldred, Eldert, Eldort or Eldren, 13, 37, 81, 93.
Forstbeen, see Forsben.
Foster, John, 85, 101, 124.
Fourniss, see Furness..
Fox, John, 220.
Framton, William, 128.
Francis, Mary, 84.
Fransen, Derick, 89.
Fransen, Hendrik, 37.
Fransen, Michall, 160.
Fransen, Oele, Olla or Woolla, 125, 160, 179, 192.
Franson, see Fransen.
French, Robert, 166, 186, 201, 219, 222.
Furby, Thomas, 99.
Furness, Henry, 122, 170.

Gardner, John, 227.
Garetson, see Gerritsen.
Garretson, see Gerritsen.
Gasper, Thomas, 192, 207, 208.
Gelping, Thomas, 82, 84, 100, 102, 123, 125, 169, 174.
Gerret, see Gerritsen.
Gerretson, see Gerritsen.
Gerrits, see Gerritsen.
Gerritsen, Abiah, 218.
Gerritsen, Cattalyntie, 31, 32.
Gerritsen, Gerrit, 7, 16.
Gerritsen, Hendrik or Henrik, 13, 37.
Gerritsen, Henry, 13, 37, 75, 83, 103, 146.
Gerritsen, Jacob, 97.
Gerritsen, John, 7, 80, 99, 119, 167, 182, 191, 218.
Gerritsen, Martin, 12.
Gerritsen, Mr., 43.
Gerritsen, Poull or Paul, 7, 37, 83.
Gerritson, see Gerritsen.
Gerritz, see Gerritsen.
Gerritze, see Gerritsen.
Gerritzen, see Gerritsen.
Gessop, William, 170.

Geuesse, see Guest.
Geuest, see Guest.
Gibbs, Edward, 149, 151, 167, 173, 174, 183, 187, 193, 203, 205, 206, 207, 210, 213, 215, 218, 224, 225, 226.
Gibbs, Judith, 149.
Gilbert, Thomas, 4.
Gillet, Thomas, 69, 77, 83, 102, 114, 122, 155, 167, 171.
Glazier, Leneord the, 169.
Goddin, see Godwin.
Godin, see Godwin.
Godwin, Peter, 156, 169, 186.
Goforth, Robert, 199, 200.
Goforth, William, 199, 200.
Goodman, Benjamin, 76.
Gouldsmith, Joana or Joanna, 195, 196.
Gouldsmith, Samuel, 195.
Grampton, see Gramton.
Gramton, John, 127, 140, 141, 147, 151, 152, 153, 154, 155, 161, 165, 181, 194.
Grant, William, 39, 43, 84, 100, 101, 123, 124, 144, 173.
Grant's Land, John on, 85, 101.
Graues, see Graves.
Graves, Thomas, 121, 171.
Green, Ann, 162, 184.
Green, Anthony, 186, 187.
Green, Edward, 86, 94, 101, 105, 106, 107, 109, 112, 122, 124, 127, 132, 133, 137, 139, 142, 145, 147, 148, 155, 157, 175, 176, 177, 178, 183, 187, 202, 206, 223, 224.
Green, Edward, Junior, 148.
Green, Edward, Senior, 127, 156, 163, 165, 172, 174, 176, 178.
Green, John, 130, 144.
Green, Justice, 130.
Green, Thomas & Company, 171.
Green, William, 59, 60, 99.
Greene, see Green.
Gregs, see Griggs.
Grigg, see Griggs.
Griggs, John, 122, 170.
Griggs, William, 122, 170.
Grub, Henry, 11.
Grub, John, 13, 103, 125, 169, 208.
Grubb, see Grub.
Guest, William, 21, 38, 69, 72, 78, 83, 95, 102, 107, 117, 118, 121, 126, 127, 142, 149, 151, 170, 180, 181, 182, 192, 227, 228.
Gulping, see Gelping.

INDEX OF PERSONS.

Gumbley, see Gumley.
Gumley, Benjamin, 84, 100, 123, 145, 174, 201, 203, 204.
Gumly, see Gumley.
Gysbert's Land, 9.

Haigh, William, 23, 79, 97, 106.
Hales, John, 169, 225.
Halliday, Engelly, 166.
Halliday, James, 91, 98, 114, 118, 120, 167.
Halliwell, see Hallywell.
Hallman, Joseph, 122, 149, 174.
Hallman, Margaret, 149.
Hallman, Peter, 103, 125.
Hallman, Peter Andries, 93, 108.
Hallyday, see Halliday.
Hallywell, Richard, 162, 165, 168, 173, 174, 177, 193, 199, 205, 208, 209, 219, 220, 222, 225.
Hambly, Richard, 187, 222, 223.
Hamilton, Josyne or Josyn, 168, 179, 193.
Hanly, William, 170.
Hansen, Hans or John, 9, 85, 99, 101, 172, 207, 208, 209, 211, 219.
Hanslo, Peter, 101.
Hanson, see Hansen.
Hard, Captain Henry, 144.
Hardy, James, 81.
Harland, George, 172.
Harman, see Herman.
Harmansan, see Hermensen.
Harmanson, see Hermensen.
Harmenson, see Hermensen.
Harms, John, 198.
Harris, John, 174.
Harris, Joseph, 84, 100, 123, 174, 177.
Harris, Thomas, 19, 79, 99, 123, 143, 174, 178.
Harrison, Edward, 218.
Harrison, Thomas, 84, 174.
Harry, Edward, 82.
Hartop, John, 199, 200.
Hartop, John's child, 123.
Hartop, John's children, 174.
Hatten, William, 99, 123, 174.
Hatton, see Hatten.
Hauge, see Haigh.
Hauke, Rand, 169.
Hay, Adam, 81, 113, 145, 149, 168, 215.
Hayly, John, 11, 101, 108, 145, 172, 173, 175, 186, 188, 190, 193, 194, 196.

Haym, Artman, 81, 89, 90, 98, 106, 120, 167, 207.
Haym, Mathew, 207.
Hayn, see Haym.
Hazell, John, 66.
Heally, see Healy.
Healy, Anna, 223.
Healy, John, 200, 202, 204, 213, 215, 216, 223, 225, 226.
Heath, Jam, 196.
Heddings, Laurens, 66.
Helm, Israel, or Isarel, 121, 170.
Hemlott, Richard, 172.
Hendricks, see Hendricksen, Hendrix, Henricks and Henrix.
Hendricks, David, 13, 125.
Hendricks, Evert or Euert, 95, 96.
Hendricks, Hybert, 80.
Hendricks, John, 71, 96.
Hendricksen, Barent, 218.
Hendricksen, Evert, 37.
Hendricksen, Hendrick, 214.
Hendricksen, Jacob, 83, 121, 170, 214.
Hendricksen, John, 7, 37, 81, 120, 145, 168, 193, 198.
Hendrickson, see Hendricksen.
Hendriksen, see Hendricksen.
Hendrix, see Hendricks.
Henrichs, see Hendricks.
Henrick, 114, 125.
Henrickson, see Hendricksen.
Henrix, see Hendricks.
Herman, Caspar or Caspares, 9, 10, 11, 12, 35, 37, 43, 48, 59, 61, 67, 77, 85, 87, 89, 92, 93, 94, 95, 100, 104, 125, 142, 156, 157, 159, 168, 172, 174, 199.
Herman, Ephraim or Epherim, 3, 11, 16, 17, 18, 22, 37, 51, 53, 56, 57, 58, 59, 60, 61, 62, 64, 65, 66, 77, 80, 84, 86, 97, 99, 119, 120, 123, 143, 147, 148, 150, 155, 159, 168, 172, 174, 199.
Herman, Mr., 42.
Hermensen, Jan or John, 13, 37, 38, 62, 69, 78, 81, 92, 97, 109, 111, 120, 132, 148, 168.
Herms, see Hermensen.
Hermsen, see Hermensen.
Hiberts, Widow, 97.
Hickman, Samuel, 166.
Hiljard, see Hillyard.
Hillyard, John, 53, 54, 55, 56, 93.
Hogg, George, 197, 211, 214, 220.
Hogg, George, Junior, 171.

INDEX OF PERSONS.

Hogg, George, Senior, 171.
Holden, see Holding.
Holdin, see Holding.
Holding, John, 73.
Holding, Joseph, 84, 85, 88, 100, 123, 155, 173, 174, 176, 201, 211.
Hollingsworth, Valentine, Valantine or Vallantine, 82, 86, 89, 91, 92, 93, 94, 95, 102, 105, 107, 110, 113, 115, 117, 118, 126, 142, 146, 165, 170, 174, 181, 190, 208, 211.
Holms, Thomas, 23.
Horsly, Ralph, 84, 99, 122.
Houlding, see Holding.
How, see Howe.
Howe, John, 116, 210.
Howston, William, 220.
Huckin, Francis, 156.
Hudden, Richard, 9, 86, 101, 109, 124, 172, 179, 181.
Hudding, see Hudden.
Huddy, see Hudden.
Hulk, John, 97, 107, 166.
Humpherys, see Humphries.
Humpheris, see Humphries.
Humphries, Ellis, 85, 101, 125, 173.
Huns, John, 171.
Hussey, John, 212.
Hutcheson, see Hutchinson.
Hutchinson, Francis, 122, 155.
Hutchinson, Ralph, 50, 72, 73.
Hutchinson, Robert, Robart or Robberd, 50, 77, 80, 86, 87, 88, 93, 96, 101, 116, 119, 124, 143, 167, 172, 182, 191.
Hutchisen, see Hutchinson.
Hutchison, see Hutchinson.
Hyam, see Haym.
Hybert, see Hybertsen.
Hyberts, see Hybertsen.
Hybertsen, Dirck, Dirk or Dierick, 19, 37, 71, 81.
Hybertsen, Hendrik, 19.
Hybertsen, John Dan, 169.

Ikey, Adam, 199.
Ingelo, Richard, 86, 100, 124.
Inloes, Abraham, 199, 214.
Iris, John, 103.

Jackson, Isack J., 196.
Jackson, Samuel, 62, 65.
Jacobson, Henry, 122, 160, 171.
Jacobson, Paul, 171.
Jacquet, Jan or Jean Paul, 37, 94, 109, 112.
Jacquet, Jan, Junior, 37.
Jacquet, John, 79, 98, 99, 106, 117, 120, 146, 167.
Jacquet, John, Senior, 105.
Jacquet, Pieter or Peter, 37, 82, 119, 167, 210, 219.
James, Duke of York and Albany, 21, 24, 56, 62.
Janes, Nathaniel, 211.
Jans, see Jansen.
Jans, Annettie, 31.
Jans, Walburg, 49.
Jansen, see Jans.
Jansen, Anna, 146.
Jansen, Arent or Aaron, 7, 71, 75, 76, 83, 102, 121, 170.
Jansen, Cornelius, 46, 81.
Jansen, Gisbert, 83.
Jansen, Jacob, 75.
Jansen, Jurian or Urian, 113, 115, 117.
Jansen, Symon, 51, 52, 146.
Jansen, Walraeven or Walrauen, 14, 15, 17, 147.
Janson, see Jansen.
Jaquet, see Jacquet.
Jaruice, see Jarvis.
Jarvice, see Jarvis.
Jarvis, John, 6, 85, 124, 173.
Jegou, Peter, 37.
Jenings, Samuel, 203.
Jerson, John, 82.
Jervice, see Jarvis.
Jessop, see Ysop and Ysops.
Jessop, William, 102, 121.
Johnso, Pieter or Peter, 10, 108, 124, 172.
Johnsoe, see Johnso.
Johnsoes, see Johnso.
Johnson, see Jans, Jansen, and Jonson.
Johnson, Bilchy, 118.
Johnson, Catharin or Catherin, 51, 53.
Johnson, Claes or Claus, 84, 100.
Johnson, Derick or Dierick, 84, 100, 122.
Johnson, Elizabeth, 98.
Johnson, Francis, 123, 174.
Johnson, Garret, or Gerret, 81, 120, 168.
Johnson, Harman, Harmen or Herman, 37, 81, 131.
Johnson, Harman, widow of, 98.
Johnson, Ould, 84.

INDEX OF PERSONS. 237

Johnson, Sybran, Sybram or Sybrant, 37, 81, 98, 119, 166, 167.
Johnson, William or Willem, 51, 53, 79, 115.
Jones, Charles, Jr., 131.
Jones, Edward, 181.
Jones, Griffith, 209.
Jones, Henry, 64, 69, 81, 98, 120, 131, 155, 157, 159.
Jones Thomas, 169, 189, 190, 191, 207.
Jonson, see Jansen.
Jonson, Clare, 122.
Jordins, Doctor, 42.
Juriansan, Christian, 106, 107.
Jurianson, see Juriansan and Urianson.
Justy, Mouns or Moens, 169.

Kemmel, William, 96.
Kennedy, William W., 184.
Kettle, Cornelius, 205.
Killingworth, Isaac, 85.
King, Ann, 215.
King, John, 46, 47.
King, Samuel, 46, 47.

Laersen, see Lawson.
La Grange, see De Lagrange.
Lagrange, see De Lagrange.
Land, Dorcas, 167, 182.
Land, Edward, 80, 99, 119, 146, 167, 182, 213.
Land, Mr., 152.
Land, Samuel or Samuell, 9, 27, 28, 47, 52, 53, 80, 83, 87, 88, 89, 90, 91, 92, 94, 95, 96, 97, 104, 105, 107, 109, 110, 119, 127, 141, 142, 153, 181.
Langshaw, Thomas, 81, 96, 102, 122, 168, 171.
Lantsom, Henry, 83.
Lareson, see Lawson.
Larson, see Lawson.
Latham, John, 218, 224.
Latts, see Letts.
Laurance, see Lourensen.
Laurane, see Lourensen.
Lauranson, see Lourensen.
Laurence, see Lourensen.
Laurens, see Lourensen.
Laurenson, see Lourensen.
Laurentsen, see Lourensen.
Laurier, Harmon or Harmen, 37, 81.
Law, see Lawe.

Lawe, John, 143, 144.
Lawe, Thomas, 101, 124, 173.
Lawranson, see Lourensen.
Lawree, see Laurier.
Lawrenson, see Lourensen.
Laws, see Lawe.
Lawson, Lasse, 98.
Lawson, Mathyas, 82, 98, 119, 167.
Lawson, Neels or Neiles, 122, 171.
Lawson, Paul, Pauell, Poul or Powell, 37, 79, 82, 112, 119, 167.
Leauesly, see Leavesly.
Leavesly, Joseph, 148.
Lefevor, Hypolitus or Hyppolitus, 211, 215, 227.
Lefevre, see Lefevor.
Legrange, see De Lagrange.
Lemens, see Lemmens.
Lemmens, Anneky, 192.
Lemmens, Hendrick, Hendrik or Henry, 19, 37, 50, 51, 52, 68, 77, 79, 82, 94, 95, 98, 107, 109, 110, 113, 114, 117, 118, 119, 127, 141, 142, 146, 148, 149, 151.
Lemmens, Widow, 167.
Lesser, Will, 83.
Lester, Peter, 219, 220.
Lester, William, 102, 115, 126, 170, 170, 200.
Letts, Francis, 99, 122, 174.
Lewden, John, 213.
Lewden, Roger, Junior, 204.
Lewden, Roger, Senior, 204.
Lindsay, see Lindsey.
Lindsey, Daniel, 88.
Lindsey, Edmund or Edmond, 13, 124, 173, 206.
Lindsey, Sarah, 110.
Lison, Edward, 211, 220, 221, 224.
Liston, Morris, 58, 61, 62, 84, 99, 123, 174.
Lite, Paul, 133, 135, 136.
Little, William, 97, 119.
Lloyd, David, 209.
Locker, see Lockier.
Lockier, Nicholas, 207, 210, 211, 213, 215, 216, 217, 222, 226.
Logan, Robert, 201.
Longshaw, see Langshaw.
Lorrain, 80.
Lott, Engelbert, 37, 79, 97, 120, 166, 168.
Loue, see Love.
Lourensen, Carsten, 19.
Lourensen, Dirk, 8, 9, 129, 130.
Lourensen, Grietie, 9.

INDEX OF PERSONS.

Lourensen, Huybert or Hybert, 9, 11, 12, 37, 81, 86, 92, 98, 101, 125, 129, 130, 173.
Lourensen, Marcus, 113.
Lourentsen, see Lourensen.
Love, Andrew, 6, 73, 84, 95, 99, 123, 174, 196.
Lovelace, Francis, 16, 62, 69.
Lovelace, Governor, 114, 185.
Lyte, see Lite.

Macdonnell, Bryan, 171.
Mac Gregory, Hugh, 177, 186, 188, 189, 191, 192, 193.
Machaeksitt, see Mechaeksitt.
Mackarty, Daniel or Daniell, 99, 123.
Mackarty, Ellen or Ellin, 205.
Mackarty, John, 173, 199, 200, 205.
Mackarty, Patrick, 218.
Mackgregory, see Mac Gregory.
Macklin, John, 85, 101.
Mackomb, see Macomb.
Mackony, John, 155.
Macomb, John, 171.
Maesland, Pieter or Peter, 37, 39.
Maitland, John, 46, 47.
Mall, Francis, 84.
Man, Abram or Abraham, 38, 43, 45, 67, 68, 75, 76, 77, 78, 83, 93, 96, 102, 122, 130, 146, 162, 164, 171, 180, 181, 187, 193.
Man, Adam, 45.
Man, William, 122, 171.
Manday, see Mandy.
Mandy, John, 19, 80, 96, 97, 107, 120, 152.
Mandy, Mary, 182.
Mandy, Widow, 168.
Mankin, Richard, 156, 182, 224.
Mann, see Man.
Marcus, see Markussen.
Markham, Captain, 80, 96, 142, 143.
Markham, William, 23, 25, 26, 35, 48, 136, 137, 168, 187, 210.
Markham, Captain William, 143.
Markham, Secretary, 160.
Markussen, Hans, 37, 124.
Marshall, Jarvis or Jaruis, 87.
Marshland, see Marslander.
Marslander, Barbara, 89, 90, 108, 110, 120.
Marslander, Hugh, 114, 122, 170.
Marslander, Willow, 81.
Martin, George, 178.
Martin, Jeffry, 209.

Maruill, see Marvill.
Marvill, William, 95.
Mash, Hugh, 123.
Massey, Samuel, 135, 136, 137, 138.
Massillant, Lymon or Symon, 217.
Masson, Gyles Barrot, 10.
Massyan, Henry, 97.
Mathews, James, 72.
Mathews, Thomas, 171.
Mathias or Mathyas, 167.
Mathiass, see Mathiassen.
Mathiasse, see Mathiassen.
Mathiassen, John, 10, 13, 98.
Mathiassen, Mathias, 6, 12.
Mathiassen, Sybrant, 7.
Mathyason, see Mathiassen.
Mattland, John, 21, 111, 116, 126.
Mattshall, Lucas, 174.
Mattshall, Richard, 81, 100, 174.
Mattson, John, 51, 53, 79, 148.
Mayl, Mary, 216.
Mayle, see Mayl.
McKarty, see Mackarty.
McKean, Thomas, 228.
Mechaeksitt, 60, 61.
Meghaeksitt, see Mechaeksitt.
Mercer, Robert, 203.
Mettland, see Mattland.
Michall, see Mattshall.
Milkes, Erasmus, 101.
Miller, Hans, 69, 91, 126.
Miller, Hans Hansen, 7, 37.
Miller, James, 224.
Mineveil, Gabriel, 72, 135.
Minveil, see Mineveil.
Minviell, see Mineveil.
Mitchell, see Mattshall.
Moensen, Jan, 37.
Moll, Christian, Christiana or Christina, 78, 106, 145, 165, 177, 201, 202.
Moll, John, 3, 8, 12, 15, 16, 19, 22, 23, 25, 26, 35, 43, 45, 48, 50, 67, 69, 70, 78, 80, 83, 88, 90, 91, 103, 106, 118, 121, 132, 145, 165, 166, 168, 172, 176, 177, 188, 189, 190, 201, 202, 209, 211.
Moll, John, Junior, 106.
Moll, John, Senior, 106.
Money, Robert, or Robart, 85, 100, 123, 173.
Monforde, John, 54, 55, 56.
Monson, John, 82, 103.
Monson, Paul, 83, 103, 189, 190, 196.
Moor, see More.

INDEX OF PERSONS. 239

Moore, see More.
More, George, 8, 10, 33, 69, 77, 80, 89, 93, 94, 96, 105, 114, 121, 127, 141, 150, 151, 184, 218.
More, Joseph, 13, 77, 79, 81, 84, 98, 99, 101, 104, 109, 123, 124, 197, 203.
Moreton, see Morton.
Morgan, John, 56, 57, 58, 59.
Morgen, see Morgan.
Morris, William, 163, 178.
Morton, Ellinor, Elinor or Elenor, 79, 100, 112.
Morton, Helena, 88.
Morton, Robert or Robart, 79, 84, 173.
Morton, Widow, 85, 123.
Mouns, John, 169.
Mouns, Peter, 169.
Mounsen, see Monson.
Mounson, see Monson.
Murrey, Widow, 169.
Myare, see Meyer.
Myer, see Meyer.
Myeres, see Meyer.
Myers, see Meyer.

Nealson, Hendrik, 48, 49.
Nealson, Jan Hendrikson, or Hendricx, 49.
Nealson, John, 49.
Nealson, Mathias, 49.
Nealson, Niels or Nieles, 37, 103, 127, 132, 169, 179, 192.
Nealson, Walburgh, 48, 49.
Neering, John Willems, John Williams or John Willemsen, 37, 62, 80, 145.
Neeterdale, Ann, 100.
Nellson, see Nelson.
Nelson, John, 136, 137, 138, 139.
Nelson, Nicholas, 83.
Nettleship, Job, 89, 99, 119, 150.
Nettleship, John, 80.
Nevill, James, 17, 129.
Nicholls, Amos, 124, 133, 173, 222.
Nicholls, Captain, 42.
Nicholls, Humphry or Humphery, 82, 98.
Nicholls, Matthias, 57, 64.
Nicoles, see Nicholls.
Nicolls, see Nicholls.
Nielsen, see Nealson.
Nielson, see Nealson.

Noble, Richard, 3, 60, 67, 77, 86, 100, 116, 125, 132, 157, 159, 169, 173, 187, 206.
Nomers, John, 16, 18, 37, 44, 75, 77, 82, 94, 103, 128.
Nomerson, see Nummerson.
Numers, see Nomers.
Nummers, see Nomers.
Nummersen, John, 13, 16, 18, 44, 122.

Oalson, see Oelsen.
Oelkens, Sick, 37.
Oelsen, Hans, 20, 21.
Oelsen, Helena, 20, 21.
Oelsen, Lasse, 108.
Oelsen, Lauranc, 82.
Oelsen, Michal or Michiel, 37, 103.
Oelsen, Oella, 223.
Oelsen, Peter, 103.
Oelsen, Sick or Sicca, 103, 115.
Offley, Michall, 84, 99, 123, 125, 174.
Offly, see Offley.
Ogle, Elizabeth, 15, 93, 122, 155, 165, 170, 198.
Ogle, John, 80, 83, 184, 198, 218, 224, 225, 226.
Ogle, Thomas, 210.
Ogle, Widow, 102.
Olle, Laurence Sick, 169.
Olson, see Oelsen.
Omella, see Omely.
Omely, Bryan, 86, 87, 101, 124, 132, 175.
Orme, Fabian, 38, 61.
Ormond, Joseph, 99.
Osborn, Basilia, or Bazilla, 85, 100, 123, 173.
Osborn, James, 53.
Osborn, William, 4, 7, 19, 123, 171, 174, 202.
Ostarhaven, Leonard, 217.
Otto, Gerrit, Gerret, or Garratt, 3, 8, 9, 10, 12, 37, 85, 91, 92, 94, 101, 109.
Otto, John, 172.
Otto, Otto, 94, 172.
Otto, Walraven, or Wallraven, 124, 209, 210.
Otto, Widow, 109.
Outhout, Fop, or Fopp, 32.
Owen, Edward, 84, 99, 123, 174, 177, 178, 188.
Owen, Lewis, 174, 196.

INDEX OF PERSONS.

Pacdvns, Thomas, 164.
Padeson, William, 100, 125, 160.
Pagg, Daniell, 3.
Parke, Robberd, 13.
Parker, William, 76.
Parks, Robert, 85.
Parris, John, 220.
Parry, John, 85.
Pash, John, 124.
Patrick, Zacarah, 171.
Patteson, see Padeson.
Paulsen, see Poulsen.
Paulson, see Poulsen.
Pead, Timothy, 33, 84.
Pearce, see Pierce.
Pearson, see Peirson.
Peirce, see Pierce.
Peirson, John, 85, 92, 129, 173.
Peirson, Thomas, 98, 114, 116, 122, 128, 132, 147, 171, 181.
Penington, John, 99, 114, 119, 167, 197.
Penn, William, 21, 22, 23, 24, 26, 35, 36, 39, 43, 45, 47, 67, 74, 76, 87, 141, 151, 180, 200, 203, 204, 205, 210, 213, 215, 217, 218, 220, 222, 225.
Penn, Governor or Gouernor, 81, 147, 185.
Perkus, Edmund, 116, 124, 133, 156, 172.
Persivall, Widow, 100.
Peters, see also Petersen.
Peters, Adam, 9.
Peters, Hans, 82, 108.
Peters, John, 124.
Peters, Samuel, 14, 77.
Petersen, see also Peters.
Petersen, Adam, 37, 85, 94, 101, 110, 124, 172, 208, 213, 219.
Petersen, Andrew, 109, 124.
Petersen, Carell, Carrell or Carl, 37, 48, 49, 50, 125.
Petersen, Charles, 68, 83, 102, 179, 190.
Petersen, Hans, 37, 68, 103, 108, 110, 114, 115, 116, 118, 126, 169, 179, 182, 189, 190, 192, 196, 200, 207, 208, 212, 218, 221, 226.
Petersen, John, 85, 91, 92, 102, 116, 117, 133.
Petersen, Lucas, 110, 114.
Petersen, Peter, 208.
Petersen, Samuel, 37, 83, 103, 118, 121, 170.
Petersen, Thomas, 48.

Peterson, see Petersen.
Philips, Ann, 161.
Philips, William, 10, 11, 85, 104, 145, 159, 161, 172.
Phillips, see Philips.
Philipps, see Philips.
Pickering, Charles, 94, 96, 114, 116, 118, 121, 170, 181, 183, 184, 187.
Picket, William, 7.
Pidgeon, Joseph, 218, 227.
Pierce, John, 101.
Pierce, Thomas, 47.
Pierce, William, 57, 58, 59.
Pietersen, see Petersen.
Pietersenproot, Jan, 37.
Pieterss, see Petersen.
Pirkeld, John, 156.
Pitt, John, Junior, 133.
Pocock, Philip, 7.
Post, Cornelius, 219.
Pouls, see Poulsen.
Poulsen, Elizabeth, or Elizabet, 5, 6, 125, 221.
Poulsen, Erick, 119.
Poulsen, Justa or Justus, 37, 82, 102, 114, 115, 118, 126, 179, 182.
Poulsen, Margriet, Margrieta, or Margret, 6.
Poulsen, Moens, 5.
Poulsen, Oele, Oella, Oalla or Olla, 4, 37, 79, 82, 91, 99, 110, 222.
Poulsen, Poull or Paul, 6, 119, 221, 222.
Powell, Davy or Dauy, 128.
Powell, John, 122.
Powell, Walter or Wallter, 99, 119, 131.
Prestner, see Priestner.
Prew, see Prue.
Price, Marget, 213.
Price, William, 213.
Priestner, John, 98, 114, 118, 120, 149, 157, 158, 163.
Priestner, Widow, 167.
Pristner, see Priestner.
Proprietary, 25, 26, 33.
Proprietary, The 24, 35.
Proprietary, The Right Honorable, 23, 33.
Proprietor, 36.
Prue, John, 103, 169.
Pruys, Claas Danielson, 37.
Pudding bag maker, Samuel, 173.

Quartermus, John, 108, 130.

INDEX OF PERSONS. 241

Quince, Richard, 100, 123, 174.
Quinch, see Quince.

Radford, John, 19.
Rakestraw, William, 106, 118, 121, 122, 171, 190.
Randall, Marmaduke, 38, 184, 185.
Rappe, Gabriell, Gabrielle or Gabreel, 78, 86, 90, 101, 118, 124, 145, 172.
Rawlings, John, 171.
Rawlings, William, 171.
Rayne, John, 213.
Read, see Reed.
Reed, James, 93, 103, 122, 170, 193, 202, 208, 209, 210, 213, 216, 220, 222, 223, 224, 227.
Reed, George, 121.
Renolds, see Reynolds.
Reynolds, Henry, 103.
Reynolds, John, 225.
Reynolds, Richard, 194, 199, 212, 214, 219.
Rice, Evan, 228.
Richards, John, 225.
Richardson, Francis, 159, 173, 179.
Richardson, John, 144, 145, 147, 155, 161, 165, 167, 201, 210, 212, 213, 216, 217, 220, 222, 227.
Richardson, Mark, 195.
Richardson, Susanah, 195.
Ridger, William, 19.
Roason, Oalla, 103.
Robinson, George or Georg, 156, 157, 159, 180.
Robinson, Richard, 121, 170.
Robinson, Robert or Robart, 90, 103, 121, 170.
Robinson, William, 158.
Roe, John, 225.
Roosemond, Marten or Martin, 16, 17, 199.
Rosamond, see Roosemond.
Rothwell, Thomas, 199.
Rotier, Jacob, 223.
Rotier, Robert, 224.
Rowland, Samuell, 110.
Rudyard, Thomas, 135, 136.
Rumsey, Catherin, 15.
Rumsey, Charles, 10, 14, 15, 16, 17, 18, 74, 75, 77, 79, 80, 94, 99, 119, 155, 167, 180, 181, 184, 188, 190, 194, 196, 197, 202, 203, 204, 206, 207, 212.
Rumsy, see Rumsey.

Saderling, see Sanderlin.
Sadler, Thomas, 92.
Salisbury, Even, Evan or Evens, 4, 5, 10, 34, 95.
Salisburry, see Salisbury.
Sallisbury, see Salisbury.
Salloway, Thomas, 172.
Samuells, Samuel, 37.
Sandelands, see Sanderlin.
Sanderlin, James, 38, 131, 158, 184, 185, 187, 204.
Sanderlins, see Sanderlin.
Sanders, Charles, 217, 218.
Sanders, Mathew, 169, 179.
Sauoy, see Savoy.
Savoy, Isaac, Isacq or Jsacq, 13, 37, 38, 125.
Scarf, William, 84, 99, 119, 123, 173.
Scarfe, see Scarf.
Schaegen, John, 6.
Scogging, Jonas, 103, 169.
Scot, see Scott.
Scott, Francis, 96, 120.
Scott, James, 86.
Scott, John, 86, 124, 156.
Scott, Widow, 101.
Screek, John, 81, 119, 167.
Scrike, see Screek.
Seaton, John, 100.
Sempil, see Sempill.
Sempill, Josyn or Joslyn, 27, 28, 31, 37, 81, 97, 120.
Sempill, Margaret, 27, 28.
Sempill, Susanna, 31.
Sempill, William, 3, 6, 8, 12, 19, 21, 23, 25, 26, 27, 28, 41, 42, 69, 70.
Semple, see Sempill.
Senecar, see Senex.
Senex, Broer or Brewer, 19, 37, 83, 102, 106, 107, 121, 147, 148, 161, 162, 170, 202, 221.
Senexen, see Senex.
Senexon, see Senex.
Sharpe, William, 61.
Sharpley, see Sharply.
Sharply, Adam, 83, 102, 126, 170.
Sharply, David, 171.
Sharply, William, 212.
Sharwood, see Sherwood.
Sherrer, William, 89.
Sherry, Margaret, 215, 221.
Sherwood, William, 35, 84.
Sickes, James, 173.
Siericx, Grietie, 12, 33.

INDEX OF PERSONS.

Siericx, John, 10, 11.
Siericx, Wybregh, 10.
Sierix, see Siericx.
Simcock, John, 23.
Simes, John, 156, 173.
Sinexen, see Senex.
Sinnexen, see Senex.
Skart, William, 13.
Slouer, see Slover.
Slover, Isack, 81, 96, 113, 120, 122, 168, 179.
Smit, see Smith.
Smith, Ann, 220.
Smith, Daniel, Danel or Daniell, 105, 106, 109, 119, 125, 167, 173.
Smith, Francis, 220.
Smith, Francis, Junior, 171.
Smith, Francis, Senior, 171.
Smith, Gerritt, Gerit, Garret, Garrit or Gerhard, 69, 70, 71, 72, 80, 98, 116, 211.
Smith, John, 7, 13, 69, 75, 80, 83, 99, 103, 121, 122, 165, 168, 171, 176, 188, 191, 202.
Smith, John, Junior, 6, 93.
Smith, John, Senior, 93.
Smith, Mary, 176.
Smith, Mathyas, 83.
Smith, Richard, 13, 38, 86.
Smith, Thomas, 3.
Smith, Walter, 173.
Smothers, James, 159.
Snelling, Thomas, 84, 88, 100, 112, 123, 174.
Snoding, see Snowden.
Snowden, Thomas, 19, 20, 85.
Snowden, Widow, 101.
Spark, Bisk &, 219.
Sparks, 101.
Sparks, Margaret, 219.
Sparks, William, 219.
Spragg, J., 137.
Spry, 11.
Spry, Thomas, 34, 46, 47, 80, 97, 107, 109, 125, 155, 184.
Staalcop, Andries, or Andrew, 14, 37, 77, 83, 102, 122, 171.
Staalcop, Carell, 37.
Staalcop, Charles, 82.
Staalcop, Christian, 108, 121, 170.
Staalcop, Jan or Jan Andriesse, 37.
Staalcop, Jan, Junior, 37.
Staalcop, John, 14, 19, 37, 83.
Staalcop, Peter, 171, 187, 197.
Staalcop, Widow, 102.

Standfield, James, 171.
Staples, Doctor's successor, 171.
Starr, Benit, 13.
Stayes, Benit, 86.
Stedam, see Stiddem.
Stedham, see Stiddem.
Stedman, see Stiddem.
Stiddam, see Stiddem.
Stiddem, Adam, 37, 102, 121, 132, 160.
Stiddem, Asman, 82, 118.
Stiddem, Benedict, 132.
Stiddem, Benjamin or Benjamen, 114, 121, 160, 170.
Stiddem, Christian, 119, 160.
Stiddem, Doctor, 119.
Stiddem, Erasmus, 37, 132, 145, 146, 160, 170, 176, 186.
Stiddem, Loalof, Lulof, Lylif, Lullof, Lolifant or Lullifant, 37, 60, 82, 114, 147, 176, 186.
Stiddem, Lucas, 37, 83, 90, 103, 121, 131, 146, 160, 170.
Stiddem, Tymen, Timothy, Timan or Timmen, 37, 102, 119, 132, 146.
Stille, Andrew, 83, 99, 102, 116.
Stilly, see Stille.
Stockdale, William, 113, 116, 162, 169, 171, 174, 181, 184, 188, 190, 196.
Stoffel, 169.
Sturkas, Nathaniel, 186.
Sute, William, 98.
Swede's Church, 226.
Swede's Church, Church Wardens, 226.
Sweet, Benjamin, 219, 223.
Sybrance, Harman, 81.
Sybrance, Hendrick, 166.
Sybrance, John or Jan, 81, 98, 118, 119, 166, 167.
Sybrane, see Sybrance.
Sybranson, see Sybrance.
Sybrant, see Sybrance.
Sybrant, 123.
Sybrantson, see Sybrance.

Tally, William, 218.
Tarkerton, see Tarkinton.
Tarkinton, 143, 144.
Taylor, George, 123, 149, 174.
Taylor, James, 13.
Taylor, Jane, 108, 112, 124, 125.
Taylor, John, 19, 20, 38, 84, 85, 99, 100, 104, 108, 112, 123, 174.

INDEX OF PERSONS. 243

Taylor, Mrs. Rebecca, 136, 137, 138, 139.
Taylor, Oliver, 171.
Taylor, Widow, 104.
Taylor, William, 136, 137, 138.
Tayne, Isacq or Isaac, 37, 69, 81, 120, 168.
Tesschmaker, Petrus (Domine), 37, 80, 96, 120, 168.
Tessemaker, see Tesschemaker.
Tessmaker, see Tesschemaker.
Test, John, 184.
Testmaker, see Tesschemaker.
Teuness, see Teunisse.
Teunisse, Philip, 10, 43.
Thirkild, John, 159.
Thomas, Oele, Oela, Oalla, Ola or Wolla, 37, 69, 75, 76, 82, 103, 121, 154, 170.
Thomason, see Thomas.
Thomassen, see Thomas.
Thompson, John, 219.
Tilly, Andries or Andrew, 13, 71, 80, 122, 165, 170, 177.
Timan, Doctor, 121.
Tine, see Tayne.
Toarson, see Toersen.
Toersen, Anniky, 115.
Toersen, Lacy or Lasse, 115.
Toersen, Lasse Olsen, 37.
Toersen, Laurance or Lawrence, 93.
Toersen, Mathias or Mathyas, 95, 115.
Toersen, Mathias Laersen, 37.
Toersen, Margrett or Margaret, 115.
Toersen, Oele, Oela, Oalla, Olla or Woola, 37, 48, 49, 50, 85, 87, 101, 103, 110, 115, 125, 145, 150, 190.
Toersen, Oele Oelsen, 37.
Toersen, Sicca, 115.
Tom, William, 12, 33, 40, 41, 42.
Tomkings, Anthony or Antony, 96, 99, 123, 174, 193.
Tomkings, Elizabeth, or Elisabeth, 193.
Toms, see Tom.
Tomson, see Thomas.
Toolson, see Toersen.
Tosson, John, 221.
Toreson, see Toersen.
Torson, see Toersen.
Tossen, see Toersen.
Touls, see Toulson.
Toulson, Henrick, 189.

Turner, Robert, or Robert, 159.
Turner, Susannah or Susanah, 184.
Tyne, see Tayne.

Urianson, Christian, 170.
Uster, Hans, 164.

Valck, John, 37, 97, 145.
Valck, Sybrant, 37, 97, 174.
Valke, see Valck.
Valkerson, Peter, 37, 98.
Van Beek, Gerrit Jansen, 37.
Vance, John, 83, 103.
Vance, Robert, 83, 170.
Van Coolen, see Vander Coolen.
Vandburg, see Vandenburgh.
Vandeburg, see Vandenburgh.
Vandenburgh, Anna, 146, 197.
Vandenburgh, Arent Jansen, 37.
Vandenburgh, Derrick, 156, 196, 198.
Vandenburgh, Hendrick, 19, 34, 37, 72, 73, 78, 80, 86, 97, 102, 106, 107, 120, 126, 132, 142, 143, 146, 148, 149, 150, 151, 166, 168, 172, 173, 179, 193, 197, 198, 205, 221, 222, 223.
Vanderburg, see Vandenburgh.
Vandercoelen, see Vander Coolen.
Vander Coelens, see Vander Coolen.
Vander Coolen, Margaret, 225.
Vander Coolen, Reynier, 16, 30, 31, 37, 56, 69, 70, 80, 81, 92, 96, 114, 118, 121, 127, 129, 141, 150, 168, 176, 177, 186, 187, 204, 216, 219, 221, 223, 224, 225.
Vander Coolen, Zachariah, 169, 182.
Vanderculine, see Vander Coolen.
Vanderheyden, Matthias, 37, 97, 144, 163, 168, 172, 217, 225.
Van der Veer, see Vanderveer.
Vanderveer, Catharine, 71.
Vanderveer, Cornelius, 6, 37, 160, 169.
Vanderveer, Jacob 5, 6, 37, 48, 50, 71, 82, 89, 103, 113, 126, 132, 146, 169.
Vanderveer, Jan, 83.
Vanderveer, William, 82, 146.
Vandiemen, Engeltie, 33.
Vandiemen, William, 33.
Vandrburg, see Vandenburgh.
Van Herre, Cornelius, 102.
Vaugans, Robart, 126.

INDEX OF PERSONS.

Verhoof, Cornelius, 54.
Verhoof, Jan Gerritsen, 7, 37.
Volckertsen, see Valkerson.
Vries, Cornelius Jansen, 37.

Walcker, see Walker.
Walker, Francis, 84, 100, 122.
Walker, John, 10, 11, 69, 85, 94, 100, 104, 109, 120, 123, 124, 130, 132, 145, 159, 161, 172, 187.
Walker, John, Junior, 9, 10.
Walker, John, Senior, 84, 87.
Walker, Joseph, 104.
Walker, Wyborough or Wyburg, 132, 210, 215.
Walliam, James, 26, 27, 28, 35, 43, 45, 48, 50, 67, 77, 80, 86, 87, 88, 89, 90, 91, 92, 93, 94, 97, 104, 105, 107, 109, 110, 113, 116, 117, 118, 120, 126, 127, 136, 137, 139, 142, 146, 148, 149, 156, 167, 168, 179, 184, 193, 199.
Walliam, John, 199.
Walliams, see Walliam.
Wallice, see Wallis.
Wallis, Anthony or Antony, 13, 86, 102.
Wallker, see Walker.
Wallkersen, John, 100.
Walraeven, Gisbert or Gysbert, 37, 102, 121, 170.
Walraevens, see Walraeven.
Wallrauen, see Walraeven.
Wallrausen, see Walraeven.
Wallraven, see Walraeven.
Wansford, Nicholas, 206.
Ward, Captain, 86.
Ward, Captain Henry, 134.
Ward, Henry, 5, 134.
Ward, Willow, 102.
Wardens, of Swede's Church, 226.
Warner, Isacq, Isaac or Isack, 19, 103, 169, 218.
Watkins, see Wattkins.
Wattkins, John, 10, 14, 15, 74, 75, 80.
Wattkinson, Henry, 14.
Watts, John, 214, 221, 223.
Webster, John, & Ryly, 172.
Weelden, see Weeldon.
Weeldon, Isack or Isaac, 84, 100, 106, 123, 154, 174, 178, 193, 198, 201, 211.
Welch, Mrs., 91.
Welch, Sarah, 120, 160, 168, 183, 184.

Welch, Susannah or Susanah, 97, 118.
Welch, William, 77, 78, 80, 86, 87, 88, 89.
Wells, Blanch, 195.
Wells, George, 195.
Wertherdale, see Westingdale.
Wessells, Dr., 109, 183.
Wessells, Doctor Gerardus, 7.
Wessells, Gerrardus, Gerardus or Garrardus, 19, 37, 38, 56, 77, 81, 92, 93, 96, 107, 116, 118, 121, 148, 150, 156, 187.
West, John, 23.
Westingdale, Ann, or An, 84, 123, 174, 203.
Westingdale, Percifull, 203, 204.
Weston, Anthony, 171.
Whale, Ann, 184.
Wharton, 114.
Wharton, Walter, or Wallter, 19, 33, 61, 105.
Wheeldon, see Weeldon.
White, Christopher, 170, 203.
White, J., 122.
White, James, 213, 214.
White, John, 47, 67, 77, 80, 83, 90, 95, 98, 103, 113, 116, 118, 119, 131, 141, 151, 153, 155, 163, 178, 183, 187, 192, 194, 197, 198.
White, Magnus, 86, 91, 92, 101, 125.
White, Richard, 174.
White, William, 47, 128.
Whitwell, Francis, 54.
Whitwell, Symon, 4.
Whyte, see White.
Wilkingson, see Wilkinson.
Wilkinson, John, 13, 77, 86, 101, 126, 177.
Willemsen, see Williams.
Willemsen, Dirk, 8, 9, 37, 129.
William, see Williams.
William, James, 13.
Williams, see Williamsen.
Williams, Dirk, Derick or Derrick, 9, 91, 92, 100, 125, 129, 130.
Williams, Henry, Hendrick, Henrik, Henricus, or Hericus, 77, 81, 84, 85, 86, 89, 90, 91, 93, 94, 95, 97, 100, 105, 113, 115, 120, 123, 127, 168, 173, 200, 204, 206.
Williams, John, 72, 73, 77, 79, 86, 87, 88, 90, 93, 94, 95, 97, 104, 110, 168, 213, 215, 216, 220.
Williams, Tuncha, 129, 130.
Williamsen, see Willemsen.

INDEX OF PERSONS.

Williamson, see Willemsen.
Willix, William, 98.
Willkinson, see Wilkinson.
Willson, see Wilson.
Wilson, John, 172, 173, 179, 181, 186, 215.
Winson, Robert, or Robart, 83.
Wodkings, John, 94.
Wollaston, see Woollaston.
Wolluerson, Gisbert, 99.
Woodhouse, William, 99, 152.
Woodland, William, 216, 225.
Woolaston, see Woollaston.
Woolaston, 154.
Woolcock, Christopher, 224.
Woollaston, Mr., 34, 153.
Woollaston, Peter, 172.
Woollaston, Thomas, 18, 38, 69, 75, 77, 82, 102, 114, 122, 127, 128, 140, 141, 144, 151, 152, 154, 161, 165, 171, 181, 194, 224.
Wooleston, see Woollaston.
Woollsen, see Woollson and Woolson.
Woollsen, Wolla, 82.
Woollson, Michall, 82.
Woollson, Sicca or Sick, 82, 115, 116.
Woolson, see Woollson.
Wootters, John, 78, 111, 112.
Wright, Henry, 220.
Wright, John, 124.
Wright, Jonas, 193.
Wruonsen, see Juriansen.
Wruonsen, Wrion, 77.

Yeates, Jasper, 210.
Yocum, Peter, 217, 218.
Yokum, see Yocum.
Young, Anna, 4, 34, 38, 39.
Young, Jacob, 86, 87, 101, 125, 151, 172, 206, 216, 222, 225.
Ysop, William, 44.
Ysops, see Ysop and Jessop.

www.ingramcontent.com/pod-product-compliance
Lightning Source LLC
Chambersburg PA
CBHW020646300426
44112CB00007B/261